POWER TOOLS

for
Pro Tools 8

Master Digidesign's Pro Audio and Music Production Application

Rick Silva

HAL LEONARD BOOKS
An Imprint of Hal Leonard Corporation | New York

Published in 2009 by Hal Leonard Books
An Imprint of Hal Leonard Corporation
7777 West Bluemound Road
Milwaukee, WI 53213

Trade Book Division Editorial Offices
19 West 21st Street, New York, NY 10010

www.halleonard.com

Book design by Kristina Rolander
Front cover design by Richard Slater
Illustrations, p. 17, reprinted by permission, Georg Neumann GmbH.

Library of Congress Cataloging-in-Publication Data

Silva, Rick.
 Power tools for Pro Tools 8 / Rick Silva.
    p. cm.
 Includes index.
 ISBN 978-1-4234-7444-9
 1. Pro Tools. 2. Digital audio editors. I. Title.
 ML74.4.P76S53 2009
 781.3'4536--dc22
                                        2009020218

Printed in the United States of America

To my grandmother, Arlene Lopez.

Table of Contents

CHAPTER 4
IGNITING YOUR PRO TOOLS SYSTEM

CHAPTER 9
MIXING AND MASTERING ESSENTIALS

ON THE INCLUDED DVD

Power Tools for Pro Tools Video Folder
    Introduction To Power Tools for Pro Tools
    DAW Basics
    A Lean, Mean Pro Tools Machine
    Igniting Your Pro Tools System
    Armed and Ready
    Making Room for Your VIPs
    Editor's Choice
    Elastic Is Fantastic
    Mixing and Mastering Essentials

Power Tools For Pro Tools Sessions Data Folder
    Audio Examples/Session Files

Acknowledgments

When I was presented the opportunity to write a book for the Hal Leonard Corporation, I was certainly honored. It was not something I set out to do, but sometimes opportunities come by way of pure circumstance and from being at the right place at the right time. Being prepared, however, allows one to take on unforeseen challenges with excitement and confidence. The idea of writing a book about Pro Tools, I must admit, made me a bit nervous. Nevertheless, I was eager to take on the challenge.

The time spent and the obstacles overcome in the writing and production of this book were greater than I ever anticipated, and for this reason, I would like to take the time to thank the various people that made the book's completion possible. First, I would like to thank my family, especially my mother Sandra Lee Achiardi, who has been unbelievably strong, positive, and supportive. Without her encouragement and consistent support throughout my life, none of this would be possible. Next is my girlfriend and love of my life, Kori Lee. She somehow tolerates without hesitation the long hours I put in while I'm working as an audio engineering instructor, studio owner, engineer, and musician. I'm not exactly sure why she does it, but I love her dearly for it. Last, but certainly not least, is Joe Testai, my very best friend of over twenty-five years. Joe, you've always been there when you were needed most and over the years probably many times when I needed you the least! You are a true friend, and that alone is worth a million thanks. You are like a brother to me; you know me better than anyone does and you still put up with me. Here's to the next twenty-five years!

The people named above are my support team, and without them in my life this book would not exist. Other people have inspired me, supported me, challenged my abilities and personal growth, and given me encouragement and maybe even a few migraine headaches along the way.

I have many "favorite" musicians, but Ross Bolton and Gary Hoey are two of the most talented, motivated, and inspiring guitar players I've ever met. They both gave me a tremendous amount of encouragement and are both excellent examples of how to make a living doing what you love to do. They were huge mentors to me. Next would have to be Orlando Rashid, T.J. Helmerich, and Paul Murphy. Orlando, you introduced me to Pro Tools, and the world of digital audio recording. Your skills are undeniable and inspiring. You opened many doors for me and I thank you.

T.J., the talented, knob twisting, mad scientist: Your tones are impeccable on every mix you touch. You reinforced my belief that being an audio engineer-musician is an art form and that long, tedious hours of dedication to one's own art are their own reward.

Paul, you were one of the most passionate teachers I've ever witnessed. You are an inspiration on many levels. Scott Pederson at Waves, you took the time to help my studio (Mixed Emotions) become one of the first Waves Certification training facilities in Los Angeles, and ultimately you introduced me to Mike Lawson and made this book possible. Thanks so much for your professionalism and enthusiasm!

Scott Church, Kyle Ritland, and Jim Metzendorf at Digidsign—thank you for all of your help, support, and all the extra goodies that helped this book. You guys rule! Mike Lawson, publisher extraordinaire—thank you so very much for giving me the opportunity to write this book and introducing me to the world as an author-instructor. I look forward to several years of friendship, guidance, and business together. Ted Greenberg—I am so grateful to have met you. We are all very lucky to have you walking the halls of Musicians Institute. You are a great guy and a seriously talented individual. You inspire everyone around you.

Also, a very special thanks to the thousands of students that I've had the pleasure of teaching during the past twenty-two years. You've all inspired me and taught me as many things as I've taught you.

Finally, to the many people at Hal Leonard who helped with the making of this book, I appreciate all of you for seeing this project to completion. It was a long grind but we made it through it.

Foreword

I have a confession to make. I am a recovering analog snob. The year was 1991, I had my own studio, did sessions around town, and tape was the only medium that I would record to. In my mind there was no other option. Later that year I started teaching at The Art Institute of Philadelphia, where they had a very good-sounding analog studio complete with a discrete console and a 2-inch tape machine. A few months later the school purchased a Pro Tools 4-track system just after the software had morphed from the 2-track Sound Tools. The flexibility was great, but the sound of the converters and the 16-bit resolution and 44.1 kHz sample rate left me cold. I honestly never thought that Pro Tools would ever catch on or replace tape. Wrong!

Over the years, Digidesign continued to improve the sound of their converters, increased the digital word length to 24-bit, and expanded their software until in 2002 Pro Tools HD arrived with sample rates up to 192 kHz. When I first heard music recorded at the 192 kHz sample rate I was amazed, but I was still an analog guy. That is, until I had the opportunity and the honor to produce, edit, and mix the soundtrack to a movie called *Standing In The Shadows of Motown*—the story of the Funk Brothers, who played on more number 1 hits than the Beatles, Elvis, the Rolling Stones, and the Beach Boys put together!

The surviving members of the original Motown band reunited and performed live with some of today's stars like Chaka Kahn, Ben Harper, Bootsy Collins, Joan Osborne, and Gerald Levert.

The concert footage was recorded to Tascam DA-88s, and I later digitally transferred the recordings to Pro Tools so I could edit the performances. The age of the musicians ranged from 68-75 years old, and their collective health was not good. One drummer had a quintuple bypass operation three weeks after the shoot, and the other drummer died from terminal lung cancer six months later. One of the keyboard players also died within a year from heart problems. One of the guitarists had not played or touched the guitar since Motown left Detroit in 1972. Needless to say, many performance and timing issues required fixing, even though these men were legends in their own time.

Pro Tools was the answer and the only system I could use to flexibly edit and resolve all the musical and technical issues. Of course, having good listening skills and the ability to play 11 instruments helped, too.

In 2003 I was fortunate to win two Grammys and two TEC awards for producing and mixing the soundtrack to the movie and help the Funk Brothers win a Grammy Lifetime Achievement Award.

I also was honored when Rick Silva asked me to write the foreword to this book, *Power Tools for Pro Tools 8*. Rick is a passionate engineer, teacher, guitar player, songwriter and producer who is a master of all the aforementioned disciplines. I have had the pleasure of observing some of his classes at the Musicians Institute in Los Angeles, and his practical, straightforward approach easily gets the point across and communicates to students of all levels.

Power Tools for Pro Tools 8 is well written and allows the reader to make the transition from version 7 to version 8 easily. I have been in the music business for 37 years and a teacher of Pro Tools at the college level for 18 years. I will be using this book myself to make the transition from version 7 and get up to speed on Pro Tools 8.

Rock on, Rick. Thanks!

TED GREENBERG

Introduction

Hello there, and thanks for reading *Power Tools for Pro Tools 8*. I wrote this instructional book to include the things I've always wanted to know about Pro Tools and what I feel are the most essential elements that make Pro Tools 8 one of the best digital audio workstations around. Digidesign released Pro Tools 8.0 just as I completed the manuscript for a book about Pro Tools 7.4. Although this presented new challenges, including long nights of re-writes and a lot of quick learning and fact checking, I'm happy the company released Pro Tools 8.0 when they did. It helped reinforce what I believe is true about knowing at least one DAW platform thoroughly: even though Pro Tools 8.0 was a big update, knowing the program really well already made it much easier for me to make the transition to using it and updating this book. The changes were intuitive and easy to learn, and there are many new I've-been-waiting-for-this features that will make all Pro Tools users smile big.

This book contains a lot of information, but not everything Pro Tools is capable of doing can possibly be covered in just one book. However, I've included enough information to get you ready for any future updates Digidesign has in store. I look forward to updating the information in this book as often as I can. Pro Tools software is ever evolving, and keeping up with the many software updates will be challenging, but we all must do it. Thank you for allowing me to share with you my years of experience as a Pro Tools user, and thanks for waiting for *Power Tools for Pro Tools 8*. Enjoy!

A Pro's Tools

For many years, Pro Tools has represented the industry standard for recording, editing, mixing, and mastering popular music. With Pro Tools 8, Digidesign has elevated that standard again. The program's latest advancements have made creating music "in the box" (by computer) easier than ever before. Pro Tools 8 introduces a group of five brand-new virtual instruments (the Pro Tools Creative Collection), almost 8 GB of high-quality audio loops, more than 20 new Advanced Instrument Research (AIR) plug-in effects, a slew of new MIDI editing features, a powerful Score Editor for MIDI production that gives you the ability to print your MIDI data as music notation, and a modern customizable graphical user interface (GUI). Elastic Pitch has also been added to the revolutionary Elastic Time features, which were introduced in version 7.4. Elastic Pitch allows you to change the pitch of your audio by cent intervals or by up to four octaves in either direction without altering the tempo or timing. To say the least, Pro Tools 8 has enhanced its role as a one-stop music-production studio in a very big way. In this book, we'll look at many of the outstanding new features in Pro Tools 8. We will also cover many standard techniques and reveal less well known, but very powerful, techniques (or "power tips") that will help speed up your work flow as a Pro Tools user.

Over the years, I've used many different recording applications while working as a professional audio engineer and instructor.

All of them have good qualities, but I almost always end up using Pro Tools for critical applications. Digidesign has consistently anticipated what professional audio engineers expect to get out of a program like Pro Tools. With each update, Pro Tools has offered more features similar to those found on traditional high-end studio gear that costs hundreds of thousands of dollars, while maintaining the program's user-friendly, two-window interface. But Pro Tools 8 has gone one step further and included several work flow templates and a plug-in bundle that provides endless inspiration.

The cool thing about working with Pro Tools is that it doesn't matter what configuration you are working with (LE, M-Powered, or HD systems), because the most important features of Pro Tools are on all of them. Digidesign systems ranging from a few hundred dollars to tens of thousands of dollars offer nearly all of the software's primary features. To top it off, Pro Tools' new software and hardware combinations keep improving sonically, and they are easier to use than ever before, especially for the musician who doubles as an audio engineer. As an instructor for one of the world's most innovative music-and-technology schools, the Musicians Institute, I like to make sure that the information I pass along to my students is not only useful but also useable—something that they can incorporate into their skill sets immediately and can continue using long after they graduate. My approach to teaching has always been not only to show students what a piece of equipment or a software program can do, but also to tell them when to use it, why it was chosen, and most important, how it can be applied to their own projects or any professional situation.

Nowadays, most software audio applications on the market do very similar things. Because there are so many things to know about any given software program, trying to learn everything about a complex program like Pro Tools on your own can be frustrating and seem nearly impossible.

This book will give you the most essential and practical information on how to become an efficient Pro Tools operator and will teach you how, when, and why to use many of the powerful features inside Pro Tools software. I hope that after reading this book you will become a confident Pro Tools user and will also better understand why the majority of music industry professionals prefer Digidesign's incredible software.

GETTING A GOOD START

Fortunately for professional engineers and educators, most people who buy Pro Tools (or any other DAW) don't immediately break out the manual and start mastering the software. In fact, most people barely make it through the setup process of the manual. The average person will usually take everything out of the box, figure out which cables go where, and just start plugging things in. Users typically slip in the installation disc and start clicking around aimlessly trying to make the software work. More often than not, the result is frustration when things don't work right away. Then come the complaints that the program is too difficult to use or that it is not user friendly.

The purpose of this book is to help you quickly become an overall better Pro Tools user and to point out important elements that can make setting up your DAW less frustrating. Throughout the course of this book, you will be given suggestions for how to optimize Pro Tools' performance when using some of version 8's new creative collection, as well as some of the additional third-party software that comes bundled with the program. In order to make the best of those suggestions, all of your software must be properly installed.

And so, as much as I dislike reading manuals, I have to suggest that you read at least the Getting Started guides, especially if you are new to installing DAW software and hardware. Making the effort to go over the Read Me files that come with each new item you install and work with will also help. Even if you are a seasoned Pro Tools software and hardware installer, you may be surprised to find that today most software and hardware products come bundled with quality tutorials (along with "light" or trial versions of other cool plug-ins or applications). During installation you may encounter problems, and in many cases, solutions are described in the documentation that comes with your new software. Even better, there may be easy solutions for "known issues" that have been driving you crazy for a long time; these bugs might be remedied by a simple update on your new installation disc. Lastly, the Read Me file might direct you to a link that could help expedite the installation process.

Knowing that you've done all you can to make things run smoothly is a good feeling, and the result will be that you can launch your new or freshly updated Pro Tools 8 software and its various hardware components with confidence.

WHAT YOU SHOULD EXPECT

Pro Tools 8 has been improved in many areas. This book can't possibly address every one of the changes, but I'll describe some of the more exciting ones. In addition to the new capabilities of version 8, I'll go over many standard functions that are deeply embedded in earlier versions of the application. Some of these functions may not be obvious to all Pro Tools users, but understanding them will provide the solid foundation you'll need before moving on to the more advanced concepts covered in this book.

Over the past ten years, I've worked on almost every kind of Pro Tools system, and I will describe some of these experiences to help you see what can be done with the software. Sometimes people don't realize the versatility of Pro Tools. Learning its secrets has made my life as an audio engineer much easier, and I can't wait to share them with you. Here is a summary of the areas I'll cover in this book.

Recording with Pro Tools

I've recorded live bands as well as numerous vocal and guitar overdubs for a wide range of artists. These recording sessions have taken place everywhere from small home studios and midsize production studios to multi-million-dollar professional studios. I've used high-end mixing consoles with a Pro Tools HD or LE system functioning exclusively as a multitrack recorder. I've also done some remote recording for television commercials with only a laptop and a Digidesign Mbox audio interface. I've even recorded band rehearsals with the same laptop and interface to help with production and arrangement ideas or to capture new song ideas that often emerge during a casual rehearsal.

Learning how to use Pro Tools as a means of capturing audio is easy. Becoming a skilled and experienced Pro Tools operator, however, takes patience, a decent understanding of music, audio engineering, and a lot of practice. In this book, I'll discuss many strategies for developing good recording technique. You will learn the basic differences between common microphones, the importance of setting good levels on a mic pre, using the right record mode for the job, getting a good headphone mix, and using the correct monitoring mode while recording. You will learn about minimizing latency, using preroll and postroll, recording multiple takes, taking advantage of the Dynamic Transport feature when writing or producing with loops, and utilizing many other tools that will maximize your recording skills.

Editing with Pro Tools

I've spent many hours editing Pro Tools sessions. The work has included everything from editing full-length, multitrack CD projects to making radio-friendly edits so mastered stereo mixes are more appropriate for commercial radio. Editing in Pro Tools is common at every stage of making music, and so there's always room to grow when it comes to the editing process. New editing techniques and shortcuts are being introduced all the time, and it can be challenging for any Pro Tools user to keep up. As a professional engineer, the faster I can work, the greater my earning potential. If I relied on only my existing knowledge, then my business might suffer, because engineers often are paid by the job rather than by the hour. I could easily find myself working twice as hard as I have to, simply because I'm not up to date with current Pro Tools features. For instance, it would be silly not to take advantage of the amazing new comping feature in version 8. If I didn't know it existed, the job would still get done, but I would be working harder, and not smarter. We need to work smarter in both the creative and professional environments, and

Pro Tools 8 makes that even easier if you are aware of all of its features and how to take advantage of them.

Today, because of the accessibility of Pro Tools, the average musician-engineer can handle most, if not all, of the audio chores on a given recording project. Digidesign has done an incredible job of making it easy to accomplish in a matter of minutes tasks that used to take professional DAW operators hours to complete.

In this book essential editing tips are given throughout the various chapters, and there is an entire chapter dedicated to developing some of the more advanced Pro Tools editing concepts. I'll go over cleaning up your audio tracks using strip silence, using sound-replacement and -enhancement techniques, working with Beat Detective in Collection mode, and turning multiple takes into one perfect performance using the new comping features. I'll also cover how to arrange your audio in the timeline using standard keyboard shortcuts and region groups and how to use Memory Locations and Window Configurations to customize view settings. You'll learn several standard keyboard shortcuts as well as some very useful advanced keyboard shortcuts in a Pro Tools mode known as Keyboard Commands Focus.

Creating with Pro Tools

Over the years, the process of recording, programming, and editing MIDI has evolved significantly in Pro Tools. Not long ago, keyboardists needed to use external MIDI interfaces and sound modules with MIDI keyboards to get their sounds. Then ReWire applications that could synchronize with Pro Tools enhanced communication between programs. In recent years, instrument tracks and a wide variety of virtual instrument plug-ins have made composing with Pro Tools more practical.

Newer USB keyboards and other plug-and-play controllers now integrate seamlessly with Digidesign's new line of virtual instruments and samplers. Pro Tools, acknowledged for years as the best audio-editing software around, finally caught up with other programs in the areas of MIDI programming and functionality. MIDI enthusiasts who had complained about the quality of MIDI capabilities in Pro Tools for years have finally been quieted by the addition of Real Time Properties, high-resolution sequencing, improved compatibility with third-party products, and brand-new virtual instruments, audio loops, and a high-quality sampler. This makes Pro Tools 8 one of the most complete and versatile self-contained creative packages on the market today.

I'll also cover some of the bonus software that comes with Pro Tools systems, such as Reason Adapted and Analog Factory, and explain how you can use them to build your creations. You can refine your ideas by using some of Digidesign's newly bundled virtual instruments and add-on Advanced Instrument Research (AIR) virtual instruments, including Strike and Velvet. Then, using some of the new Pro Tools 8 creation templates, you can create some custom templates of your own, featuring more plug-ins such as Digidesign's Eleven, Native Instruments' Guitar Rig, and other sounds from NI's Komplete 5 bundle.

Mixing with Pro Tools

Pro Tools has taken the art of DAW mixing to a completely new level. Depending on the type of system you are using, it is possible to mix everything from music demos to full-length feature films, all in Pro Tools.

Whether you're using an Mbox or a Pro Tools HD system, you can get the job done with quality results if you know how to maximize your system. The amount of mixing power you can expect to get from a Pro Tools LE system, for example, is determined by your computer's processing power and the amount of RAM you have installed. In Pro Tools 8, the track count has increased to 48 stereo or mono tracks on an LE system, and can be greatly increased if you have purchased one of the Toolkit upgrades. Obviously, the more CPU power and RAM you have, the better performance you can expect to get from your system.

Some third-party software companies have developed their own DSP cards that you can install on your computer. These cards greatly increase the processing power and mixing capabilities of your system but are not compatible with every computer. I'll describe several ways to achieve the best possible performance and results when using a Pro Tools LE system. I'll also give you mixing tips on equalization and compression, sidechain signal-flow routing concepts, information about how to create width and depth with time-based effects, how to synchronize those effects, and how to lock them to the Pro Tools transport. I'll also touch on some of the various new AIR plug-ins that come bundled with Pro Tools 8.

Mastering with Pro Tools

The mastering process is the final stage in the recording process before your music is finalized. Having the final say on the way a track sounds before it's released is a powerful feeling, but it can be a heavy responsibility. I've mastered several projects, ranging from Christmas albums to contemporary indie-rock CDs. I've also mastered instructional CDs and television commercials as well as the audio for this book and others like it. With the versatility of Pro Tools and the many great mastering plug-ins to choose from, it is easy to understand why mastering in the box has become so widely used and commercially accepted.

I'll discuss how to set up a mastering project, why using frequency and peak meters is so important, and how to set the best output level without overcompressing or "slamming" the track. I'll give you tips about using reference CDs, taming the low end, shaping your final frequency curve, and using dither options for your final mixes that are to be sent off for mass duplication.

WHAT YOU SHOULD KNOW

Many times, the most frustrating part about working with Pro Tools (or any music software) is the installation, setup, and optimization process. Although this book will not cover details about the setup process or how to make sure that everything in your system is functioning properly, I will point out some tips that make the setup process less painful.

This book assumes that you have an above-average knowledge of computers and generally know how to properly optimize yours for pro-audio applications. You should also have a basic musical background that includes some knowledge of music theory, and having a fair amount of skill with your primary instrument won't hurt. A basic understanding of signal flow and a working knowledge of fundamental audio-engineering terms, techniques, and concepts will also help speed your journey through this book.

If you haven't developed these skills yet, then you may find this book a bit challenging. On the other hand, if you are an intermediate to advanced Pro Tools operator who has some decent musical ability, you'll find that the end-of-chapter questions and tips contain useful information that will definitely enhance your Pro Tools skills. This book will give every Pro Tools user something new for their audio toolbox.

ABOUT KEYBOARD SHORTCUTS

The keyboard shortcuts used in this book are based on the Macintosh key layout. The following table lists Mac modifier and execution keys with their Windows equivalents.

MAC OS	WINDOWS
Command (Apple) key	Ctrl (Control) key
Option key	Alt key
Ctrl (Control) key	Start (Win) key
Return key	Enter key on main keypad (not numeric)
Delete key	Backspace key

Back to DAW Basics

2

ESSENTIAL ELEMENTS

This chapter will provide you with the essential elements you need to use Pro Tools software and hardware effectively. You don't have to be a professional audio engineer to achieve high-quality results from Pro Tools. However, having a good understanding of the basics of audio engineering and knowing the fundamental process of digitizing audio for recording, editing, and mixing will increase your chances for success dramatically. If you feel you already know most of this information, I suggest taking the Pro Tools Tune-up Test at the end of this chapter. This test will serve as a good gauge to use to determine if you should skip over this chapter. It will inspire you to either move ahead in the book or go back and gather the information you need before continuing with it.

SOUND ADVICE

Many of us take for granted the sounds we hear around us every day. Even right now, you may be hearing birds chirping, phones ringing, cars going by at a distance, or even the hum of the refrigerator, air conditioner, or any other electrical appliance that is turned on within earshot of wherever you are. More than likely you are so used to these sounds that you tune them out without even realizing it. If you want to get better at capturing audio with any recording medium, start by simply listening to every sound you hear and realize how each one of those sounds has its own distinct character that makes it uniquely its own. If you are wondering how that is supposed to help, try thinking about it this way: Let's say you have four pets—two cats and two dogs. When one of them makes a sound, it is easy to tell whether it was one of your dogs barking or one of your cats meowing. A dog sounds like a dog and a cat sounds like a cat, right? The exciting part about this simple analogy is not that dogs sound like dogs and cats sound like cats; rather, it is how easily we can tell exactly which one of our dogs or cats has just made a sound. Knowing how sounds are created and why we perceive each sound as being unique provides an invaluable insight on how to go about recording it. The more you know about sound, the better you will get at recording it. The better you get at recording it, the more you'll understand how to mix it within the context of the other instruments. The cycle is endless, and one always feeds the other. Therefore, knowing the most you can about the sounds you are working with is sound advice.

THE SOURCE

When we hear a sound, what we are actually experiencing are the changes in the sound pressure around us. These changes are created by the vibrations of any particular object. When an object vibrates and it completes one back-and-forth motion, it is referred to as one *cycle*. This cycle of vibration creates an audio event. If the vibration cycle that caused the audio event falls within a given range, our ears can perceive it as sound. The range at which humans perceive sound is between 20 and 20,000 vibration cycles per second. So, determining exactly which one of our cats or dogs made a sound depends on three factors contained in the vibrations created by the pet's voice box: the amplitude, frequency, and waveform of its "voice." Simply put, *amplitude* is the volume, or strength, of the sound. *Frequency* is the pitch of the sound in terms of high and low. And *waveform* is the shape of the vibrations that caused the sound. One goal of this chapter is to break down the science of sound into a more digestible concept. Another is to help you understand why you should have an overall awareness of the basics of sound as they apply to recording and mixing audio.

Amplitude

Our ears perceive the magnitude or strength of the variations in sound pressure as overall volume or loudness. Amplitude is also referred to as *sound-pressure level*. This volume or sound-pressure level is measured in decibels. The decibel (one-tenth of a bel) is based on a logarithmic scale that indicates the ratio between the amplitude of a sound and that of a standard reference. This standard reference is known as the *threshold of hearing* and has been assigned a value of 0 dB. Most people can initially perceive sound at 0 dB. All other sound-pressure levels are expressed in relation to that reference. To put this into perspective, an average conversation measures in at approximately 60 dB, while 120 dB is commonly referred to as the threshold of pain. Here are a few examples of common sounds as they relate to decibels. These are approximations, but they help put things into context.

LEVELS OF COMMON NOISES IN DECIBELS

Threshold of hearing	0 dB
Rustling of leaves	10 dB
Average recording studio	20 dB
A quiet bedroom at night	30 dB
A library	40 dB
An average home	50 dB
A normal conversation	60 dB
A vacuum cleaner	70 dB
Heavy traffic	85 dB
Average club before the band starts playing	100 dB
Chainsaw at around five feet away	110 dB
Threshold of pain or discomfort	120 dB
Average rock concert	125 dB
Jet engine	160 dB
Rocket engine	195 dB

Frequency

Frequency refers to the number of cycles that pass a fixed location over the period of one second. Since we now know that the perception of sound is created when an object completes one vibration cycle, we can determine that the pitch of that sound is a reflection of how many cycles pass our ears (or a microphone) in one second. Frequencies are measured in units called hertz (abbreviated Hz). One thousand cycles per second is equal to one kilohertz (kHz). Previously, I mentioned that the range of human hearing is between 20 cycles per second and 20,000 cycles per second. Therefore, we can also say that the range of human hearing is 20 Hz to 20 kHz. This does not mean that a source is not able to create sounds above and below this range; it means that we usually do not perceive the vibration cycles out of this range as sounds. It is safer to say that we feel them rather than hear them.

So how does all of this relate to music? Well, as the frequency or rate of vibration increases, so does the pitch of the sound; similarly, as the frequency or rate of the vibrations decreases, the pitch of the sound gets lower. Each time the frequency doubles, it increases the pitch of a sound by one octave. For instance, an A note played on the second fret of the third string on a guitar vibrates at a rate of 220 cycles per second, or 220 Hz. Playing an A note on the fifth fret of the first string produces vibrations at 440 Hz, which is one octave higher. The same thing applies in reverse. If you were to pluck the fifth string, which is an A note one octave lower than the A note at 220 Hz, its frequency is 110 Hz. Hopefully, this will shed some light on why knowing the fundamental frequencies and range of frequencies of various instruments will help you when you record or mix audio.

Waveform

A waveform is a visual representation of a sound's vibration cycle and its amplitude, or sound-pressure level. A simple waveform such as a sine wave gives us a great visual account of sound. A simple sine wave will have an intelligible pitch, and when you look at it in an audio-editing program, you can see how a particular frequency repeats itself back and forth over the zero-crossing while keeping the same distance horizontally with each cycle. Not only can you see it repeating itself in length, but you can also get a visual representation of the amplitude as the waveform decreases in size as the sound fades out.

Simple sine waves are usually created by things such as a tuning fork after it's been struck, or an oscillator that is built into a professional recording console. Simple sine waves are used for many reasons in a recording studio. For example, sine waves are used when aligning a two-inch analog tape machine or printing a tone reel for analog recording. Sine waves are used to calibrate the inputs on a professional DAW interface such as a Digidesign 192. Musicians can tune their instruments by listening to a 440 Hz sine wave (an A note) from a synthesizer. You can even use sine waves with triggered noise gates to fatten up a kick drum or "make the cars go boom."

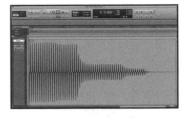

Sine waves also are a great aid to visualizing frequency and amplitude on a computer screen; however, they definitely lack character in their sound. Most of the sounds we hear on a daily basis consist of much more complex waveforms that are well defined and unique to themselves in sound. Their appearance tends to be jagged and far less symmetrical than a simple sine wave. Complex waveforms provide us with an audio fingerprint that allows us to discern one sound from another, enabling us, for example, to not only hear one of our dogs barking, but also to distinguish exactly which one of them is barking. Almost every sound we hear vibrates differently, creating complex waveforms and giving each sound its own unique identity.

MICROPHONES

Even though this book is not about microphone technique or how microphones capture sounds, being aware of the basic elements of audio engineering and having a fundamental knowledge of microphones is very important. The role of a microphone is to react to and properly translate the changes in air pressure, or the amplitude, frequency, and complex waveforms that make up a sound. Microphones help us capture, interpret, and convert a sound source into an electrical output that can be recorded. The continuous electrical energy produced by a microphone is key to accurately reproducing the original acoustic information and maintaining the integrity of a particular sound source. There are many types of microphones out there, so please become familiar with your options.

Dynamic Microphones

Dynamic microphones are equipped for handling loud sound-pressure levels and generally have a darker, less defined sound. They are very durable and usually more affordable. They are great for guitar and bass amps and the kick, snare, and toms of a drum kit.

Condenser Microphones

Condenser microphones typically require 48 volts of phantom power and have an extremely fast transient response. Some have multiple polar-pattern selections, various highpass filters, and a decibel pad to protect them from damage caused by high sound-pressure levels. High-quality condenser microphones reproduce an accurate "top end" of any source. They are great to use on acoustic instruments and are known especially for capturing great vocal performances.

Frequency Response and Frequency Curve

Every microphone has a *frequency response*, meaning the lowest and highest frequency they are able to capture. Many microphones manipulate the frequency curve and have bumps or dips at set frequencies, either by design or as the result of the manufacturer trying to keep costs down. When using or selecting a microphone, keep in mind the fundamental frequencies of the source and what kind of representation of the sound you are trying to get. It is equally important to know the limitations of any given microphone. Knowing these things will help you achieve acceptable results, even on the most modest budget. Always try to use the right tool for the job if you can, and when cost is an issue, learning as much about the microphone and the source you are trying to capture will allow you to make better recording decisions.

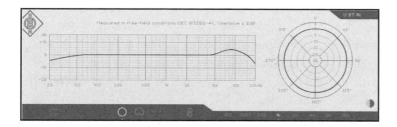

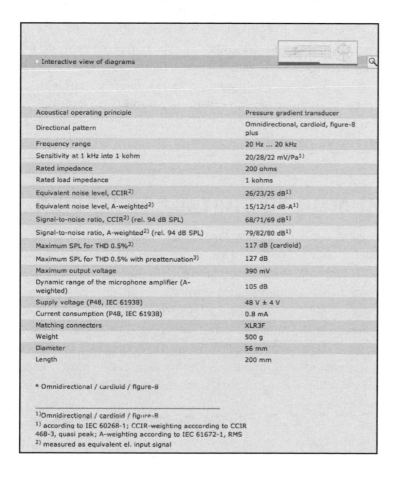

> Interactive view of diagrams

Acoustical operating principle	Pressure gradient transducer
Directional pattern	Omnidirectional, cardioid, figure-8 plus
Frequency range	20 Hz ... 20 kHz
Sensitivity at 1 kHz into 1 kohm	20/28/22 mV/Pa[1]
Rated impedance	200 ohms
Rated load impedance	1 kohms
Equivalent noise level, CCIR[2]	26/23/25 dB[1]
Equivalent noise level, A-weighted[2]	15/12/14 dB-A[1]
Signal-to-noise ratio, CCIR[2] (rel. 94 dB SPL)	68/71/69 dB[1]
Signal-to-noise ratio, A-weighted[2] (rel. 94 dB SPL)	79/82/80 dB[1]
Maximum SPL for THD 0.5%[3]	117 dB (cardioid)
Maximum SPL for THD 0.5% with preattenuation[3]	127 dB
Maximum output voltage	390 mV
Dynamic range of the microphone amplifier (A-weighted)	105 dB
Supply voltage (P48, IEC 61938)	48 V ± 4 V
Current consumption (P48, IEC 61938)	0.8 mA
Matching connectors	XLR3F
Weight	500 g
Diameter	56 mm
Length	200 mm

* Omnidirectional / cardioid / figure-8

[1] Omnidirectional / cardioid / figure-8
[1] according to IEC 60268-1; CCIR-weighting acccording to CCIR 468-3, quasi peak; A-weighting according to IEC 61672-1, RMS
[2] measured as equivalent el. input signal

Microphone Preamplification

When recording with a microphone, never just plug it into the interface and try to record. The levels would be too low to use and recording them would be pointless. In order to boost the signal that the microphone captures, you need to use a microphone preamplifier to bring the level up high enough so that the A/D converters can capture a good "picture" of the sound. A high-quality preamp will improve the sonic quality of your recordings and is always a key ingredient in professional recordings. However, good results can be achieved with just the basic preamplifiers on an Mbox or on any other interface compatible with Pro Tools LE or M-Powered that has microphone preamps built in. The important thing is to make sure that you get a good level at the mic-pre stage, so that you can optimize your signal-to-noise ratio and ultimately maximize your resolution (bit-depth). Be careful not to set the mic-pre level too high, or you will experience digital distortion. There is nothing pleasant about digital distortion. Getting a strong level at the microphone preamp is definitely important, but it is even more important that you do not overload the input to Pro Tools and record digital distortion.

ANALOG-TO-DIGITAL CONVERSION

Analog-to-digital conversion is the final stage before your analog source becomes digitized or converted to digital bits or binary numerical information (also known as "ones and zeros") that is archived and ultimately read and manipulated by a computer. Regardless of which platform or operating system you are using, the sound source must be converted from acoustical energy to electrical energy by way of a microphone, a guitar pickup, or some other input device, and then translated into ones and zeros so that information can be used by the computer's software. This process is commonly called A/D conversion. Limitations of this process are defined by sampling rate and quantization.

Sampling Rate

Sampling occurs when an electrical signal enters an electronic circuit known as a sample-and-hold circuit. This circuit suspends the incoming signal, takes a "snapshot" or "sample," and analyzes the signal's voltage level at that instant. Once analyzed, it is then sent to the A/D converter to be converted into a digital number. This digital number represents the voltage level, or amplitude, at that specific instant. The *sampling rate* is how many times this process happens in one second. The sampling rate required for digital audio is based on the fundamental law of A/D conversion called the Nyquist Theorem.

The Nyquist Theorem states that in order to properly translate the frequency of a sound, a digital recorder must have a sampling rate that is at least two times greater than the rate of the source's highest frequency. If the sampling rate is any lower than that, an audio anomaly called aliasing, which is caused by frequency distortion, will occur. This is definitely an unwanted artifact in digital recording. However, since we have already established that the range of human hearing is 20 Hz to 20 kHz, then it follows that since the highest vibration rate we can perceive is 20,000 cycles per second, any sampling rate greater than two times that amount (40 kHz) is acceptable and can capture full-frequency audio.

Almost all digital recorders have a sampling rate of at least 44.1 kHz, and more often, 48 kHz. These days, it is common to have an interface that offers sampling rates of 88.2 kHz, 96 kHz, and often as high as 192 kHz. If you are using a higher sampling rate, be aware that higher sampling rates take up much more hard-drive space and greatly decrease the number of audio tracks that can be recorded and played back simultaneously. When choosing a higher sampling rate, you should choose one that is divisible by the standard rate used for audio CDs (44.1 kHz). The mathematical equation is easier on your computer's processor and can actually result in better sound quality. Professional compact discs that we buy off the shelf are stored at a standard sampling rate of 44.1 kHz.

Bit Depth and Amplitude Resolution

The dynamic range of any given sound is the difference between its lowest and highest amplitude. The useful range of dynamics for music and speech is considered to be from 40 to 105 dB. To successfully capture this range, an A/D converter needs to be able to accurately represent differences in amplitude of at least 65 dB. The relative loudness of a sample is captured by a process known as *quantization*. In simple terms, this means that each sample is quantified as, or assigned to, the amplitude value that is closest to the sample's actual value. Computers use bits to quantify each sample that is taken. The number of bits used to define a value is referred to as the *binary word length,* or *bit depth*. This means that the range of value represented by a word length is defined by a binary word length and is the equivalent of 2 to the *nth* power. A 4-bit recording, for example, is equal to 2 to the 4th power (2^4), which is equivalent to saying $2 \times 2 \times 2 \times 2 = 16$. This word length (bit depth) would be able to capture and define only 16 levels of amplitude to represent your recording's dynamic range. That is not so good. On the other hand, a 16-bit recording is equal to 2^{16} and would be able to define 65,536 amplitude levels. This results in a huge improvement in the accuracy of your recordings. If you do the math for 24-bit resolution, you'll find that a 24-bit digital word length can define 16,777,216 discrete amplitude levels, and is therefore clearly the best choice for recording any sound source. For many years a 16-bit digital recorder was considered the standard for recording digital audio and was widely accepted. However, it was also subject to criticism; there was constant debate about how accurately it was able to reproduce its original sound source. Today, a 24-bit recording crushes the accuracy of its 16-bit counterpart. The superiority of analog versus digital recordings is still fiercely debated, but current-day 24-bit digital recordings are getting so much better at maintaining the integrity of the original sound source that it is becoming more a matter of taste than audible quality.

Dynamic Range and Headroom

An important thing to understand is that with each additional bit of information recorded, the dynamic range of your system will increase by 6 dB. Therefore, if an 8-bit recording has a dynamic range of 48 dB, this means a 16-bit recording has a dynamic range of 96 dB. Consequently, a 24-bit recording has a dynamic range of 144 dB, which is far more than enough to accurately reproduce the dynamic range of the original sound source and better than many high-end analog multitrack recorders. When a system is capable of capturing such a large dynamic range, it means that the signal-to-noise ratio potential is exceptionally good. But remember that just as when you use a higher sampling rate, using a larger word length or bit depth takes up more hard-drive space. Therefore, a 24-bit recording generally uses approximately one and a half times the space that a 16-bit recording does. If you can spare the hard-drive space, using a higher bit resolution is well worth it.

Number of Tracks and Length	16-bit at 44.1 kHz	16-bit at 48 kHz	24-bit at 44.1 kHz	24-bit at 48 kHz
1 mono track, 1 minute	5 MB	5.5 MB	7.5 MB	8.2 MB
1 stereo track (or two mono tracks), 5 minutes	50 MB	55 MB	75 MB	83 MB
1 stereo track (or two mono tracks), 60 minutes	600 MB	662 MB	900 MB	991 MB
24 mono tracks, 5 minutes	600 MB	662 MB	900 MB	991 MB
24 mono tracks, 60 minutes	7 GB	7.8 GB	10.5 GB	11.6 GB
32 mono tracks, 5 minutes	800 MB	883 MB	1.2 GB	1.3 GB
32 mono tracks, 60 minutes	9.4 GB	10.4 GB	14 GB	15.4 GB

THE VIRTUAL CONSOLE AND MULTITRACK RECORDER

After the source passes through the microphone and the signal goes through the A/D conversion process, your source finally reaches your computer's hard drive and is ready to be manipulated in any way your creativity and DAW knowledge allow. At this point, you should have an understanding of how an analog signal is recorded by a microphone or any other transducer, then translated to electric energy, and finally digitized to be Pro Tools ready.

Before getting into using Pro Tools, I want to explain a few more things about what is waiting for you inside the digital domain. It is essential you realize that in the scheme of signal flow, Pro Tools acts as a virtual recording console that makes professional recording easier than ever. Pro Tools software and hardware combinations have all the elements of high-end recording consoles. Once the source travels through the interface and is recorded onto the hard drive for storage and manipulation, you have the same options available as with an analog board. One main difference is that the internal dynamic processing and time-based effects used in Pro Tools are primarily nondestructive. This means you can change the parameters of these processors at any time, save them at any stage of the session, and recall the settings within a matter of seconds.

To better understand how to use all the features that Pro Tools has to offer, it is vital that you are aware of some common terminology and some of the limitations you may encounter with your computer. Not everyone has the same computer; therefore, it is impossible to tell you here what the best way to set up your particular system would be. It is your responsibility to know the specifications of your computer; this knowledge will help you understand its capabilities and help you recognize its limitations. However, it is safe to say that it is always wise to purchase as much RAM as your computer can accommodate. Doing so will allow you to use Pro Tools at your computer's full potential.

Here are some of the key terms you should know. Throughout the rest of this book, I will be adding more terms and their definitions to your vocabulary. As you go through this book, you will realize that audio engineering isn't just about twisting some knobs and letting the computer fix things. The computer doesn't think; therefore, it is up to you to tell the computer what to do. What you tell it to do is directly related to the amount of knowledge you have about digital audio workstations and what they are capable of doing. Knowing the following terms will help you get the most out of Pro Tools and your computer.

ESSENTIAL DAW TERMS

AMS. Audio MIDI Setup lets you set up audio and MIDI devices connected to your Mac. You can select the audio input and output devices, configure output speakers, set clock rates, and control levels. If you are using Windows, you will need to use the MIDI Studio Setup to create specific MIDI configurations for your different MIDI devices.

authorization. The term *authorization* refers to the process of activating a software product by registering it with the manufacturer and confirming the validity of the purchase. This process is usually transacted over the Internet. Sometimes this process can be tedious, but it is required with the majority of today's plug-ins. Therefore, if you want to use the plug-ins that come bundled with Pro Tools (or any other plug-ins) to enhance your system, you need to learn how to go through this process. It will also allow you some form of technical support and make you eligible to receive free updates and, in some circumstances, free upgrades.

CPU. The central processing unit is the main chip inside your computer that makes it run; it is the brain of the computer. The fundamental operation of a CPU is to execute a sequence of stored instructions. The speed of your CPU will relate directly to how efficiently Pro Tools runs on your computer: the higher the speed, the better the performance.

DAE. Digidesign's Digital Audio Engine is a proprietary real-time operating system for digital audio recording, playback, and processing. It is installed automatically when Pro Tools software is installed.

DAW. A digital audio workstation is a system that has audio and sequencing software, and hardware that adds functionality to the system.

external hard drive. A storage medium for audio and data files used for computer applications. For DAW application, an external hard drive that runs at 7,200 rpm or faster and has a seek time of less the 10 ms is preferred. Firewire or E-SATA connections are the fastest and most stable connections for pro-audio and video applications.

host application. Plug-in processors do not operate by themselves; they function within larger programs. A host application such as Pro Tools is a program in which plug-ins operate.

host platform. Macintosh and Windows are examples of host platforms.

iLok. A small plastic "dongle," or key, that connects to your computer via USB. It serves as an authorization storage place to ensure that your software plug-ins and applications are properly authenticated and can be used on your computer. An iLok is portable, so it allows you to take your plug-ins with you wherever you are working.

interface. The device used for the analog-to-digital conversion process. It sometimes acts as a mixer to route audio playback from an audio software program to speakers or headphones.

latency. A delay in audio throughput caused by digital-recording process. Latency is most noticeable, and is the most troublesome, when processing a track in a multitrack session or when tracking a live performer. If, for example, a plug-in's latency is excessive, the resulting track will be out of time with the rest of the music and must be offset.

native. Applications, such as Pro Tools LE or M-Powered, are called native if they use the host platform's processing power to perform all DSP functions. Native plug-in formats for Pro Tools include RTAS, Audio Suite, and VST (if you have the right conversion software). No external processing devices are needed, although an external I/O device may be necessary to run the host application.

Playback Engine. A menu within the Pro Tools software that allows you to modify various parameters to get the best performance out of your computer for that particular session.

plug-in. A plug-in is a software add-on that enhances a software program's capabilities. Think of it as a software accessory that provides extra tools for shaping the sound of any source. Plug-ins usually do not function as standalone applications; instead, they are accessed from within the host software.

RAM. Random access memory, to which your computer has instant access for performing various computer tasks. The more RAM you have, the quicker your computer can process information. Pro-audio applications have minimum RAM requirements to run their software, but having the most RAM that your computer can accommodate will greatly increase your computer's ability to function with pro-audio applications.

RTAS. Real Time Audio Suite, a common type of native plug-in. Plug-ins use the power of your computer's processor rather than the dedicated DSP (digital signal-processing) chips on an audio-processing card. They are far less expensive, and if used properly can be very effective. There are many third-party plug-ins for Pro Tools.

TDM. Time-division multiplexing. This refers to dedicated DSP hardware for Pro Tools HD systems. TDM plug-ins use the processing power of TDM hardware, rather than that of the host computer. Many TDM plug-in packages include their native counterparts, but native products do not contain TDM components. Having the power of dedicated DSP hardware greatly increases the power of your Pro Tools system.

OPTIMIZING YOUR COMPUTER FOR PRO TOOLS

I highly suggest that you set up your operating system properly before installing Pro Tools. Certain functions on your computer's operating system need to be set up a specific way to take full advantage of Pro Tools keyboard commands and to optimize the performance of the software on your computer.

It is important to read the *Getting Started* guide that comes with your Pro Tools system. It gives specific information about the best way to optimize both Mac- and Windows-based systems. If you have misplaced your guide or you have recently upgraded your Pro Tools software version, you can find the information on the Digidesign Web site (digidesign.com).

PRO TOOLS TUNE-UP FOR CHAPTER 2

1. When any source vibrates, that vibration is made up of three primary components that allow us to interpret them as sound. Those three elements are _____, _____, and _____.

2. Amplitude is the sound-pressure level or volume of a particular sound. Sound-pressure levels are measured in _____ and are commonly abbreviated as "dB."

3. The threshold of pain usually occurs when the amplitude of a source reaches _____ dB.

4. The number of vibrations that a source produces in one second is referred to as cycles per second, The term *cycles per second* is referred to as _____.

5. Frequencies are measured in _____ (abbreviated "Hz").

6. When there are more than 1,000 frequencies in one second, the frequency is measured in _____ (abbreviated "kHz").

7. The frequency range of human hearing is _____.

8. Higher frequencies represent sounds that are high in pitch, and lower frequencies represent sounds that are _____ in pitch.

9. Each time a frequency doubles, it goes up in pitch by one octave. Each time a frequency is cut in half, the pitch of the frequency goes down by _____.

10. A visual representation of a sound's vibration cycle and amplitude is called a _____.

11. There are two main categories of waveforms; they are _____ and _____ waveforms.

12. A _____ waveform provides us with an audio fingerprint that allows us to distinguish one sound from another sound.

13. The terms *dynamic* and *condenser* refer to typical types of _____.

14. A _____ microphone requires the use of phantom power.

15. The lowest frequency and the highest frequency that a microphone can capture is called its _____.

16. Bumps and dips in the _____ of a microphone can cause a misrepresentation of the pure sound source once it has been recorded. This is neither good nor bad. Simply being aware of this fact will help you make better microphone selections when you are trying to capture a particular sound.

17. The final stage before your analog source becomes digitized is referred to as _____.

18. Currently, the most common sampling rate for audio in the music industry is _____. The highest sampling rate available in a Pro Tools LE system is 96 kHz, and the highest sampling rate in an HD system is 192 kHz.

19. The Nyquist Theorem is the fundamental law stating that in order to properly translate the frequency of a sound, a digital recorder must have a sampling rate of at least _____ greater than the rate of the highest frequency produced by the source. If the sampling rate is too low, you can expect frequency distortion known as *aliasing* to cause strange artifacts in your audio.

20. One of the most important things to take into consideration when choosing a bit depth is that each bit represents 6 dB of dynamic range. Therefore, a 16-bit recording has _____ dB of dynamic range, and a 24-bit recording has _____ dB of dynamic range.

21. Macintosh and Windows are two types of operating systems; however, they are both referred to as _____ platforms.

22. A software add-on that enhances a software program's (host application's) capabilities is called a _____.

23. Native applications such as Pro Tools LE or M-Powered use plug-ins that use the host computer's CPU. This type of plug-in is referred to as a _____ plug-in. Pro Tools TDM plug-ins use the resources of dedicated DSP hardware found on HD systems.

24. *Latency* is a fancy term for _____. It is most noticeable when tracking live instruments and when the system's hardware buffer size is set to a high number.

25. The process of activating your software product is sometimes done by a challenge-and-response method, but it is much more common to use an iLok to _____ your software.

A Lean, Mean Pro Tools Machine

3

TRIMMING THE FAT

This chapter is for those of you who already know your way around Pro Tools and want to fill in any gray areas you may have in your fundamentals. Sometimes it is easy just to use what you already know. Using techniques that you are most comfortable with and simply staying with the software version of Pro Tools you have used for years is quite common, especially when it has been effective and you've achieved some level of success. However, any time that Digidesign announces a significant update for Pro Tools, many new tools become available to you.

In a little over two years, Pro Tools has had four major updates that were "paid" upgrades. If you have been using Pro Tools for a while, perhaps you converted from version 6.9 and updated to some version of Pro Tools 7 not long ago. If so, you probably found that there were many changes made between just those versions. Pro Tools is currently at version 8, and version 7.3, 7.4, and 8.0 were paid upgrades, just like version 7. Before you upgrade to the most recent version of Pro Tools, make sure you check for compatibility with your computer's operating system and that your computer's processing speed and the amount of RAM you have will meet the minimum requirements suggested by Digidesign. Both Mac and Windows operating systems are ever-changing, usually for the better, but even with better processors and more memory, advancements that can truly enhance Pro Tools' performance can do so only if the current version of the program is compatible with your computer's operating system and its performance specifications.

In this chapter, we will trim away some of the comfort-zone fat you've picked up since your last Pro Tools update and make sure that you have all of the essential knowledge to run a lean Pro Tools session from start to finish using the most current version of Pro Tools. No bells and whistles per se, just everyday information and knowledge that the average engineer would need to possess to be considered an asset in the creative environment. We will touch on many of the things you will need to start making music quickly. Two of the most important elements necessary for being a confident Pro Tools user are having a good mental and visual understanding of the program's two main windows and knowing how to access all of the basic Pro Tools functions. Most of the topics covered in this chapter should already be familiar to you, but if they are not, understanding the information here will be key to your getting the most out of this book and out of Pro Tools in general.

If you are a frequent Pro Tools user who has had some training or done well with the program on your own, it is often easy to overlook some basic elements or concepts that can instantly make you a better Pro Tools operator. This book explores many of these overlooked tips that will help you improve your skills, and I highly suggest you take the Pro Tools Tune-up quiz at the end of each chapter to see how you measure up before moving on.

CREATING A NEW SESSION

Before you can create a new session in Pro Tools, you have to launch the program by clicking on the Pro Tools icon.

You will see the program begin to start up, initialize your interface, load your installed plug-ins, and verify that they are authorized.

Once the process is complete, a new pop-up window will appear. This Quick Start window is one of the new features of Pro Tools 8, and offers several types of templates from which to choose. These templates are just fine if you are a musician-songwriter who simply wants to lay down some ideas and get some decent "canned" sounds in order to demo a song. Otherwise, these templates can give aspiring audio engineers a false sense of security.

In other words, just because these templates have been set up by professionals doesn't mean that your music will instantly sound professional. The templates simply provide typical settings to get you started and headed in the right direction. The engineers who set them up have no idea what sounds you are hearing in your head or what sounds you are hoping to replicate. If you want total control over your sound, you have to dig deeper into professional audio engineering and ask yourself some questions. Why is it important to know the reasons a particular chain of plug-ins was used on a given instrument or why everything is routed a particular way in each of the templates? These templates give you a good place to start, and they all can be customized further once they are open.

Look at the settings that are used, try to understand what was done, and ask yourself why they were done. Then, change things up a bit; experiment by making some changes to the templates. Try to set up a session with your own custom routing scheme from a blank session. Doing these types of exercises will introduce you to new methods or ideas for signal routing and sound shaping. They will help inspire your songwriting and production sessions while using Pro Tools and also bring you closer to achieving the sounds that are in your head.

At first, these premade templates may be awkward and clutter up your screen a little bit, but once you realize how much work has already been done for you, you may find yourself pleasantly surprised. The main point is to try to use this new Quick Start feature as a learning tool and a jumping-off point for further study. There are many great templates to choose from, and I suggest you take a look at all of them. Some may be very useful, especially if you are new to Pro Tools or migrating from another software platform such as Logic.

However, if you are a professional audio engineer and longtime Pro Tools user, you will want to have total control over your session templates and may find these new templates annoying. If so, you can simply deselect the Quick Start option from the lower left corner of the Quick Start dialog box. The graphic at left shows some of the template options in the Music category. Other categories include Songwriter, Guitar, Record + Mix, and Miscellaneous.

Once you've selected one of the new templates or chosen the Create Blank Session selection, click on the arrow next to Session Parameters, and a more familiar dialog box will appear. This is where you choose your Audio File Type, Sample Rate, and Bit Depth. Make your selection and then click OK.

Finally, you will be prompted to choose where you would like to save your new session. It is at this stage that users often make file-management mistakes: forgetting to name your session and where you're storing it. Make deliberate choices at this stage. Give your session a specific name, and choose the exact location where you would like it to be stored. You should choose an external hard drive or a partition created on your primary drive that is dedicated to audio. The name and location you choose is important, because you don't want to come back to your computer to continue your work and realize that you don't know where your work has been saved. Since Pro Tools typically defaults to saving your session in the Documents folder on your primary OS drive on a Mac, you may be in luck.

However, let's say you remember where your session is saved, but you have forgotten what you named it. If being consistent about naming your sessions is not one of your finer qualities, you may see a long list of generic folder names and not know exactly which one to open. To avoid this kind of unnecessary stress, practice good file-management habits from the start.

After naming and selecting a destination for your session, making the right choice about your Audio File Type, Bit Depth, and Sample Rate options is very important: the options you choose should be determined by the type of project you are working on. You could, for example, simply be putting down scratch tracks for a song idea and you want to do that quickly, so sampling rate, bit depth, and file format may not be that important to you at that moment. However, if you are recording what may become final tracks and you would like the option of using your scratch tracks as "keepers," you should be deliberate with your choices.

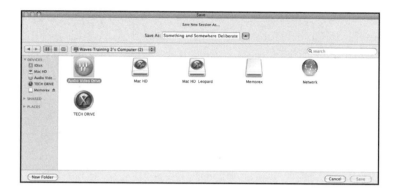

If you would like to always have the option of using any idea you've recorded, you should get into the habit of selecting 44.1 or 88.2 kHz as your sampling rate. (Numbers divisible by 44.1 kHz are the best choices unless the project is for broadcast audio or film; otherwise, 48 kHz or 96 kHz is more common). Select 24-bit depth as the preferred bit depth. Even though your final stereo mix will be converted to 16-bit, it is still better to record at 24-bit because you will get better sonic results, and minimize quantization error. If you don't have enough disk space to accommodate 24-bit recording, then use 16-bit; just realize that you'll be sacrificing a certain amount of sound quality.

The default file format for both Mac and PC is BWF (.wav). This is the standard file format for cross-compatibility. For many years, the SDII file type was the default Pro Tools audio format; it is still an option but is not very common and supports only up to a 48 kHz sampling rate. The AIFF format is another option and is still commonly used.

FILE MANAGEMENT

As soon as you launch your Pro Tools session, a folder with the name you gave it is simultaneously created on your hard drive in the location you selected to store it. Inside this folder are several file folders that contain important information about your session. These folders are created automatically, as needed, and are continuously updated as you work on your session. Pro Tools saves new information in specific folders with each manual save, or as often as you tell it to automatically save. While working with any DAW, it is always good to know where your program stores important information. Pro Tools makes that easy by putting everything neatly in its own place. In the next section, I will cover what you can expect to find in a typical Pro Tools session folder.

Pro Tools Session File

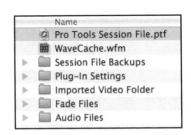

Pro Tools files are named with a PTF extension. A PTF session file contains a map of all audio tracks, video files, edits, and user settings that belong to that session. Different versions of the same session can be stored by using the Save As or Copy options and giving them a different file name. It's important to remember that all saved versions and copies of the session will get their audio files from the same source audio in the original Audio Files folder unless the Save Copy In option is chosen and you direct Pro Tools to copy all audio files.

WaveCache File

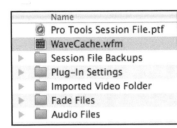

The WaveCache.wfm file saves all waveform information about your session and helps the computer quickly load the information. Pro Tools also stores this information in the local Digidesign Databases folder, where it stores data for all Pro Tools files on your system. If for some reason these WaveCache files get deleted, Pro Tools will rebuild the waveform data when it recognizes the file is missing, but the session will take noticeably longer to open.

Audio Files

The Audio Files folder is where Pro Tools stores all audio information for the corresponding session files. All relevant recorded, converted, and imported audio is stored in this folder. The default file format used for cross-platform compatibility purposes with Pro Tools is WAV. Pro Tools also recognizes several other formats including AIFF, and SDII (Mac OS only). If the files in this folder are deleted, your Pro Tools session will open up, but you won't be able to locate any of the audio files. Pro Tools does not regenerate lost or deleted audio files.

Sometimes the data indicating the location of your audio files may become inaccurate if, for example, you remove the files from the Audio Files folder or you make a copy of the session and try to open it on another computer. If this happens, Pro Tools will automatically try to find the files and relink to them. You will know if this happens, because you will be prompted to choose how you want to address the missing files in a session. Choosing the Automatically Find And Re-link option usually does the trick.

Fade Files

The Fade Files folder stores all fade file documents that are generated during the editing process for volume fades-ins, fade-outs, and crossfades. If this folder is missing, Pro Tools will automatically rebuild the information.

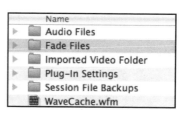

Region Groups

The Region Group folder is the default directory that Pro Tools uses for all region groups that are exported from your sessions.

Session File Backups

When you enable the AutoSave function, Pro Tools saves backup session files with user-defined parameters. All session backups are stored in the Sessions File Backups folder.

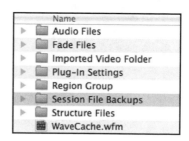

Video Files

A Video Files folder is created only when you digitize a movie into Pro Tools using the AV option or Avid Mojo. If a movie is already in a digital format such as QuickTime before you import it into Pro Tools, your session will reference the movie from its original location but will not copy it to your Session folder. For

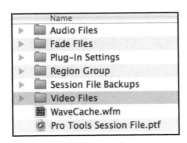

maximum portability, create a video-file folder and copy your video data to the new folder before importing the movie into your Pro Tools session.

WHAT'S ON THE MENU?

Once your session opens, you will notice that there are several menu items across the top of the screen in Pro Tools. Understanding the menu structure ultimately helps you navigate Pro Tools in a way that is intuitive and convenient.

Throughout this book, I'll point out many keyboard shortcuts that will allow you to access certain menu options without having to select from the actual menu. In the meantime, try to memorize which menu you need to access to perform various tasks. Having the ability to find any function that a situation calls for will allow you to work with confidence. If you get used to using the menus first, you can always learn the various keyboard shortcuts by quizzing yourself about what a particular keyboard shortcut would be, and then checking your answer by looking at the shortcut that's listed to the right of the function in the menu. Before you know it, you will have a plethora of keyboard shortcuts at your command. Here are brief descriptions of each of the menus found in Pro Tools. Users of previous versions will notice that all of the menu items in Pro Tools 8 (and Pro Tools LE 8) are the same as those in version 7.4.2. The main differences between the menu items in Pro Tools 7.4.2 and those in version 8 are in the Windows menu. (Other subtle differences will be pointed out in later chapters.) These menu items haven't changed much from version to version, and so learning them should prepare you well for future releases.

File Menu

The File menu is used to maintain your session. It is also used to access some of the most commonly used functions in Pro

Tools, such as Save, Close Sessions, Save Session Copy, Import, Export, Send, and Bounce To files, and to get to important session data.

Edit Menu

The Edit menu holds the functions commonly used to manipulate selected information in your timeline such as Cut, Copy, and Paste and region operations such as Duplicate, Repeat, Trim, Separate Regions, and Heal Separations. Throughout this book, we will be using many of the functions in this menu.

View Menu

The View menu controls the display of Pro Tool's windows, tracks, and track data. Selecting the submenus of some of these commands will display certain components or data such as Transport, Disk Space, and Narrow Mix views. Deselecting them hides the component or data previously selected. Many of the features in this menu can be accessed from within one of the two main windows in Pro Tools, but knowing where they are located in the menu is just as important.

Track Menu

The Track menu commands allow you to create and maintain the tracks in your session. You will use this menu when creating new tracks, grouping tracks, duplicating tracks, and selecting important monitoring modes and other valuable track settings.

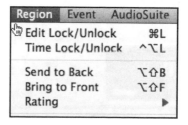

Region Menu

The Region menu is used to modify regions and region settings. Many commonly used commands that relate to working with regions for arranging, grouping, looping, and quantizing can be found in this menu.

Event Menu

The Event menu is where you have access to many of the important MIDI operations found in the Pro Tools software, including the MIDI Real-Time Properties and the MIDI Event List. Time- and tempo-related options such as Identify Beat and Beat Detective are also found in this menu.

AudioSuite Menu

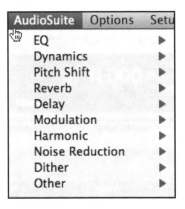

The AudioSuite menu allows access to all AudioSuite plug-ins currently installed and authorized on your Pro Tools system. Using this menu allows you to use a proprietary file-based processing (not real-time) format to permanently apply effects to selected audio files. The original file remains unaffected, but a duplicate file with processing applied to the audio replaces your selection. Pro Tools' time compression and expansion algorithm automatically uses this type of processing. Learning to use the AudioSuite plug-in menu will allow you to save a lot of CPU power when working with larger Pro Tools sessions.

Options Menu

The Options menu lets you choose from several recording, playback, editing, monitoring, and display options. Also included in this menu are several other important functions such as Pre/Post-Roll, Midi Thru, and Pre-Fader Metering.

Setup Menu

The Setup menu is mainly used to configure Pro Tools hardware and software parameters. It includes options for setting up your peripheral devices such as surface controllers, synchronization devices, and all other MIDI devices. It gives you access to other key features in Pro Tools such as the Preferences configuration menu, I/O setup, and Disk Allocation functions.

Windows Menu

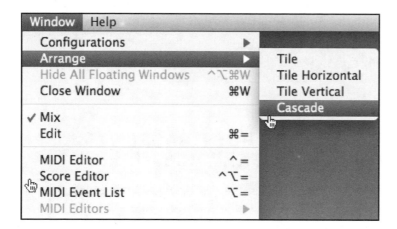

The Window menu is used for various Pro Tools window and palette arrangements. Important functions such as Memory Locations, Big Counter, and Automation functions are found in this menu. It also includes commands for toggling the Edit, Mix, and Transport windows, the Pro Tools Task Manager, and the Workspace, Project, and Browsers windows. Pro Tools 8 added a few new arrangement features for your window views. For instance, the Arrange submenu gives you three tile options and one cascading view option. You can also gain access to the new MIDI and Score Editors from this menu.

Help Menu

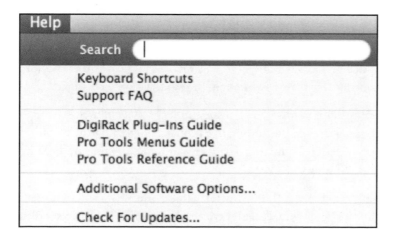

The Help menu is used to quickly access links to important Pro Tools documentation. All Pro Tools manuals are easily referenced from this window. Also, you will find some subtle yet handy new options from this menu, such as Additional Software Options and Check For Updates. Remember to check for compatibility issues before automatically updating your software.

OPTIMIZING HOST-BASED PRO TOOLS PERFORMANCE

For many Pro Tools sessions, the default system settings are fine for processing most tasks, but Pro Tools allows you to customize the way it uses its resources for better performance depending on the application. In other words, a demo-style, preproduction session may have a lot of virtual instruments and only a few audio tracks with minimal overall plug-ins. The Playback Engine options you'd use for this situation would be much different from the ones you'd use if you were tracking a live band and recording with 20 microphones at once or if you were editing or mixing a session with 48 tracks of audio and trying to use Elastic Audio. This is one of the reasons that Digidesign has added new features in its Playback Engine drop-down menu.

After you have opened your new Pro Tools session, before you dive right in and start tracking, creating, or importing audio to manipulate, take a moment to optimize the way you want Pro Tools to utilize its resources. To do this, go to the Setup menu and select the Playback Engine option. Changing the hardware buffer size and CPU usage limit appropriately will allow you to optimize your host-based processing capability. Pro Tools has added some new options in this menu that give you even more control over the way your system resources are distributed.

Using lower hardware buffer size (under H/W Buffer Size) reduces the latency when recording live inputs. A higher hardware buffer size is better for mixing and using more Real-Time AudioSuite (RTAS) plug-ins.

The CPU Usage Limit option affects the way the computer's processing power is assigned to do specific Pro Tools tasks.

Lower settings are helpful if you are experiencing a sluggish system response time when you are running other applications simultaneously with Pro Tools. A higher CPU usage limit is better to use when you are playing back large sessions (high track count) or using several instances of RTAS plug-ins.

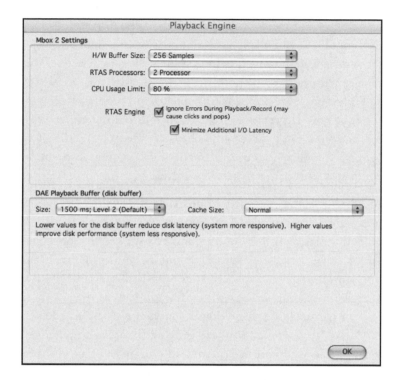

Since all computers have different processors with different speeds and various amounts of RAM, it is up to you to find the best settings for your system. You will still find yourself changing these settings from time to time depending on the circumstances. Each session you work on will be different from the previous one and will require you to select the appropriate system settings. Try to get used to considering this every time you open a new or existing session.

Furthermore, it is not a good idea to use your system drive for recording or playing back your audio; you should have a dedicated audio drive for this purpose. It is recommended to have an external hard drive connected via FireWire 400 or 800 for the best results. Many current external drives have an exceptionally large storage capacity. It is common to see drives that are 500 gigabytes (GB) and up to one terabyte (TB). For drives of this size, it is a good idea to partition them. Making a few partitions on a large storage drive is convenient for a few reasons. When a computer searches for audio on a hard drive, it scans the whole drive. If you have a very large drive with several different sessions that contain an abundance of audio files, your computer has to sort through all of those files until it finds the ones it needs. This can sometimes create a problem if the session can't access the audio fast enough because it isn't able to find it quickly enough. If one of your larger drives is partitioned into different sections, the computer can perform a much faster scan of the audio drive because you have put custom-size boundaries on each partition and it sees each partition as its own drive.

Another advantage of having one external drive that has a few partitions is that it allows greater portability. Many Pro Tools users have large custom sound libraries with various loops and samples that they use frequently. If you use one of the partitions on your external drive to store your loops and samples, you can bring your custom sounds with you. You can also save a copy of your personal plug-in settings folder and plug-in installers in this drive. If you fancy yourself as being the freelance-engineer type, having your custom sounds and plug-in settings with you at all times is invaluable and sets you apart from the average user. It is also great if you are traveling and would like to bring along your laptop but still have all of your familiar resources readily available.

While we are on this subject, it is important to go over some etiquette for traveling with plug-in installers. In order to bring your plug-ins with you from studio to studio, sometimes you have to install them on a computer that you are using as a guest. When you leave and take your iLok authorizations with you, you also leave the owner of the computer to deal with your plug-ins popping up with demo or authorization reminders every time they launch Pro Tools. Since this can be very aggravating to the owner and it makes you look careless and inconsiderate, you should create a "plug-ins unused" folder and move the plug-ins you installed to

that folder when you leave, so the owner doesn't get the reminders. It is a simple courtesy and will be greatly appreciated. Pro Tools 8 added another new feature that automatically creates a "plug-ins unused folder" and brings to your attention that some plug-ins that are installed were found and are not authorized, and gives you the option to move these plug-ins automatically. Nice feature, but when you find yourself working on someone else's system and they are using an earlier version of Pro Tools, just remember to be aware of the plug-in etiquette suggestions mentioned above.

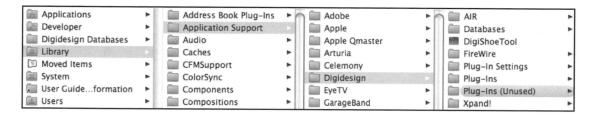

One last suggestion for optimizing hard-drive performance for any Pro Tools session is to set the parameter for how long it can continuously record new audio. To do this, click on the Setup menu and select Preferences. Click on the Operation tab in the Preferences menu. In the Open-Ended Record Allocation section, select the Limit To option and choose the longest duration you think you will need while recording your audio files. This allows Pro Tools to allocate only the amount of memory it requires to perform this function.

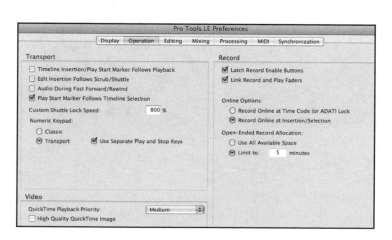

Remember that maintaining your drives properly will help your computer's performance as well. This means you should occasionally defragment your drive or back up all of your information on a separate drive, reformat your audio drive, and then copy the information back onto the newly reformatted drive.

MIX AND EDIT WINDOWS

These two windows are the primary windows for accomplishing almost every task imaginable in Pro Tools. A big reason that Pro Tools has dominated the audio-engineering industry for so many years is because of the incredible functionality and accessibility you have to all Pro Tools functions from just these two windows. This is where you can really see the changes in the look of Pro Tools 8: it is much more modern, with better colors and an overall sleek look. The Toolbar is now fully customizable, allowing you to choose the arrangement of your tools and basic transport functions. In the upper-right corner, you will find a new Edit window Toolbar menu that allows you to see different toolbar views with any option, in any combination, including MIDI and Synchronization options.

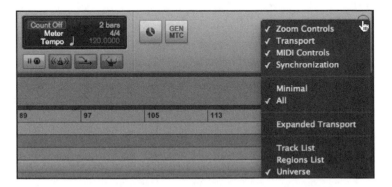

Pro Tools 8 has introduced two additional windows, the MIDI Editor and Score Editor windows. Some people would probably consider these to be "main" windows. I agree that they are great improvements for MIDI users and composers alike, and are very similar to windows on many other DAWs on the market.

However, even though these are considered major "new windows," I still think it is very important that you learn to view Pro Tools 8 as a two-window program with a couple of new optional view settings—powerful new workflow options or features that were added to the Edit window.

The redesigned Transport window is another important floating window in Pro Tools. We'll take a closer look at the functions it provides in the next chapter, but first, study the main Mix and Edit windows in detail.

EDIT WINDOW FEATURES

The Edit window gives you a graphic representation of your audio waveforms. Your tracks are arranged from top to bottom (the top being track 1). It is nice to get a good visual understanding of this window, but awareness of everything else surrounding the waveforms within this window is equally important. Along the top of this window, you have access to the different editing modes, your editing tools, the main and sub counters, and a basic transport window. This area is called the Toolbar. Since there are so many features available to us from this window, let's start at the Toolbar and move on from there.

EDIT MODES

Pro Tools has four edit modes: Shuffle, Slip, Spot, and Grid. You can select any of these modes by clicking on the mode buttons located in the upper-left area of the toolbar. You can also select the different modes by using the function keys (F1 through F4) on your computer keyboard. Each mode has a different effect on the movement of the audio and MIDI regions (and individual MIDI notes) in your playlist, and each also has an effect on how each tool interacts with the audio or MIDI data. Therefore, it is vital to know which mode you are in at all times.

Shuffle Mode

Shuffle mode allows you to make regions line up next to each other without their overlapping or having space between them. You can rearrange the order of your regions, but you cannot separate them. They will simply "shuffle" around each other. Each trim, cut, and paste edit you make in Shuffle mode affects the placement of the other regions surrounding it. Watching the supplied QuickTime examples on the accompanying CD-ROM will make this much clearer.

Slip Mode

In Slip mode, you have the freedom to move audio and MIDI regions freely without affecting any other regions in the timeline. You can overlap regions and create space between them if you choose. Unlike Shuffle mode, Slip mode allows your tool's edit functions to work without any restrictions to placement in time.

Spot Mode

Spot mode allows you to put regions exactly where you would like them placed in the timeline using precise numerical values. When this mode is enabled, Pro Tools prompts you with a dialog box whenever you click on a region with the Grabber tool or drag a region in from the Regions List or DigiBase browser. It is often used in postproduction to place regions exactly where you want the dialog or sound effect to start. To do this, simply enter the desired location in the pop-up menu, and Pro Tools will snap that region to the specified location. Spot mode is also useful when you have moved a region from its original location and the timing of that particular region is now out of time with the rest of your tracks, and you would like to put it back to its Original Time-Stamp location.

Grid Mode

In Grid mode, regions that are moved, trimmed, or inserted into the timeline will snap to the nearest increment set by the selected grid value. Precise time-interval editing is very useful. In Grid mode, Absolute Grid and Relative Grid positioning are your choices.

When using Absolute Grid mode with the grid value set to a quarter note, if you move a region somewhere on the timeline in between the quarter-note beat, the region will snap to the nearest absolute quarter note.

When Relative Grid mode is selected, you can move a region that does not start on the absolute quarter note or downbeat. It will still snap to the nearest quarter-note value, but the region will maintain its relative value to its nearest absolute beat.

Another nice new feature in Pro Tools 8 is called Snap To Grid. Previously, you could only use one edit mode at any given time. In Pro Tools 8, you can now choose to snap to the grid in any edit mode by combining two edit modes at a time. This feature allows you to implement specific "mode" tasks and adds increased functionality for editing. I suggest turning these functions on and playing around with them to see how they may suit your particular needs and how they can enhance your current skill set. To activate these features, select Grid Mode, and then hold down the Shift key and select one of the other three modes. You will notice you are basically in two Pro Tools editing modes at the same time and they work in concert with each other in different ways.

EDIT TOOLS

Pro Tools editing tools are located on the upper-left side of the toolbar. Almost every editing option you will ever use in Pro Tools will be executed by using one of these editing tools. They are the Zoomer tool, the Trim tool, the Selector tool, the Grabber tool, the Scrubber tool, the Pencil tool, and the combination Smart tool. If you are new to Pro Tools, watching the QuickTime demos a few times will help you get the hang of how these tools are used. If you don't know what the functions of these tools are yet, read about them in the Pro Tools help menu to get a more thorough explanation on how to use them. Briefly, here are how the tools function.

Zoomer Tool (F5)

The Zoomer tool is used to zoom in and out on a waveform anywhere in the timeline. It is useful when doing precise editing, and it has quite a few options allowing different levels of zoom that can be set to your own specifications. In normal Zoom mode, the Zoomer tool stays a Zoomer tool after the zoom selection is made. In Single Zoom mode, the Zoomer tool reverts to the previously selected tool after the zoom selection is made. You can also zoom in horizontally or vertically by holding down the control (Ctrl) key, and then dragging it up and down or side to side. To zoom out, click-and-hold the Option key.

Trim Tool (F6)

The Trim tool allows you to trim excess audio or MIDI from a region's start or end point. The action is nondestructive and just hides the trimmed selection. You can trim a region back and forth, allowing you to decide on how much of a particular region you would like to hear. Its movement is directed by the mode or grid value of your Pro Tools session. Your Trim tool also allows you access to Pro Tools Time Compression and Expansion trimming functions. These are more advanced features that will be covered in later chapters of this book. You will also find yourself using the Trim tool for MIDI edit functions and automation features that will be discussed later in this book.

Selector Tool (F7)

Use the Selector tool to set the playback cursor anywhere in the timeline or waveform overview to play back from the chosen spot with a single click. You can click-and-drag horizontally or vertically to make an edit selection. You can add or take away from that selection by holding down the Shift key and clicking-and-dragging to the left or right. You can also use the Shift + Tab keys to snap to the nearest value set by the grid, time-scale increment, or audio transient.

Grabber Tool (F8)

A single click with the Grabber tool selects the whole region, which can then be moved anywhere in the timeline or to any track in the tracks display area by clicking-and-dragging the region to the desired position. With the Grabber tool, holding down the Option key and clicking-and-dragging to a new selection in the timeline on any track makes a copy of the selected region while leaving the original region in its original location. Many other useful features for the Grabber tool, including the Object Grabber tool, will be covered in the following chapters.

Scrubber Tool (F9)

By selecting the Scrubber tool and dragging back and forth over an audio track, you can hear the playhead "scrub" over the audio as if you were slowly winding the analog tape over the playhead. This is how edit points are cued up for editing analog tape. Using the Scrubber tool allows you to listen for the exact edit point, and it mimics the technique used for "splicing tape" when using analog recorders. Since we have the Zoomer tool and a digitized audio waveform to look at in Pro Tools, the Scrubber tool is not the most frequently used method chosen to perform edits, but it is still a cool feature to have around.

Pencil Tool (F10)

When using the Pencil tool on an audio waveform, you can "redraw" the waveform. This tool is normally used to fix unwanted pops and clicks in the audio that appear as hard spikes in the waveform. There are some pretty good plug-ins that make this tedious task much quicker these days, but the Pencil tool has many other features for MIDI and automation functions that will be covered in more detail later in this book.

Smart Tool (F6 + F7)

The Smart tool has a new look in version 8 but still gives you instant access to the Selector, Grabber, and Trim tools and allows you to perform fade-ins and fade-outs as well as crossfades. It is a real time-saver when you get used to using it.

You can access all of these tools by using the function keys on your keyboard (F5 through F10), provided that they were set up properly in your operating system's Preferences and your Pro Tools Preferences menus. Consult your Pro Tools *Getting Started* guide for the correct preference settings. For now, it should be a goal of yours to get a solid visual recognition of what Pro Tools features you have access to in the Edit window without the use of keyboard shortcuts.

MAIN COUNTER AND SUB COUNTER

The Main counter is located in the upper right-hand side of the toolbar. The Main counter determines the time format used for transport functions and the Grid and Nudge values. You'll now find the Grid and Nudge values just to the right of the Main and Sub counter indicators on the toolbar. The Sub time scale is an additional timing reference for you to use. The Main counter defaults to minutes and seconds (Min:Secs), but both the Main and the Sub counters can be set to Bars|Beats, Min:Secs, and Samples. You can choose the options by selecting the Main counter option under the View menu or by clicking on the Down Arrow next to the individual counters from the fully expanded transport and making a selection from the drop-down menu.

The Main counter window also allows you to see the selected start and end times as well as the duration of the selection.

BASIC TRANSPORT

A basic transport with all the standard features of any tape deck is provided for you on the toolbar. Stop/start, play/pause, fast-forward, and rewind functions can be accessed from this basic transport. In Pro Tools version 8 you can choose to view the fully expanded transport from the Toolbar as well.

MAIN TRANSPORT — FULLY EXPANDED

Unlike the basic transport located only in the Edit window, the main transport can be viewed from both the Edit and the Mix windows. To bring up the transport, you can use either the keyboard shortcut (Command + 1) on the numeric keypad or navigate to the Window menu and select the Transport option. If the transport is not fully expanded when it appears, go to the View menu and select Transport or use the newly added drop-down menu in the upper right-hand corner of the main transport. Make sure that the counters, MIDI Controls, and Expanded options are selected. Even if the transport comes up with counters and MIDI controls, you still should navigate to this menu or pull-down window and check things out. When the fully expanded transport is in view, you can access a number of important parameters. Here are some key features about the transport. First, notice that the MIDI Controls view shows the following:

Wait For Note

When the Wait For Note button is engaged and Pro Tools is record enabled, nothing will be recorded until Pro Tools sees the first incoming MIDI event. This feature is generally used when Pro Tools' transport functions are being controlled by another "master" controller or even another computer running another program.

MIDI Merge

Use this function when you would like to record a MIDI part while having a loop selected. The MIDI data will not be erased

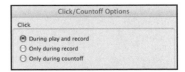

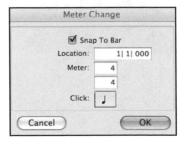

after the selection loops, and you can keep adding MIDI events or parts as the selection loops. This function is on almost all the time while programming MIDI drum parts, but not so much for live MIDI performances.

Metronome On

When the Metronome is selected, it turns the click track on. Change the settings of the Metronome by double-clicking on the Metronome icon, and set up your click parameters. You can also select the number of bars to be counted off before you hear the selection. If you select the During Play And Record option, you can hear the click any time the track is playing.

Conductor

The Conductor determines if Pro Tools uses the tempo map set in the Tempo Ruler. When the Conductor is on, you can have tempo changes throughout the song that are set up from the Tempo Ruler. We will explore this feature later in the more advanced chapters of this book. For now, the important thing to know realize that if the Conductor is not on, you can type in or tap in the desired tempo at any time during the production.

Tempo Resolution Selector

This button allows you to set the note value that gets the click. When it is set to quarter notes (the default setting), you will hear the click on every quarter note. If you click on the Tempo Resolution selector box and choose eighth notes, you will hear the click and your MIDI data in half-time. If you choose a half note, you will hear the click track and MIDI data in double-time, or twice as fast. The default setting usually works best.

Meter Change

The Meter Change display shows the time signature of the song. Use this to customize the time signature if your production is in anything other than common time (4/4).

Tempo Field

The Tempo field shows the current tempo or beats per minute (bpm) of your track. You can type in the tempo by highlighting the field and entering a number, or you can tap in the tempo by highlighting the field and then manually tapping on the T key on your QWERTY keyboard.

Pre-Roll and Post-Roll

The Pre-roll and Post-roll functions are located just under the standard transport controls (play, stop, rewind, fast-forward). The Pre-roll and Post-roll functions determine how many bars and beats Pro Tools will play before and after the selection (when this option is turned on). The time value you set for this function is directly related to the Main time scale; this is why most users prefer the Main counter to be set to Bars|Beats. To use the Pre-roll and Post-roll functions, click on either the Pre-roll or the Post-roll button to toggle the function on and off.

You'll use Pre-roll and Post-roll a lot when doing recording overdubs. A quick and easy way to turn each of these functions on and off is by using the (Command + K) keyboard shortcut, which can also be accessed through the Options menu.

Transport Time Scale

In the center of the transport, you will notice the Main and Sub counters. You can select either of the time scales from the transport by clicking on the Down Arrow located next to the respective counter and then selecting the desired value. When the time scale is set from either the basic or the main transport, the chosen time scale is applied to the entire session and not just the transport from which you select the time scale.

RULER VIEWS

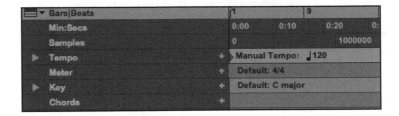

The Ruler view provides an additional way to help navigate along the timeline. All time formats can be viewed from the Ruler, not just the time formats set in the Main and Sub scales. The Ruler view is located in the timeline just above the Edit window. You can choose exactly what you would like to see above the timeline by going to the View menu and selecting Rulers. Or you can click on the Ruler view located just underneath the mode selector buttons and select desired ruler views from the pop-up menu. Certain Ruler views listed below will not be included in the graphic for this section because they only come with upgraded additions of Pro Tools LE or they are included with HD systems only. I've included them in the text to give you an awareness of some of the upgrade features that are available to you.

Bars|Beats

This view is primarily for musicians, music editors, and composers who like to have quick reference to the bars and beats by looking just above the timeline.

Min:Secs

This is for people who like to use absolute time. It is commonly used in radio. Using the Min:Secs function in the Sub counter is usually efficient for having quick reference to absolute time, but use whatever works best for you.

Samples

This is an uncommon view for most music applications. This is Pro Tools' highest resolution for editing and comes in handy when doing some tedious editing functions and fixing track offsets to compensate for plug-in latency.

Timecode

This function is used for professional music applications when synchronizing multiple machines. Its main use is for video and film postproduction. It is a standard option for HD systems and comes with the DV Toolkit upgrade. It is not a feature of the LE and M-Powered Pro Tools.

Feet + Frames

This is another view used primarily in video and film postproduction and is available or HD systems or as an LE DV Toolkit upgrade.

Tempo

This ruler view gives a visual representation of the custom tempo map settings. With each tempo change in the session, you will notice a visual confirmation of the change within the Tempo Ruler view.

Meter

This indicates changes in the time signature and tempo changes in the timeline of the session. Pro Tools software refers to time signature changes and tempo changes as "meter changes." If you are coming from a musical background and are using tempo changes or time signatures changes that are not considered "common time," or 4/4 time, realize that both Meter and Meter Change imply time signature setting and tempo changes. They are the same thing.

Key

The Key ruler added in version 7.3 allows you to import and export key signatures into your session using either the add button, located just to the right of the key signature ruler, or by Control-clicking directly in the ruler. Once you make this selection, the Key Change dialog box appears. From this window, you can select the major or minor key. Using the Snap To Bar option is nice, and you can select the Edit Pitched Track option. Both MIDI and instrument tracks have a pitch-track feature, which allows them to be transposed to accommodate any key changes that may have been added to the song after the parts were already played and recorded in the session. You can also choose to transpose your pitched tracks up or down in pitch and apply pitch function either diatonically or chromatically. When using this feature, make sure your MIDI drum tracks have this option disabled so that no transposition of the drums will occur.

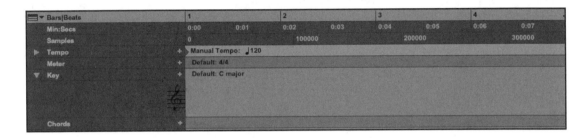

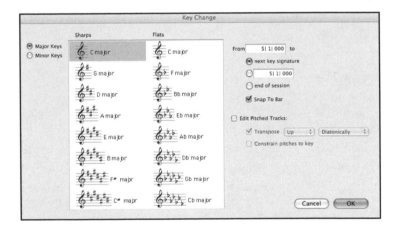

Chords Ruler

The addition of the Chords ruler in version 8 allows you to add, change, move, and delete chord symbols along the timeline. You can specify the root note of the chord, its quality, the voicing or inversion of the chord, and even a desired chord fingering configuration diagram if you wish.

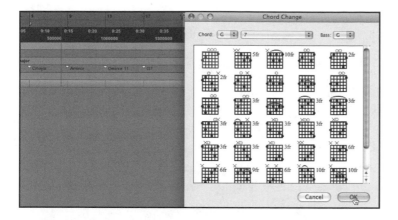

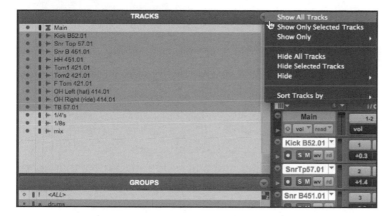

EDIT WINDOW SIDE COLUMNS

Side columns can be found on the left and right side of the Edit window, and they provide additional view and display options for your session content. The left side column shows information regarding the tracks. The track list shows all tracks in the current session, their type, and their Show and Hide status. Each track can be shown or hidden by clicking on the desired track. You can choose several other options by clicking on the track's pop-up menu at the top of the track list. Just underneath the Tracks, you will find the Groups. Groups also has several options to choose from by clicking on the Edit Groups pop-up list menu located at the top of Groups.

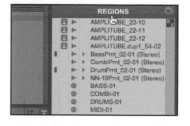

Along the right side of the Edit window, you will see a side column that shows the Regions list. This column shows audio

and MIDI files, and all file segments (regions) that are available in the current session. You can collapse these columns by clicking on the double arrows located near the bottom of the columns allowing you more Edit window coverage. If you would still like to see some of the column views, you can customize the width by positioning the cursor over the column separator. When you see the double-headed arrow, just click-and-drag it to the desired width. New zoom features in Pro Tools 8 have vertical and horizontal zoom buttons that can be found in the lower-right corner of the Edit window. Audio and MIDI Zoom In and Out buttons are in the upper-right corner of the Edit window.

MIX WINDOW

This window will be most familiar to audio engineers because of its mixer and multitrack combination environment. The tracks are displayed from left to right and look like traditional channel strips, with common options such as inserts for dynamic processing, sends for time-based effects and independent headphone mixes, input and output routing, automation mode selectors, pan sliders, and volume faders. In addition, users have access to solo and mute toggles, record enable, track names, voice assignments, and mix group assignments. You can even use color selections to organize your tracks to the highest level. Here is a brief description of each section in the channel strip in the Mix window. We will start at the top of the strip.

THE CHANNEL STRIP

Inserts

There are now ten insert points per channel in Pro Tools 8. These are used to insert dynamic processors such as EQ, compression, gating, and many other plug-in choices. Clicking on the Up and Down Arrows will activate the plug-in drop-down menu. This is where you will see a list of plug-ins that have been installed and authorized on your computer. You can set them up to be viewed by category, manufacturer, or both. They can also be viewed as a flat list.

Sends

There are ten sends per channel strip. Sends are typically used for busing (sending) an extra output of a dry signal on a channel into the input of an aux track that is set up to receive the input on the same bus. The aux track usually has a time-based effects processor such as reverb, delay, or chorus effect on its insert. The volume output of the effect is controlled by the aux input fader's volume position. Sends are also commonly used to send independent headphone mixes to artists when you are recording them. In this configuration, the sends are sent directly to one of your interface's outputs and routed to a headphone amp, and then sent to the artist. As with any professional aux send, they can be sent prefader for true independent mixes or when using creative effects-processing techniques.

Input and Output Selectors

The input and output selectors are chosen based on the type of track and how they are being used. In their simplest form, the input and output selectors allow you to set which input will receive live audio and which channels will be used to send audio to a mixer, a control room, or a headphone amplifier. They can be also used as independent outputs that are used for internal submix routing. If you look closely, you will see a little minifader. This is your audio window button. Click on it and a floating fader pops up with a few more options for panning.

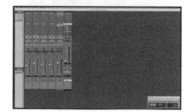

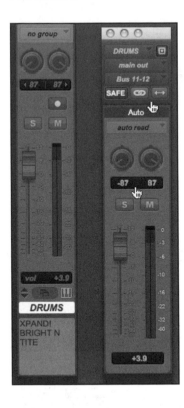

Automation Status Selectors

This is where you choose the type of automation you will be using and where you record enable the automation features in Pro Tools.

Pan Sliders

The pan sliders are used to select the output positioning of the audio in the stereo field. Simply click-and-drag them to the desired position and enjoy the wonders of stereo panning. Holding down the Command key while dragging to the left or right allows you to fine-tune the positioning of the audio in smaller increments. If you have selected the floating-fader window option, notice the chain-link and the double-arrow icons. When selected, they will link panning or imaging perfectly. The importance of taking the necessary time to listen closely to where you place various instruments in your mixes is really underrated. You should take the time to audition several panning arrangements and stop when you feel you've achieved the right placement for the song.

Record Enable, Solo, and Mute Buttons

These buttons activate common features found on traditional multitrack recorders and mixing consoles. Simply click on them to activate either their on or their off status. Solo a track when you would like to isolate that particular instrument in the mix. Mute the track when you do not want to hear it while all other tracks are playing. Record enabling is used when recording live instruments, instrument tracks, or MIDI tracks.

Volume Fader

The volume fader position determines how much of the signal in the channel is being sent to its selected outputs. You can always set the fader to unity gain by holding the Option key and clicking on the fader. Holding the Command key while moving the fader up and down allows minimal gain adjustments of the output level of the channel.

Also located near the bottom of the volume-fader section are track type indicators, active, and inactive track selection. At the very bottom of the channel, you have a place to name the channel and select a color scheme for that channel or group of channels. There is also a comments box. This box is for making channel-specific notes regarding information about mic choice, effects choices, performance notes, or whatever else will help you keep organized during your session. Make a mental note of the various right-click functions that have been added. You access these features by right-clicking on the channel's name.

MAKE ROOM FOR DESSERT

Now that I have gone over the major components of the Transport, Mix, and Edit windows, it is important to go over just a few more things to get you off to a good start and finish up this crash-course chapter right. If you are comfortable and familiar with everything up to this point, that's great. If you feel a little bit behind, feel free to reread the previous chapters until you understand them and can answer all of the questions in the Pro Tools Tune-up section at the end of each chapter. Try to learn all of the information in these chapters inside and out, but if you can ace the Pro Tools Tune-up questions and have watched the QuickTime demos that apply up to this point, it is safe to say that you can move on with your training.

CREATING NEW TRACKS

Creating new tracks is as simple as clicking on the Track menu and selecting New Track. A menu will come up, and you will need to decide not only how many tracks to use but also what type. You can also use the keyboard shortcut Command + Shift + N.

TRACK TYPES

Various types of tracks can be created in any given Pro Tools session. The track types supported in Pro Tools 8 include the following:

Audio Track

The Audio Track allows you to import, record, and edit audio files as a waveform. Audio tracks can be mono, stereo, or any other multichannel format in Pro Tools 8. You now have up to 48 mono or stereo audio tracks on an LE system, or with the Music Production or DV Toolkit 2 installed, you can have up to 64 mono or stereo audio tracks at 48 kHz or 48 mono or stereo tracks at 96 kHz. Pro Tools 8 also supports mixed audio file formats, and LE can give you up to 20 5.1 surround tracks with the new Music Production Toolkit 2.

Pro Tools version 7.4 added the ability to treat audio as if it were MIDI, allowing you to slow down or speed up the tempo of an audio file without affecting the pitch. It even quantizes audio with great results. You will notice that in the Track Control area of an Audio Track in Pro Tools 8, you can choose from the original four Elastic Audio algorithms as well as one brand-new algorithm. All of the Elastic Audio algorithms have improved sonically. We will take a closer look at these awesome features in the Elastic Audio section of this book.

Aux Input

The Aux Input option can be used in a number of ways, including to monitor the input of a live track or the destination of internally routed submixes, or as a standard effects return. Auxiliary inputs can be in mono, stereo, or any supported multichannel format (HD only).

Master Fader

The Master Fader controls the overall output of tracks that are being routed to it. Master faders are postfader outputs, so changing the level of the master fader changes the volume that is sent to its selected output. It also changes the amount of output being sent to the processing inserted on its channel. This can be a nuisance when you are mastering projects and you need the output of the track to be processed all the way through its fade-out. I'll go over certain techniques on how to work around this situation in the section of this book about mastering.

MIDI Track

The MIDI Track option stores and records note and controller data. You can import and export MIDI and edit it in a variety of ways. MIDI tracks are data only and contain no audio, so there is no need to specify a track format. Pro Tools 8 has some incredible new MIDI editing features and a brand-new MIDI and Score Editor window to work from.

Instrument Track

The Instrument Track combines the function of Aux Input and MIDI Track. Using the Instrument Track option provides the quickest way to record MIDI information with soft synths, virtual instruments, sound modules, or any other type of MIDI controller. Later in this book we will cover some of the new bundled virtual instruments from AIR and dig into the new creation possibilities with Pro Tools 8.

CLICK TRACK

You can use a mono aux track to set up a click track by clicking on an Insert, selecting the Instrument category, and then choosing Click Track. You can also simply go to the Track menu and select Click Track. You can change the default sound of the click track by clicking on the factory default option on the click plug-in.

You can also change the sound of the click track by using the plus or minus tabs next to where it says "factory default." You can set the tempo of the click track by turning off the Conductor in the transport and entering your own value in the beats-per-minute area. If you do not know the tempo of the song, you can tap the tempo in by leaving the Conductor turned off, highlighting the BPM box, and tapping on the T key at the desired tempo. There are many other things to know about how a simple click track works in Pro Tools. Knowing a few handy features of the Click Track will often prove significant when you encounter songs with different tempo changes or with time-signature changes within the song.

MEMORY LOCATIONS

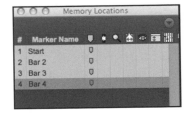

Memory locations are used for a number of reasons and are commonly referred to as "markers." Markers are usually set for the different parts of a song such as the intro, verse, and chorus. You can use markers to quickly access these parts in the song, create loops for overdubbing, and use specific custom views. You can access the Memory Locations by using the Windows menu and selecting Memory Locations or by using the keyboard shortcut Command + 5.

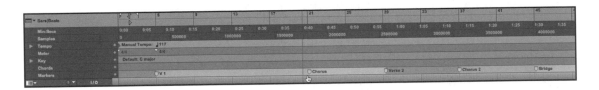

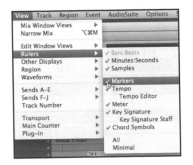

You can also use the Markers Ruler view by navigating to the View menu, selecting Rulers, and choosing Markers.

From either view, you can click on the markers you created and the play-head will snap to that location. Clicking on a marker and then holding the Shift key while clicking on a second marker will highlight the selection between the chosen markers. You can quickly loop this selection by holding down the Ctrl button and clicking on the Play button on the transport.

Memory locations are very underrated, and their powerful navigation and viewing assistance is commonly overlooked. We will go over the many benefits of using memory locations in many different ways in various chapters of this book.

SCROLL OPTIONS

Pro Tools offers a few choices when it comes to scrolling options. LE and M-Powered systems do not have as many options as do HD systems, but here are the ones you need to know on an LE or M-Powered system.

No Scrolling

The No Scrolling option means that when the cursor moves off the screen in the Edit window, Pro Tools does not reposition the waveform.

After Playback

When you use the After Playback option, no scrolling will take place while the track is playing or being recorded. When playback is stopped, Pro Tools will reposition the waveform display to match the point in the file at which playback stopped.

Page

When the Page option is selected, Pro Tools will update the Edit window each time the cursor reaches the far-right end of the window. The Edit window follows the cursor, turning the page.

POWER TIPS SUMMARY FOR CHAPTER 3

1. Get into the habit of selecting 44.1, 88.2, or 176.4 kHz (HD only) as your sampling rate. Sampling rates that are

divisible by 44.1 kHz are the best choices for audio sessions. If your project is for broadcast audio DVD or film, then 48, 96, or 192 kHz (HD only) is the best way to go. The idea is to have the computer perform the easiest mathematical calculations possible during the conversion. Some experts say that there is an audible difference.

2. If you have a large hard drive (250 GB or more), consider dividing it into a few partitions. Since the computer sees each partition as a separate drive, Pro Tools can perform a much faster scan of the audio drive to play back or record audio because there have been custom size boundaries set for each partition.

3. If you use one of the partitions on the external drive to store your loops and samples, you can bring your custom sounds with you. You can also save a copy of your own personal plug-in settings folder and plug-in installers in this drive. If you are the freelance engineer type, having your custom sounds and plug-in settings with you at all times is invaluable and sets you apart from the average user. Just remember proper "traveling plug-in etiquette."

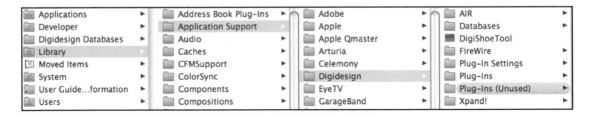

4. Another way to optimize the performance of a hard drive for Pro Tools is to go to Setup menu, select the Preferences option, and then click on the Operation tab. In the Open-Ended Record Allocation section, select the Limit To option and choose the longest duration you think you will need while recording your audio files. This allows Pro Tools to use only as much RAM as necessary for this function.

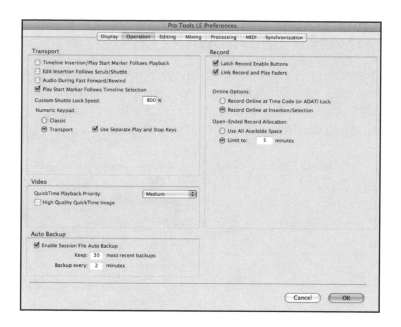

5. There is a small Mixer icon in the lower left-hand side of the Mix window. If you click on this icon, you have the ability to quickly select the configuration of the channel strip. This is a useful function when you want to customize your view of the channel strip.

6. When you are starting a creative session and you would like to record in Grid mode, it is very important that you record your instruments to a click track. If you do not know the tempo of the song yet but you have a feel for the song's bpm, you can tap in the tempo. This is done by turning off the Conductor in the Main transport, highlighting the BPM Tempo box, and using the T key on your QWERTY keyboard to manually tap in the tempo of the song. The grid will conform to the tempo you tap into the sequencer.

7. It is handy to work with the Scroll options set to No Scrolling. However, the Edit window does not update when the curser passes the end of the window. If this is bothersome for you, click on the Left Arrow on your keyboard to update the screen once playback has stopped.

KEYBOARD SHORTCUT SUMMARY FOR CHAPTER 3

Here is a list of some of the Pro Tools keyboard shortcuts that were mentioned in this chapter. There are also some shortcuts on this list that were not covered in the text, but that will be used in the QuickTime tutorials accompanying this chapter.

KEYBOARD SHORTCUT	FUNCTION
Spacebar	Starts and stops playback
0 (numeric keypad)	Starts and stops playback
1 (numeric keypad)	Rewind function of the transport
2 (numeric keypad)	Fast-forward function of the transport
3 (numeric keypad)	Starts and stops recording
4 (numeric keypad)	Loops playback of selected area
Command + S	Saves Pro Tools session in its current state
Command + X	Cuts the selection
Command + C	Copies the selection
Command + V	Pastes the selection
Command + N	Creates a new session
Command + =	Toggles between Mix and Edit windows
Command + 1 (numeric keypad)	Toggles Transport window
Command + 3 (numeric keypad)	Toggles Big Counter on and off
Command + 5 (numeric keypad)	Toggles Memory Location box on and off

PRO TOOLS TUNE-UP
FOR CHAPTER 3

1. To create a new, empty Pro Tools session, you must first launch the program, then choose the _____ option from the Quick Start menu.

2. Your first priority after creating a new session should be to give the session a name and specify where it should be _____.

3. When storing your Pro Tools session, it is best to store it on a hard drive that is _____ for audio recording and playback.

4. The final three options that you must choose to successfully create your new Pro Tools session are

    a. _____

    b. _____

    c. _____

5. The lowest sampling rate that is most commonly used for music applications is _____.

6. The most standard file format in Pro Tools for cross-compatibility is _____.

7. All Pro Tools session files are saved in your Session folder and are easily identifiable by the Pro Tools Session icon and the _____ extension.

8. The folder inside your Session folder that contains all of the audio for that particular session is called the _____.

9. The folder that contains all of the information about volume fade-ins, fade-outs, and crossfades is called the _____.

10. When experiencing an intolerable amount of latency or delay when recording live input sources, you should go to the Setup menu, choose Playback Engine, and _____ the Hardware Buffer Size.

11. Use a higher hardware buffer size when your session has a very high track count or there are quite a few instantiations of _____.

12. _____ the CPU Usage options in your Hardware Setups is a good idea when you are running other software in addition to Pro Tools.

13. The _____ menu is used to save, close, create copies of your work, and execute many other valuable session options.

14. The _____ menu is used to create new tracks, delete tracks, group tracks, and many other valuable session options.

15. The _____ menu is used to quickly access important Pro Tools documentation.

16. The _____ window and the _____ window are the two main windows in Pro Tools.

17. Name the four edit modes in Pro Tools.

    a. _____

    b. _____

    c. _____

    d. _____

18. Out of the four available edit modes, _____ mode is the most useful when the Main or Sub time scale is set to Bars|Beats.

19. There are a total of seven edit tools available in Pro Tools. The Smart tool is a combination of which three main edit tools and is capable of performing which commonly used editing function?

    a. _____

    b. _____

    c. _____

    d. _____

20. The Main Transport can be accessed by going to the
    _____ menu.

21. Controls to expand the Main Transport (for showing the
    counters along with other Pro Tools MIDI functions) can be
    accessed in the _____ menu or by selecting
    the Transport option.

22. The Edit window contains two columns located on the left
    and right sides. The column on the left side shows information
    regarding the _____ and the
    Groups List. The column that is located along the right
    side of the Edit window shows information regarding the
    _____.

23. There are a total of _____ inserts per
    channel.

24. There are a total of _____ sends per channel.

25. There are a total of five Track Types that can be created in a
    Pro Tools session. They are

    a. _____

    b. _____

    c. _____

    d. _____

    e. _____

Igniting Your
Pro Tools System

4

ONCE AROUND THE BLOCK

In the previous chapter, I gave a thorough analysis of Pro Tools'
two main windows and pointed out some of the changes that
have been made to them in version 8. All the essential elements
of a basic Pro Tools session were covered and explained. It is
important that you understood what you read and were able
to answer the Pro Tools Tune-up questions at the end of the
chapter. In this chapter, I'll show you how to open up a session,
create several track types, and do a system check. Think of this as
taking your system once around the block. It is very important
that all of the right connections have been made and that the
software, computer, and its peripheral devices are responding
properly and are set up for maximum efficiency.

Pro Tools, now more than ever with version 8, is designed to
be a creative environment, and nothing kills a creative moment
more than having to troubleshoot every five minutes or work
with a session that's so disorganized that it impedes the creative
work flow. Pro Tools comes bundled with plenty of third-
party plug-ins that have almost every Digidesign hardware and
software configuration available. I am using an Mbox 2 for the
production of this book, and it came with the Ignition Pack 2.
Most of you have probably recently upgraded to Pro Tools 8 and
want to learn about all the new virtual instruments that come

with the upgrade, but it would be a shame if you didn't take advantage of the bonus software you already have, too. Although I'll cover the new Creative Collection additions in Pro Tools 8, I suggest that you put in the extra effort to get the most out of the Ignition Pack you already have. When you register all of your software, check to see if it is authorized, connected, and working properly; you will save yourself from many frustrating moments that would only have a negative impact on your creativity and perhaps even your bank account.

If you are trying to earn a living as a recording engineer, you'll find that many artists will be using different versions of Pro Tools software, and your studio should therefore be set up to accommodate sessions that use typical third-party software that comes bundled with Pro Tools. Remember, your goal is to be an extension of the artist's creativity and to capture them "in the moment." You should be able to organize things "on the fly"—that is, quickly and effectively. It can be embarrassing if an artist comes to your studio to do some recording or mixing, and they have to wait a long time while you stop and fix something or set something up every time they make a simple request. However, if you can fulfill their requests without any hang-ups in your system and you have the chops as a Pro Tools operator to provide them with what they want, when they want, there is a good chance they will keep coming to you for your engineering skills. You never know what an artist will ask you to do when they are working, so it's wise to make sure that every aspect of your system is functioning and your basic skills are up to speed before a client ever steps into your studio. Studying the information in this book will give you more knowledge to draw on when you run into a difficult situation. Even if you don't have memorized all of this information, remember that you can always use this book as a quick reference on such occasions.

Throughout this chapter, you will continue to learn more ways to navigate the Pro Tools software using keyboard shortcuts. You will develop troubleshooting skills and organization habits that should be in your skill set regardless of your Pro Tools skill level.

With that in mind, it is time to get back to learning about the essential elements in Pro Tools that are required to run a Pro Tools session and how to use some of the bundled software that comes with it.

OBJECTIVES FOR THIS CHAPTER

- Optimize session settings
- Understand Grid mode setup
- Create and use various track types
- Set up a MIDI keyboard using AMS
- Set up USB MIDI controllers
- Use sounds with Xpand
- Use Reason with Pro Tools via ReWire
- Troubleshoot common problems when using controllers

OPTIMIZING YOUR SESSION AND DOING A SYSTEM CHECK

Whether you are setting up your own Pro Tools system for the first time, updating your existing system, or setting up a Pro Tools studio for a client, you will want to develop a setup "checklist" or routine that is thorough, but not so boring that you hate doing it. Pro Tools can always be fun, even when you are doing a boring, periodical system update. In this next section, I will show you a basic routine to use when setting up a typical, small production studio that includes an LE system, a MIDI controller, and a MIDI keyboard. You can expect to have some problems that will need to be solved, but using this method will allow you to have a little fun while you are solving them, because you are basically creating a new session and making sure everything you would need for the session works properly. Having a setup routine that you do the same way every time will not only make you faster at it, but you'll find that there will be less frustration because you will start anticipating potential problems before they come up and you'll be prepared for them. You'll notice your trouble-shooting skills and your confidence will increase the more you do it.

Start by launching Pro Tools. Select the Create Blank Session option from the new Quick Start feature in Pro Tools 8 and set up the session for a standard music production. Name the session "Igniting Pro Tools," and make sure it is being stored on your external FireWire drive. Choose BWF for the file type, 44.1 kHz as the sampling rate, and 24-bit for the bit depth. Once the session opens, navigate to the Setup menu and select the Hardware option. Verify that your interface is being recognized, the Clock Source is set to Internal, and the Sampling Rate is set at whatever was selected earlier (in this case, 44.1 kHz).

Next, go to the Playback Engine from the Setup menu and set your H/W Buffer Size. A good number to start with is 256 MB. You can always adjust these settings as the session progresses if you need to. Select the number of computer processors you would like to use for RTAS processing. I am using an iMac with a 2 GHz Intel Core 2 Duo processor and 4 GB of RAM for all material in this chapter, so I will select a two-processor configuration. Since I have decent processing power, I will set the CPU usage limit to 75 percent. This allows the Pro Tools software exclusive use of 75 percent of my computer's resources and leaves the other 25 percent for other computer programs I may have running in the background. I generally use the default settings for the DAE Playback Buffer size. These settings vary from computer to computer, so use the settings that work best for your system.

New enhancements to the Playback Engine were introduced in version 7.4, and they enabled you to dial in custom settings that would improve your system's performance. All options in the Playback Engine menu are typically determined by the type of session you will be setting up. For instance, if you are recording several virtual instrument parts, select the RTAS Engine box. You will get better performance out of your computer, but the quality of your audio will decrease. That is okay, because after you capture the performance of the artist, you can regain the audio quality by turning this option off.

You will also notice that the DAE Playback Buffer Size now shows in milliseconds the amount of audio that is buffered when your system reads from the hard drive. Suggested settings for the DAE Playback Buffer can be found at the bottom of the dialog box; the suggested settings will help you choose wisely for the type of session you are working with.

The last option is the Cache Size. This is important if you are using Elastic Audio features in Pro Tools. If you select the Minimum setting, the performance of your Elastic Audio features may decrease, but it will free up memory for other system tasks such as your RTAS processing. On the other hand, if you are using a lot of Elastic Time in your session, you may want to choose a higher cache size to take advantage of the new Elastic Time features. Keep in mind that your RTAS performance will decrease at higher cache settings. Since this session is being done primarily to make sure that everything is set up properly (and therefore, there won't be any Elastic Time features being used), simply go with the default settings. After the Playback Engine and Hardware settings are in order, dig in a little deeper and optimize the hard drive. To do this, go to the Setup menu again, choose the Preferences option, and select the Operations tab. Under the Record settings, set the number of minutes you'll need Pro Tools to record at any one time. I find that a setting of five to eight minutes for this type of session is plenty.

While you are still in the Operations tab, enable the Session File Auto Backup feature. This is a very valuable feature and takes up only a small amount of your system resources. I usually set it to keep 30 of my most recent backups every two to five minutes. This assures me that I will have access to my last one to two-and-a-half hours of work in case anything unexpected such as a power failure or computer crash happens. Setting up the number of sessions and the regularity of your auto backup is a matter of personal preference. The important thing is that you set it up and turn it on. I was a victim of many sessions that unexpectedly quit back when this feature wasn't an option. There is no excuse not to use this safety precaution.

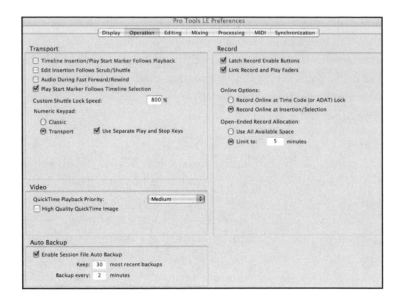

GRID LOCKED

In this next section, make sure that you are in Grid mode, and then configure some of the settings that support it, such as the Grid Value and Nudge Value settings. Although you are primarily running a systems connection-check session for our Audio MIDI setup and USB controller connections, you will be using Grid mode a lot in this book. By starting with this session in Grid mode, you will begin to see the power of working with the grid right away.

Grid Mode

From the Edit window toolbar, choose Grid mode by clicking on it, using the F4 key, or pressing the tilde symbol (~) located below the Escape key on your computer keyboard to toggle through the modes until Grid is selected.

Grid Value

To select the grid value, use the Grid Value drop-down menu located just to the right of the Main And Sub Counters window, choose the Bars|Beats view option, and then select the note value you would like to use. This means that if you select a grid value of quarter notes, you will see four subdivisions between every bar line in the Track Display area. If for some reason you do not see any grid lines, first make sure that you are in Grid mode. If Grid mode is confirmed and you still have no grid lines, you may need to click on the Bars|Beats selection box just to the right of the Track Lists drop-down menu on the left-hand side of the Edit window. Clicking on this box toggles the status of the grid lines on and off.

I generally go with a grid value of 16th notes when I'm starting a new session. You can either follow along with what I do or choose the settings you prefer. You will also notice that you have a few choices for grid values. In addition to Bars|Beats, you have Min:Secs, Samples, and Regions/Markers. Music productions tend to work well with the grid values set to Bars|Beats or with the Region/Markers functions selected. If you haven't used Grid mode much in the past, I highly recommend that you start using it now. Almost everything you do for music production in Pro Tools should be based around the grid.

Nudge Value

The nudge value represents the horizontal movement of a selected region when using the plus and minus keys on the numeric keypad. This is a nice function to use when you are arranging or editing in Grid mode. There are a few options to choose from in the Nudge Value drop-down menu. You can select Bars|Beats, Min:Secs, Samples, or Feet:Frames (in Pro Tools HD only). Once again, Bars|Beats is great to use when working in Grid mode. Even if you are in any mode other than Grid, the nudge value still maintains movement, using the chosen note value.

Most of the other options available are for film and postproduction types of editing and mixing, in which they are lining up to frames or things need to be based on absolute time. For now, I'll use a nudge value of 16th notes to match the grid resolution.

CREATING THE TRACKS

Once your session is optimized and set up in Grid mode, it's time to create some tracks. In this chapter, we will create several tracks and make sure that all of their basic functions are in fine working order. You can always use the File menu to create new tracks, but try getting used to the keyboard shortcut (Command + Shift + N) and the suggested keyboard shortcuts for your choice of track type and format. When creating your new tracks, notice that if you use the plus sign located on the far right of the New Tracks dialog box, you can add more than just one track type, format, or time base simultaneously. For an even quicker way of creating multiple track types and formats, look at the QuickTime video example associated with this chapter.

Track List

Let's start by creating the following track list:

- 4 stereo instrument tracks
- 1 MIDI track for an external MIDI keyboard
- 1 mono aux input
- 1 stereo master fader

Naming and Organizing Your Tracks

After creating your new tracks, it's good to get into the habit of naming them, making any necessary comments for the tracks, and arranging them properly to create a nice workflow. You can do this from either the Edit or the Mix windows. To name the track, double-click on the track name, type in a new name, and then click on OK. If you would like to name all of the tracks without having to double-click on the track name every time, simply double-click on the first one, name it, then hold down the Command key and select either the Left or the Right Arrow key on the computer keyboard to go to either the next track or the previous track. Continue naming the additional tracks until you are finished. You can also click on the Comments box and enter track notes. If the Comments box is hidden, you can add it to the Mix window by clicking on the Mini Mixer icon on the lower-left side of the Mix window. If you are in the Edit window, select the Edit Window option from the View menu, and choose Comments.

To arrange or move a track, single-click on the desired track's name and drag it left or right. Let it go where you would like the track to sit. You can select and move multiple tracks by clicking on the first track, and then holding the Shift key and clicking on any additional tracks. If the tracks that you would like to select are more than one track away from each other, you can Command-click to highlight any track, in any order.

Since several track types and formats have been created at one time, you should get used to using the track indicators to identify one track type from another. Here is an example of each of the track indicators. You should have no problem identifying any track type or format.

If you go to the Edit window, you will now notice the track list located on the left of the Track Display area. You can also see the Track Indicator icons next the names of the tracks on the track list. Remember, clicking on any of the tracks from the Tracks list will show or hide any of the tracks in the Track Display area and from the Mix window. Note that when you hide a track, it does not mean it will not be audible just because it is hidden. If you would like the track to be hidden and not be heard, you must make sure to mute or make the track inactive before you hide it.

To make the track inactive from the Edit window, simply right-click on the track name and select the Make Inactive option. Notice that you can choose Hide and Make Inactive in one shot. From the Mix window, you can click on the track indicator. From there, you will have the choice to make the track active or inactive, depending on the status of the track, or you can simply right-click on the track name again and choose Hide and Make Inactive from there.

When you have created more tracks than you need, you can delete any track by using the Track menu and selecting Delete, but since version 7.3, the right-click functionality makes this even easier. Just right-click on the track name and choose Delete. It is important to have only the desired track or tracks highlighted when deleting, because any track that is highlighted will be deleted when you choose this function. Since we aren't going to use the Mono Aux Input we made earlier, let's delete that track now.

Okay, now that you have created your tracks, you should have an external MIDI keyboard or other controller to record MIDI data onto the MIDI and instrument tracks you just created. I will talk about entering MIDI data without a controller in later chapters, but for now, I'll talk about MIDI keyboards and controllers and how to make sure they are ready to use with your system.

AUDIO MIDI SETUP

Mac OS X–based computers use what is referred to as the AMS or Audio MIDI Setup, which is located in the Utilities folder inside the main Applications folder. You have access to it from inside Pro Tools by going to the Setup menu and selecting MIDI, and then choosing MIDI Studio.

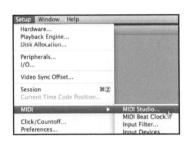

There you will see a few icons that confirm the MIDI devices connected to your system. Since I am using an Mbox 2 and an M-Audio/Axiom 49 Keyboard controller, you can see these listed in my AMS.

If you have been making music using DAWs for a while, you may still have your favorite MIDI keyboards, with sounds you are used to and patches that you like use. To use your keyboard inside of Pro Tools, you must add it to your AMS by doing the following things.

From the Audio MIDI Setup dialog box, select Add Device. A new external device will be created, and now you need to set up your device Properties and customize your keyboard's functionality. To do this, you must double-click on the new External Device icon, and the Properties for that device will appear. In the Device Name field, type in the name (My MIDI Keyboard). Next, from the Manufacturer drop-down menu, you can choose the manufacturer of your keyboard. For example, I am using a Triton Studio, and so I will select Korg. Next, I will choose the model (Triton Studio), and then click on the Icon Browser and select the icon that resembles a Triton.

To further customize the functionality of the newly added device, click on the tab that says More Information. This opens up a dialog box that allows you to select various functions that are vital to the keyboard's operations with Pro Tools. From the Transmit and Receives sections, apply the specific channel numbers on which you would like your keyboard to transmit and receive MIDI data. Selecting all of the channels is a good idea, so that you can send and receive MIDI data over any channel at any time. Selecting the MIDI Beat Clock (MBC) and MIDI Time Code (MTC) options in both areas is also a good idea. This allows you to synchronize your keyboard with Pro Tools in both directions.

For instance, if you have a sequence stored on your keyboard and you would like to record the MIDI data into Pro Tools and have it locked to the Pro Tools Grid, you will need these functions turned on in the Transmit section. On the other hand, if you would like to press Play in Pro Tools and have it control the start/stop function of your keyboard's sequencer, you will need these options on in the Receive area.

Last, you need to use the In and Out arrows from your new device to connect it to the MIDI Interface icon. To do this, click on the

Up Arrow of the newly added device and, while holding the mouse down, drag it to the Up Arrow of your MIDI interface. Also, test your system to make sure that the MIDI cables going to and from your MIDI interface and keyboard are connected properly.

To test your connections, navigate to the Test Setup icon in the upper-right section of AMS and click on it. Once it is activated (indicated by turning blue), press a key on your MIDI keyboard and you should hear a General MIDI tone that indicates the device is connected properly. Keep in mind that various MIDI keyboards have their own set of global menu MIDI functions that allow them to communicate with other MIDI devices. You have to make sure that you know how to use these functions on your keyboard if you want it to work properly with Pro Tools. If the setup you've just gone through isn't successful, delete the device in AMS and start the process over. If your keyboard still doesn't respond properly with AMS for functionality in Pro Tools after the second or third time, you probably need to refer to your keyboard's manual. Try looking under the MIDI functions, transmitting data, or channel off and on information.

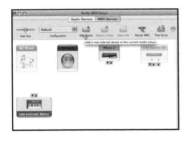

USB CONTROLLERS

There are many MIDI controllers around these days, and nearly all of them are plug-n-play. You plug the controller in, and start playing it to record your music. MIDI controllers in today's market come in many configurations, from simple keyboard controllers to keyboard controllers with trigger pads, assignable knobs, faders, pitch-bend and mod wheels, and transport controls. There are also many fine MIDI guitar controllers for those of us who are keyboard-challenged guitar players, and there are even breath controllers for humanizing your wind-instrument parts.

Making the USB Connection

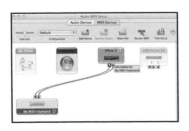

Connecting a USB MIDI controller can't get much easier. Simply connect it to the computer using a USB cable, and make sure that the keyboard powers up. Some USB controllers have an on/off switch, so make sure it is turned on. Others turn on automatically when they receive power. For controllers that do not require an adapter and use the power of the computer, it is always best if you connect through a powered USB hub or a dedicated USB port on your computer. Stay away from connecting it using your keyboard or monitor if possible. If your controller requires an external power supply, use the one that came with your controller or make sure that you buy the one made specifically for your model. A CD with drivers usually comes with your new controller, but is hardly ever required for installation. Pro Tools recognizes a wide range of various controllers these days, but in the event that it doesn't recognize your device, you can use the CD that came with your controller or download the most current driver from the manufacturer. You will need to go to the Web site for information on availability and instructions on how to do this for your specific controller.

Once the connections have been made and your controller is powered up, you are ready to start enjoying the sounds of some of the software that comes bundled with Pro Tools.

XPANDING YOUR HORIZONS

The original Xpand plug-in, is a virtual instrument that used to be included with all Pro Tools systems and featured 1,000 factory sounds usable in any genre of music. The original Xpand engine had sample playback and frequency modulation (FM), wavetable, and virtual-analogue synth architecture that was capable of creating some very cool sounds quickly and easily. Xpand also featured integrated effects and the ability to play multiple simultaneous patches. Pro Tools 8 comes with Xpand[2], which comes with a hefty 1.5 GB of content—from keyboards to rhythmic loops, guitars, basses, and so on. This book uses the original version of Xpand, but its functionality is almost identical to the new version. I'll take you through the original version, and you can experiment with the new version on your own. Now, let's get started!

Since an instrument track acts as a MIDI track and an aux input simultaneously, instrument tracks are very convenient when you're using plug-in instruments such as Xpand. To

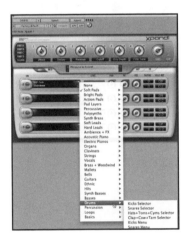

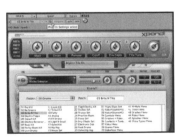

load the Xpand plug-in, go to the Mix window and click on the insert of the first stereo instrument track. Select the Multichannel Plug-in option, and then choose the instrument bank and select Xpand.

Once the plug-in is loaded and appears on your screen, you will notice that it has four synthesizer banks, labeled A though D. Click on the A bank, and it will turn blue; this lets you know the bank is active. Just to the right of the part-name indicator is a Down Arrow that gives you access to all of the user presets the come with the Xpand plug-in. The new version also gives you a MIDI-channel selector just to the right of the bank on/off selector.

When you are selecting a drum kit, it is very convenient to navigate to the top of the plug-in and click on the Patch List browser next to the Librarian menu, just to the right of the plus and minus tabs. If you click on the Folder menu, you will see a long list of categories from which to choose. Select the Drums folder, and select one of the kits from the Patch List menu. In the graphic slightly below at left, you will notice I have selected the Brite N Tite kit.

At this point, you should be able to play your MIDI controller and hear the drum kit you have chosen. If you have a small MIDI controller keyboard that doesn't have a wide range of keys, sometimes certain patches load properly but are not within the range of your controller's default settings. If you load the drums patch and you don't hear anything, find the transpose function on your controller and scroll up or down a few octaves; there is a good chance you will find the range of keys that works for the patch settings you are trying to use. If you still do not hear any sound, go to the Options menu and make sure that MIDI Thru is checked.

If this is not selected, your virtual instrument may detect input but will not let any sounds pass through its output. If you don't see any input on the selected virtual instrument, go to the Setup menu and select MIDI, and then select Input Devices. When the dialog box appears, you should see your controller and any other active controller or MIDI port connected to your computer.

Make sure that there is a check mark next to the controller you are trying to use.

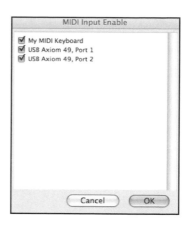

Once your controller is verified and selected, you should be able to hear the drums. Once your drums are loaded on track 1, name the track "Drums" and type in the name of the drum patch you used in the Comments box. Now you can set up the second stereo instrument track. This time you will use the plug-in Copy function to instantiate it on the track. To do this, hold down the Option key, and then click-and-drag the Xpand plug-in that is on the first track over to the second stereo instrument track. The drum kit will still be loaded on it, but now you can go to the second Xpand plug-in on track 2 and change it to a bass patch using the same selection method that you used for choosing your drums patch. Once you find a bass sound you are happy with, name the track "Bass" and type the patch name into the Comments box. Naming the track is obviously a good thing to do to organize your session, but it really comes in handy to enter the specific patch name in the Comments box. This way, if your system loses the sound that is on the track, you can quickly find the sound again. It's much quicker than going through bank after bank and trying to guess which sound is the correct one. If you make a note in the Comments box about which sound you were using, it is easy to remember what it was and where you can find it.

A REASON TO KEEP READING

Reason Adapted for Digidesign software by Propellerhead is a very powerful tool for creating music, and it integrates perfectly with Pro Tools via ReWire. It consists of synths, samplers, drums, and effects that can really jump-start your creativity.

I am assuming that you have taken the extra time to install and activate your Ignition Pack plug-ins; therefore, I will go over a few things inside the Reason software that are helpful when setting up your system. I will discuss how to make sure that your controller will work with Reason, and I will give a few Pro Tools tips on how to set up independent audio channels for each

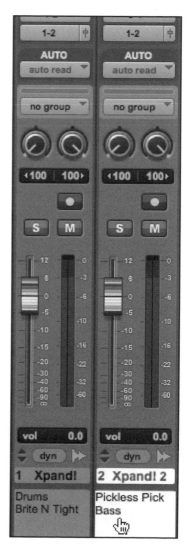

Reason instrument by using multiple ReWire outputs. This will allow you to have greater flexibility when it comes time to mix the track.

I'll start with the MIDI controller setup. To use your MIDI controller with Reason, you should be sure that your controller is being recognized by Reason. To do this, go to the Reason Application window, select the Reason Adapted For Digidesign menu, and select Preferences. There you will see a dialog box with a few selectable options.

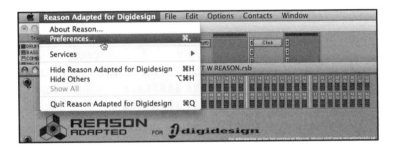

Next, click on General, and choose Control Surfaces And Keyboards.

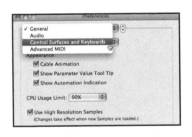

Click on the Auto-detect Surfaces button, and when your controller appears select it to be the master keyboard and check the Use With Reason box.

Your controller will now be able to function with Reason.

Using Reason with Pro Tools

After your controller is functioning properly with Reason, load Reason into the third instrument track the same way you did for Xpand. Reason automatically loads up and engages the ReWire software. Once you are in Reason, you can start adding parts to your session immediately by programming the various Reason instruments from inside the Reason software. However, if you would like to use your MIDI controller to record MIDI directly into Pro Tools, you have the option to do that as well. To use this feature, simply go to the Instrument view on an instrument track and assign its output directly to

Reason, giving you the ability to record MIDI into Pro Tools straight out of Reason with your MIDI controller. To do this, go to your View menu, select the Edit Window Views option, and choose Instruments.

When you can see the Instrument view in the Edit window, click on the MIDI Output selector for the instrument track (where it says None by default), and assign it to the Combinator. Record enable the Combinator track, and you should see MIDI input and hear the Combinator.

Next, create one more Reason instruments on the next stereo instrument track so that you can understand how routing works with ReWire. Select the NN-19 sampler in the Reason software, and choose a sound. Notice that when you play the sound, it is still coming through the instrument track for the Combinator. This is because all instruments in Reason are routed to its mixer by default and are assigned to outputs 1 and 2. You need to take the outputs of the NN-19 sampler and assign them directly to ReWire outputs 3 and 4. To do this from Reason, use the Tab key to get to the back of the virtual rack. There you can see that the outputs of the NN-19 sampler are connected to the mixer, and the mixer is being output to ReWire inputs 1 and 2. Click-and-hold on the outputs of the NN-19 sampler until you see a drop-down menu. When the menu appears, assign the outputs of the NN-19 to Hardware Interface Inputs 3 and 4. Now go back to Pro Tools and click on the second Reason plug-in on the NN-19 instrument track. When the ReWire dialog box comes up, set the outputs to Channel 3–Channel 4.

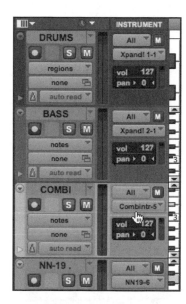

Now you should hear and see your NN-19 sounds on the correct instrument track. Remember to assign the instrument output to NN-19 so that you can record the MIDI data directly into Pro Tools, just as you did for the Combinator earlier in this section.

If you are still unclear about how to do this, the supplied QuickTime tutorial will give you a demonstration on how this works. If you were able to follow along in your "Igniting Pro Tools" session, go ahead and name the Reason tracks and make comments on the patches you used. Then go to Reason and

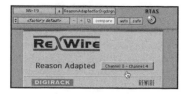

save the Reason session the same way that you save a Pro Tools session: go to the Reason File menu and select Save.

Reason will ask you to name the session, and you will need to tell it where to save your Reason file. I suggest that you save the Reason file in the same folder where your Igniting Pro Tools session is, and that you name your Reason file "Igniting PT w Reason."

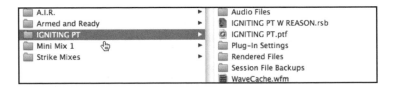

After you save your Reason file, go back to Pro Tools and save the "Igniting Pro Tools" session and get ready for the next chapter.

FINAL THOUGHTS

Keep in mind that the Ignition Pack 2 bundle comes with a few other virtual instruments and plug-ins. When using Analog Factory, BFD Lite, or Digidesign Live, use the same routing techniques with them, too. The same thing applies to Digidesign's complementary Structure Free sampling plug-in. If you find yourself running out of system resources after using several virtual instruments in one session, we will address ways on how you can conserve your CPU power and maximize your system resources.

POWER TIPS SUMMARY FOR CHAPTER 4

1. Using the Ignore Errors During Playback/Record selection is great when you are recording live tracks and using several virtual instruments; the sonic quality goes down a little bit but performance picks up quite a bit. Once you are done recording, you can deselect this option to bring back the

tracks' original sonic quality. This option is selected by going to the Setup menu, choosing the Playback Engine, and selecting the Ignore Errors During Playback/Record in the RTAS engine section.

2. Choosing a higher cache size from the playback engine will increase the functionality of Elastic Audio. Lower settings will allow more RTAS processing.

3. Use the Tilde key located just below the Escape key to toggle through the Edit modes in Pro Tools.

4. Click on the Bars|Beats Ruler view indicator to toggle the on and off status of the grid lines. I know this seems like a simple one, but if you forget about it and you can't see the grid lines when you are editing or doing anything in Grid mode, not knowing how to turn them back on will make you insane.

5. When you are creating new tracks in Pro Tools using the keyboard shortcut Command + Shift + N, you should continue to hold down the Command key and use the Left and Right Arrows to change from stereo to mono tracks. Then use the Up and Down Arrows to select the track type. If you would like to add several track types in a single visit to the New Tracks dialog box, then hold Command + Shift while using the Down Arrow to add more of the next type of track. You can create as many as you need, and using the Command + Up Arrow will take them away. Holding down the Command key and the Option key and using the Up and Down Arrow toggles the Time Base option from Ticks to Samples.

6. Remember to use the Patch List browser when selecting patches in Xpand. It gives a much better view, and the layout is easier to scan in an instant. The Patch List browser is located just to the right of the Librarian menu in the upper-left side of the plug-in.

7. When instantiating the same plug-in on a different track, you can hold down the Option key, click on the plug-in, and drag it to its new destination. You can also make the plug-in inactive

by holding down the Command and Control keys, and then clicking on the plug-in from the Mix window. To bypass it, hold down Command and click on it. The difference between bypass and inactive is that when a plug-in is bypassed, you do not hear it, but it still uses CPU power. If a plug-in is inactive, you don't hear it and it frees up processing power.

8. When using a MIDI controller, make sure that you go to the Setup menu and select MIDI to see if your controller is a listed input device. Also, double-check that the MIDI Thru function is on in the Options menu.

9. If you are selecting drum kits from various plug-in instruments, sometimes the patches load properly but your MIDI keyboard is set up in the wrong MIDI zone or range. Use the Transpose function on your controller to scroll through the different octaves, and you will probably find the drum patches that weren't triggering. This happens a lot with controllers that have very few keys.

10. You can record MIDI into Pro Tools straight out of Reason with your MIDI controller. To do this, go to the View menu and select the Instruments view from either the Mix or the Edit window, set the outputs of the instrument track to the desired Reason instrument, and you are on your way. Remember, if you want to hear the Reason instruments individually, you have to assign them in Reason to individual hardware-device outputs and assign ReWire to the corresponding outputs.

KEYBOARD SHORTCUT SUMMARY FOR CHAPTER 4

Here is a list of some keyboard shortcuts that are either mentioned in the text or used in the QuickTime tutorials that accompany this chapter. Try to memorize as many of these commands as quickly as you can. Knowing the menus is valuable, but knowing the shortcuts saves you time and is a real convenience once you get used to them.

KEYBOARD SHORTCUT	FUNCTION
F1	Selects Shuffle mode
F2	Selects Slip mode
F3	Selects Spot mode
F4	Selects Grid mode
F5	Selects Zoomer tool
F6	Selects Trimmer tool
F7	Selects Selector tool
F8	Select Grabber tool
F9	Selects Scrubber tool
F10	Selects Pencil tool
Command + Shift + N	Creates a new track
Command + Left or Right Arrow	Toggles track format in New Track dialog box
Command + Up or Down Arrow	Scrolls through types in New Track dialog box
Command + Click on Track	Selects track names in any order
Command + Shift + W	Quits session without closing Pro Tools

PRO TOOLS TUNE-UP FOR CHAPTER 4

1. When setting up the playback engine, selecting the RTAS Engine options increases your computer's performance when recording several MIDI parts using virtual instruments, but it decreases the quality of the _____ until the option is turned back off.

2. If you choose a small cache size from the Playback Engine dialog box, that decreases the Elastic Time performance but increases the performance for your _____ processing.

3. To customize your auto backup feature, navigate to the Setup menu, choose Preferences, and then click on the _____ tab.

4. The two main settings that support Grid mode functions can be found in the Edit window and are called Grid Value and _____.

5. To quickly select Grid mode, you can click on it from the Edit window toolbar, use the F4 key on your keyboard, or scroll through all of the modes by using the _____ key, just below they Escape key.

6. If you are in Grid mode and you do not see any grid lines, you can toggle on and off for this function by clicking on the _____ Ruler view, just to the right of the Tracks List drop-down menu.

7. The most common grid values used for music production are the Bars|Beats value and the _____ / _____ value.

8. The nudge value represents the vertical movement of regions in the timeline. To nudge a region either back or forward in time, use the _____ keys on the numeric keypad.

9. When creating new tracks, you can create multiple track types and formats by clicking on the _____, located on the far right of the New Track dialog box.

10. To name a track, simply double-click on the _____, and type in the desired track name and comments.

11. To arrange the order of the tracks in the Mix window or the Edit window, make sure that only the tracks you would like to move are highlighted; then, _____ to the desired position.

12. Please identify the following track types using the screen shot on the next page..

    a. _____

    b. _____

    c. _____

    d. _____

    e. _____

13. If you hide a track, it will still be audible unless you mute it before you hide it, or you can right-click on the track name and select the _____ and _____ options.

14. To quickly delete a track, you can go to the Track menu, or you can _____ on the track and choose Delete.

15. When setting up a MIDI keyboard that is not USB, you need to go to the audio MIDI setup and add the desired keyboard. AMS is located in the Mac OS Utilities folder, but to access it from Pro Tools you can use the Setup menu and choose the _____ option.

16. To allow your keyboard to synchronize with Pro Tools, you must make sure that you check the MIDI Beat Clock option or the _____ option, depending on the type of synchronization required.

17. An instrument track is very convenient when using virtual instruments because it acts as a _____ track and a _____ input simultaneously.

18. To use Xpand as a stereo plug-in, go to the insert of a channel and choose the Multichannel Plug-in option, and select the _____ bank.

19. The Xpand plug-in can trigger or play _____ sounds simultaneously.

20. When selecting patches from the Xpand plug in, you can either use the Down Arrow just to the right of the Bank On and Bank Off selector or go to the top of the plug-in and use the _____, just to the right of where it says "factory default."

21. When choosing a drum patch, if you have a small MIDI controller with a small range of keys, you may need to use the keyboard's _____ function and find the "zone" that is active for the chosen patch.

22. If you are using a MIDI controller and have selected and set up everything the right way but still do not hear sound, go to the Options menu and make sure that the _____ is selected. If that is turned on, then check MIDI in the Setup menu and choose _____ to see if your keyboard is being recognized by your computer.

23. When using Reason with Pro Tools, you can use your MIDI controller to record MIDI data into Pro Tools directly out of Reason. To do that, you must go to the Instrument view on an instrument track and _____ directly to Reason.

24. If you would like to use multiple instruments in Reason but you want them to play back in Pro Tools on individual instrument tracks, make sure you go to Reason and connect each Reason instrument to its own hardware interface. Then set the _____outputs to the corresponding individual channels.

25. In order to use your MIDI controller with Reason, you must make sure that Reason is recognizing your controller. You can do this by going to the Reason Adapted For Digidesign menu and selecting the _____ option. From there you can click on the General tab and choose Control Surfaces And Keyboards, and then use the Auto-detect function. Once your MIDI controller is recognized, set it to Use With Reason.

Armed and Ready 5

A PRO TOOLS CREATION

In the previous chapter, you took your Pro Tools system "once around the block" to do a systems check. The idea was to make sure your entire system was up and running, allowing you to keep the creative juices flowing once they start. You made sure your MIDI controllers were working, and that you understood the basics of using a virtual instrument or a ReWire device without being lost in the land of technology. I also covered some "need to know" troubleshooting tips and went over why Playback Engine settings are important, when they should be changed, and under what circumstances. By now, you should be starting to realize that you control your computer and what it does. It does not control you. In order to make sure you remain in control of your sessions, it is important to be aware of and learn as many functions as possible in Pro Tools. So do your best at making it a habit to be armed with knowledge and ready for any situation you may encounter in a Pro Tools session.

RECORD MODES AND MONITORING MODES

There aren't many record modes in Pro Tools, but they all function slightly differently. You should always make deliberate choices when there is an option. There are also modes for monitoring while you record in Pro Tools. This is something that needs to be completely understood and well reviewed. In this chapter, you will continue to build your Igniting Pro Tools session by opening it, going to the File menu, and saving it as Armed and Ready. Then you will create a click track, record some MIDI using an instrument track, and record some audio on an audio track. First, I'll go over the different ways to record in Pro Tools. Listed below are all of the alternatives to standard Record mode.

Destructive Record

To select different recording modes in Pro Tools, use the Options menu. Destructive record mode is the first option you can choose. Part of the beauty of Pro Tools is that almost everything you do is nondestructive. One of the exceptions is Destructive record mode. I've been working in Pro Tools a long time, and I have used the Destructive record option fewer than a handful of times. However, if disk space is a concern or if you refuse to have anything other than "keepers" recorded to your hard drive, go ahead and choose Destructive record. However, be aware that anything you record on top of either MIDI data or an existing waveform will be overwritten on your hard drive, and it will be gone forever. You can verify that you are in Destructive record mode by going to the Options menu and seeing if there is a check mark next to the option. A quicker, more convenient way to tell what mode of recording you are in is to simply look at the transport. The Record button will indicate which of the record modes have been selected. Destructive record mode is indicated by an uppercase D superimposed on the Record button.

Loop Record

Loop recording is nice when the artist is improvising a part or simply wants to record multiple takes consecutively. When this mode is selected and you start to record, the selected area cycles. Every time the selection loops or cycles, the recorded information is stored to a new playlist. Before you start recording in this mode, select the new Automatically Create New Playlists When Loop Recording option from the Operations tab under Preferences in the Setup menu. This new feature in Pro Tools 8 makes it easier than ever to use multiple takes to build one final-take track by using a compilation of all of the best parts from each of the takes. This technique will be covered in the later chapters of this book. Loop record mode is selected either from the Options menu by pressing the number 5 on your numeric keypad or by using the keyboard shortcut Option + L. The arrow around the Record button in the transport is the indicator for Loop record.

QuickPunch

Other than the standard Record mode in Pro Tools, QuickPunch is probably the most commonly used recording mode in the program, and it is certainly the most convenient. It has many built-in safety features and is indicated by an uppercase P on the Record button in the transport. Anytime a record-enabled track is playing, you can punch in and start recording new material from that point forward until you punch out or playback is stopped. If for some reason the punch-in was executed late, you can use the Trim tool to trim the new recording and recover the first few missing notes. When in QuickPunch mode, the recording actually starts the instant that playback is started. This is a very cool feature, because if the artist asks you to play the track so they can practice their part and you realize a minute or two into the song that they are really playing well, you can discretely punch them in and start recording. When they finish and say, "Man, I should have had you record that," you can simply trim from their punch-in point all the way back to the beginning, and now you have the whole take. Sometimes this comes in very handy and is quite often an overlooked feature of QuickPunch mode.

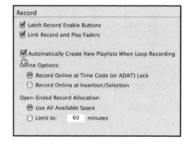

You can select QuickPunch mode from the Options menu, using the keyboard shortcut Command + Shift + P, or you can simply press the number 6 on your numeric keypad. You can also toggle through all of the record modes in Pro Tools by holding down the Control key while clicking on the Record button. To execute a manual punch-in or punch-out, make sure you are in QuickPunch mode, play the track, and use the number 3 on your computer's numeric keypad to punch in and punch out of the record-enabled track. You can also use any of the other standard methods such as the keyboard shortcut Command + Spacebar or the F12 feature.

PUNCH IN AND PUNCH OUT

Every artist I know, myself included, prefers to capture his or her part in just one take. Something about the overall continuity, feel, and conviction always shines through on a full-take recording pass. However, even the best takes may contain some things that the artist may wish that he or she did a little bit differently. Perhaps the timing could have been more precise, or maybe a note should have been played differently. Many people believe that those subtle imperfections are what give these "flawless" takes their character. However, it is inevitable that you, as the engineer or the artist, will have to clean up some of the unacceptable takes that have great potential. This means punching in has to be done on the track to make an otherwise unacceptable take worth keeping.

To do a good job when punching in and out, you should be familiar with the musical part you're working on and learn to execute this function the way an audio engineer had to back in the day. Meaning, you tap along with the beat of the song, and when the part comes up that requires an overdub, you manually punch in and start recording and then punch out when the desired fix has been made. When you perform a punch-in this way, you can stay in Grid mode and still make an exact punch-in and punch-out that won't snap to grid at the punch-in or -out points and sound unnatural. If you get good at this, you should feel good about yourself. The ability to execute flawless punch-ins and punch-outs manually is one of the many qualities of a good engineer that has fallen by the wayside since the introduction of the automated punch-in functions of DAWs. If you try this manual way of punching in and out, you will quickly realize that a true audio engineer had to have good musical timing in the days prior to DAW recording.

If you realize that you need some practice with your timing and your punch-in skills need a little help, Pro Tools makes it easy for you to seamlessly punch in and out of a track like a pro. If you are just punching in full verses or a certain number of measures, you can stay in Grid mode and use the Selector tool to select the desired section to punch in. Once the selection has been made, you should turn on the Pre-roll/Post-roll function and set it to either 2 bars or 4 bars. Some artists may have a preference, so just provide them with what they like. Once these selections are made, you can start the transport into QuickPunch by using one of the many standard record commands such as the 3 key on the numeric keypad, the keyboard shortcut Command + Spacebar, or the F12 function key. Or you can just manually click on the Record button, and then click on the Play button on the transport. Pro Tools will start playing back the track and automatically punch in and punch out in the selected area.

If you are doing short, tedious punch-ins and you need to be very precise, you can set Pro Tools to Slip mode, zoom in close to the area that you would like to fix, and highlight a sample accurate selection. Once you make the selection, you can punch in automatically just as described above for automatic punch-ins, and Pro Tools will punch in and punch out exactly where you have made your selection without being constrained to the grid values. This is a great feature to use when fixing one or two notes or words at a time that would otherwise be difficult to execute. Once the punch-in is made, remember to go back into Grid mode to resume working as you were prior to the punch-in.

MONITORING MODES

Input-only monitoring and auto-input monitoring are very simple concepts that have been around for many years on professional multitrack tape machines. For some reason, many people are confused by their function or purpose. To make things simple, apply the following basic set of rules and use them while you record, and you will quickly understand their purpose. These functions are found in the Track menu. You will see only one or the other mode: if you see Auto Input Monitoring as a choice, the status of monitoring is already in the Input Only Monitoring mode. You can toggle between the two modes by using the keyboard shortcut Option + K. The main transport has an Input Only Monitoring indicator just to the right of the Record button, making it easy to tell which mode you are in at any time.

Input Only Monitoring

If this option is selected, it means that a signal will pass through the record-enabled channel any time there is a signal present, regardless of whether the track is playing. Using Input Only Monitoring mode is great when you are having an artist play along to the track while the track is record enabled. By having the artist play to the track as though they were actually recording their part, you can get an accurate mic-pre level.

I've found that when you simply record enable a track and have the artist check the mic by randomly noodling on their instrument or doing their favorite voice impersonation, they don't play or sing the way they would if they were actually recording their part. In this scenario what usually ends up happening is that you do your mic check, set the levels, and think you are ready to record. You tell the artist to stand by, you roll the track, and they play or sing a lot louder or softer, and you end up having to readjust your levels while they are playing and then stop them half way through. This can be frustrating to both the artist and the engineer. Since it is the engineer's job to be an extension of the artist's creativity, you should learn to use Input Only Monitoring to set good levels the first time while the artist plays to the track they will be recording to. Once the recording levels are good, you can adjust the monitoring functions back to Auto Input, and record them for real the first time.

Auto Input Monitoring

Auto-input monitoring is used when the artist is done recording their part and they want to go back and punch in at a particular spot in the song. If you are still in Input Only Monitoring when you play back the track, the artist will not be able to hear what they just recorded and won't be able to tell where they are at in the song. However, if Auto Input Monitoring is selected, you can tell the artist they have some preroll and should play along with their previously recorded part, and they will hear their old take until the punch-in is executed. The moment the track is recording again, the artist will be able to hear live input and automatically monitor input or hear himself while he is recording the new part or overdub.

HEADPHONE MIXES

Now that you know the modes of recording and how the monitoring system works, I'll go over some of the ways to set up a headphone mix. Sometimes when you are recording directly, without a microphone, the artist can sit in the control room and overdub his or her part while listening to the main control-room speakers. If you are using microphones, however, this isn't an option because the music coming out of the speakers will "bleed" into the microphone that is recording the source and will be recorded to the same track. If the speakers are too loud or the mic-pre is turned up too much, you can accidentally create a feedback loop. This could result in damage to your equipment or your ears, and neither one is a good thing. Most of the time, the artist will be using headphones. Here's how you set them up.

Stereo Bus Mixes

If you are using an Mbox series interface, simply plug into either one of the headphone jacks (one is located on the front of the interface, with another on the back). There is a level or volume control for the headphone output so you can select the desired listening level. On the Mbox series of interfaces, you will notice a knob labeled Mix. This knob is used when you are recording. It determines how much of the input signal is being blended with what is coming out of the Pro Tools mixer. Since there is latency caused by the A/D conversion and host-based processing, using the Mix knob may help the performer tolerate the amount of latency they hear when they are recording with the track. I suggest that you mess around with this knob when overdubbing to fully understand its purpose. Using the extreme values set all the way to Monitor or Mix will make the function of this knob more obvious and help you to better understand what it does.

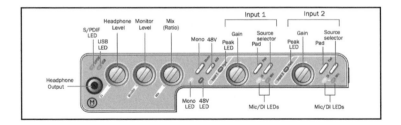

Independent Headphone Mixes

While you are recording, you must realize that the musicians will also hear whatever changes you make to the mix while they are recording. This is very distracting to the artist, so you shouldn't mix while recording. In the professional environment, it is common to send the artist an "independent" headphone mix. This means that they get a headphone mix that is completely independent from the mix that is being heard in the control room. When you are using the Mbox series of interfaces, this is not an option. To have this option available to you, you must have an interface with more than two outputs. Having the additional outputs will allow you to create an independent headphone mix from the auxiliary sends in the channel strip in Pro Tools.

This is much easier to set up if you are looking at the extended view of the send you are using. If you are looking at the Mix window, go to the small mixer icon located at the bottom left side of the mixer and click on it.

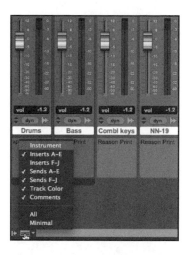

Choose to view all but the instrument settings, and you will notice that you have all ten sends in view. Click on Send J on all channels you would like to use for the headphone mix, and then choose an unused stereo bus combination from the sends list. In the example figure below and at right, the send has already been named "HP Mixes." Then create a new stereo auxiliary track, name it "Headphone Mix," and set its inputs to receive from the same stereo send you selected for your headphone mix. Now set the outputs from this auxiliary track to an open stereo pair on your interface.

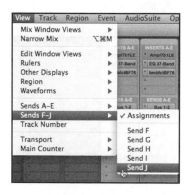

When the new outputs are chosen, the signal from the auxiliary will be sent to the outputs of your interface. Those outputs on your interface need to be connected to a headphone amplifier or mixer so that the signal can be distributed to one or more sets of headphones; the overall master volume for the headphone mix is usually selected from there.

Now, go to the View menu, select Sends F–J, and choose to view Send J.

You will notice that in the channel's send section there is a small fader with a few choices such as the panning arrangement, Mute selector, Send Level indicator, and the Pre/Post fader selector. To set up an independent headphone mix, adjust the level of each of the sends on all the faders you have assigned to Send J. At this point you can send the exact mix the artist would like to hear in their headphones. An important step in setting up an independent headphone mix is making sure that you send the headphone mix prefader.

What this means is that the headphone mix you send through the auxiliary is sent to the artist before the mix gets to your main fader in the mixer. That way, even if all of your instrument faders are completely turned down, the auxiliary send is still sending the headphone mix track, out to the interface, to the headphone distribution mixer/amplifier, and finally to the artist. This allows you to give the artist exactly what they would like to hear to help inspire their performance, and you can tweak your mix at the same time. To make the auxiliaries a prefader send, simply click on the small box that says "pre" on it. When the auxiliaries are in prefader status, you will notice the box is highlighted. Remember, if you are sending an independent headphone mix, the changes you make to the main faders and pans will not be heard, but any changes you make to any inserted plug-ins will be heard. Just because you have an independent headphone mix being sent using auxiliaries doesn't mean that you can tweak everything in the mix—just the faders, pans, and mutes of the main faders.

RECORDING AN INSTRUMENT TRACK

Finally, it's time to do some recording. When recording in Grid mode, or any mode for that matter, you should set up a click track so the audio that is recorded will be synchronized with the grid in Pro Tools. There are several approaches to setting up a click track, but for this exercise we will start by going to the Track menu and choosing the Create Click Track option. This automatically creates an aux input that has a click plug-in inserted.

Once the click track is created, make sure that the Metronome icon is selected in the transport, then single-click on the click plug-in and choose the desired click sound (as described in chapter 3). Once the click is set up to taste, you are ready to record.

We are going to start our recording by creating a 4-bar drum loop. To do this, look at the first stereo instrument track from the Edit window, go to the Edit window view selector, and choose the items you would like to see in the Edit window. I like to view everything but the comments, inserts, and sends. If you are following along with your own session, choose what works for you, but at least select the instrument view. In the I/O box of the instrument view of the Xpand channel, the drum kit should still be loaded from when the connections were being checked in the "Igniting Pro Tools" session. Now all we have to do is record enable the track and start recording parts for our session. However, before you start recording, please use the Save As function and name your session "Armed and Ready."

To record your first 4-bar loop, select standard Record mode, and then put the cursor at measure 9 to leave some space at the beginning of the track. You can use the Selector tool and drop the cursor at measure 9 in the timeline or use the keyboard shortcut Equal sign + the respective measure number. In this example, once the cursor is on measure 9, you can add to the selection by holding down the Shift key and clicking-and-dragging the selection to measure 13.

An even quicker way to select a 4-bar loop is to use your numeric keypad and enter the keyboard shortcuts that allow access to the Main Counters, Start Time, End Time, and Length selections. To do this, use this sequence of keyboard shortcuts from the numeric keypad:

Press the forward slash symbol (/) in the numeric keypad to scroll through the three options. The first time you press the / key, it highlights the Start Time so you can enter a specific bar number from which you would like the selection to start playback in the timeline. Then, by pressing the / symbol two more times, the highlighted option will be the Length selection box. From there, you will enter the number of bars you would like to loop. For instance, if you enter 4 and press play, you will have a perfect 4-bar selection from the Start Time measure you entered previously. This is a very convenient method for navigating to any place in the song and setting a perfect loop, so when your time scale is Bars|Beats, this navigation tip should almost always be used for navigating the timeline.

Once your 4-bar selection is made, turn on the Pre-roll/Post-roll function (or use the Count Off feature from the transport), make sure that the Metronome is selected so the click track will play, and start the transport. Set up your metronome so the click track is heard during play and record. Press Play to verify that your selection is looping and you can hear the click track at the desired level. I suggest you play along to the click for a few seconds to set your levels properly.

When recording a drum loop with MIDI, make sure that you select the MIDI Merge function. This will allow you to tap in your kick drum pattern during the first loop pass, then tap in your snare track next, then your hi-hat, and so on. If you do not have MIDI Merge on, you will become quickly frustrated at how every time the section loops, it records over what you just tapped in. MIDI Merge allows you to build the loop one sound at a time until you are through.

Real-Time Properties

If you find yourself having trouble playing "in time" to the click to create your loop, there's a cool feature called Real-Time Properties. Since we are in the Edit window, go to the View menu, select Edit Window Views, and choose the Real-Time Properties option. You will see the Real-Time Properties appear just to the left of the track height selector.

There are five options you can select from the Real-Time Properties box: Quantize, Duration, Delay, Velocity, and Transpose. For this example, you want to help your "timing" while entering your drum parts, so the Quantize function needs to be selected.

The cool thing about this function is that it doesn't actually change the timing of the notes that were entered into the Pro Tools sequencer; it simply plays them back "in time." If you are wondering why you would ever want to keep things if they were out of time, well, sometimes even though a player isn't in perfect time with the click track, the music has a great "feel." If you want to fix the feel of the performance, you can do this with Real-Time Properties without having to commit to the changes. In earlier versions of Pro Tools, if you wanted to quantize something, you had to be very careful because it was a real pain, if not impossible, to get the original performance back—unless of course, you saved the original version first. But now, with the addition of Real-Time Properties, you can audition powerful MIDI quantize functions without the possibility of losing the original performance. I suggest playing with all of the parameters to see what they do. They are there to primarily re-create feel after quantizing the original performance. When things are quantized exactly to the grid, they can start to sound too mechanical, and it can hurt the performance more than it helps it. By varying the duration, delay, and velocity of the MIDI notes, you can "humanize" the parts. Humanizing the performance by playing around with the Real-Time Properties values can be the answer, especially if the player is no longer there to record the part over. If you decide that you like the changes you've made with Real-Time Properties, you can write them in permanently by going to the Track menu and selecting the Write MIDI Real-Time Properties function.

Make sure that the desired part you want to quantize is selected on the MIDI track; otherwise, the computer won't know which part to write the Real-Time Properties on. There are many more ways of editing MIDI parts in Pro Tools to your exact taste, and we will cover more of those functions in later chapters of this book. In the meantime, make sure you can record your MIDI drums and bass with the Xpand plug-ins on the first two stereo instrument tracks, and then program the second two stereo instrument tracks using Reason. If you have any problems recording your MIDI parts, remember to go over the related QuickTime tutorial associated with this chapter.

RECORDING AN AUDIO TRACK

Recording an audio track is similar to recording a MIDI or an instrument track. The main difference lies with where the source is being generated. MIDI and instrument tracks need to receive input from some form of MIDI controller so that they can record the MIDI data into the Pro Tools sequencer. The recorded data from the sequencer is sent to a virtual instrument that is instantiated on in an insert, a MIDI keyboard's local sound bank, or a rack-mounted sound engine so they can trigger the relevant audio sounds assigned to the MIDI notes they received.

Then we can ultimately hear the sounds via an aux input or on an instrument track in Pro Tools.

A live audio track is recorded using a hardware interface that is compatible with Pro Tools. A direct source or a microphone can be used to record the audio. Since I am using an Mbox 2, I have two available inputs. Both of them have a line, mic, and DI input. The examples used in this book will be based on this hardware configuration. There are several interfaces that are compatible with Pro Tools LE and M-Powered software on the market, and I will assume here that you can use the configuration in this book as a reference, and will apply it when setting up your particular interface for recording.

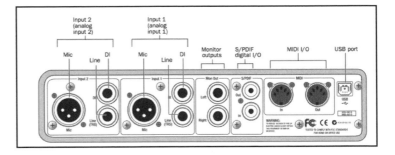

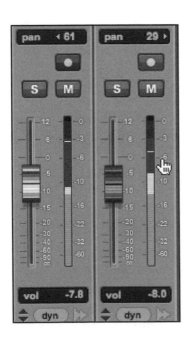

If you are using a microphone, you need to determine if it is a condenser microphone or a dynamic microphone. For condenser microphones, you'll need to turn on the 48V option on your interface to supply phantom power. Select the input on the interface to be a mic (not a DI) setting. Make sure that the mic control knob is all the way down before plugging in the microphone. Position the microphone, create one new audio track, set its input to the corresponding input number you are using on your interface, *arm the track* (another term for record enabling the track), and start to play the source instrument or speak into the microphone. Slowly bring up the mic control until you have a nice input signal on the channel's input meter in Pro Tools.

If you do not see any input, make sure that you are properly connected and go to the Track menu and make sure you turn on the Input Only Monitoring function. Remember, you can toggle this feature on and off by using the keyboard shortcut Option + K.

A Direct Approach

Many times, you don't have the luxury of working in a well-isolated studio to record at loud volume levels. However, instead of the traditional method of using microphones to record loud guitar or bass amplifiers and cabinets turned up to "11," Pro Tools gives you the option of recording direct and then reamping the guitar or bass signal using RTAS plug-ins. There are several plug-ins compatible with Pro Tools that are made specifically for recording guitar and bass. Pro Tools Ignition Pack 2 comes bundled with the Amplitube plug-in by IK Media. Pro Tools 8 has included the relatively new Eleven plug-in for recording direct guitar and getting excellent amp and speaker emulation. These plug-ins are just a couple of the many amp-modeler plug-ins available today that re-create some nice amplifier sounds without your having to own the hardware or turn them up really loud to get them to sound good. This is a very simple process, and here is how it works.

Making the Connection

To record direct, simply plug the instrument cable from your guitar into the DI input on your interface, then select the source to be DI (not Mic) on the interface. Record enable the correct mono audio track and adjust the input to the desired level. Insert the Amplitube plug-in by going to the insert and clicking on the plug-in option, choose the Harmonic category, and select Amplitube. When the plug-in appears, you have several options to create the sound you are looking for. There are three amp types and three cabinet types. You can use any combination and use the standard amp settings such as gain, bass, mids, treble, presence, and master volume. You can select separate overdrive, delay, reverb, and wah effects, plus this plug-in comes with a built-in tuner on its interface. If you are unsure of what sound you are going for or would like to use for your recording, you can click on the factory default setting in the upper area of the plug-in and use one of the factory presets.

One of the best things about using an amp-modeler plug-in is that the hard drive records the clean, uneffected guitar sounds. This allows you to set the plug-in for any sound that inspires you to record the part, but you can still go back and make any adjustments you want. This ensures you of having total tonal control over how the guitar part sits in the mix all the way to the final mixdown. None of the effect is recorded permanently to the hard drive unless you print the track. I will go over printing plug-ins to save CPU power in the next chapter.

So far, I've covered how to set up a headphone mix, record parts using microphones, and do direct recording using an amp modeler. Now you need to create two mono audio tracks to add to your Armed and Ready session, name them "E gtr" and "A gtr," and record an electric guitar part with the Amplitube plug-in and an acoustic guitar part with a microphone. By now you should have the MIDI drums, bass, keys, and sound-effects tracks recorded, so hopefully you are starting to hear your production tracks beginning to come together.

If you don't play guitar or have access to one, try to find someone who does. You don't have to use the same instrumentation that I suggest in each chapter, but you will get more out of your Pro Tools training if you at least follow the theme. To be efficient in a creative situation, you need to apply the concepts you read about, hear about, or discover on your own while dinkin' around in Pro Tools.

As long as you have used a MIDI controller to record the Xpand and Reason tracks, recorded an audio track using the direct recording approach with an amp emulator, and recorded a second audio track using a microphone, you will be in good shape if you are trying to get the most out of this book. Pro Tools 8 comes with a couple of choices for guitar-amp emulators. If, however, you would like to hear some of the others that are out there, go to the manufacturer Web site of any plug-in you would like to audition, and you can usually download a demo or trial version of it. The trial period for most plug-ins is usually anywhere from 7 to 30 days, which gives you plenty of time to work through the sessions we are creating with this book. There are no excuses, so let's get some recording done and then move on!

USING INSERTS FOR DYNAMIC PROCESSING

So far we have used the inserts only for virtual instruments, amp modeling, or setting up a click track. Most commonly, inserts are used for dynamic processing. Dynamic processing involves anything that has to do with changing the amplitude of a sound. Equalization, compression/limiting, and gate/expansion are the main categories of dynamic processing. We will go a little bit deeper into these subjects in chapter 9, but for now I'll show you how to insert them into a track. Pro Tools 8 now features ten inserts for additional creative control. The additional inserts also give you a reason to try out the new AIR plug-ins. There are more than 20 of them, so be sure to check them out.

To insert a dynamic processor, go to the Amplitube guitar track, click on the insert, and choose Plug-in. EQ and Dynamics will be listed as two separate categories. They are still both considered dynamic processing, but they are listed separately. Choose the EQ category and select the 7-band EQ III by Digidesign. This is a good stereo EQ algorithm that ships with every Pro Tools 8 system. This EQ can be used to reshape the frequency curve of any instrument you apply it to, and it is very clean and flexible. It has a phase-reverse option and high- and lowpass filters that can be selected from a first-order to a fourth-order filter by choosing the rolloff rate, which is determined in decibels per octave. There are four bands of parametric EQ, and the highs and lows can be selected as peak or shelving EQ. Remember to always check the input and the output to make sure that neither of the signals are coming in or going out, or are overloading and causing digital distortion.

This EQ plug-in has a nice graphical view of the frequency spectrum and illustrates how your EQ'ing technique affects the frequency curve. I suggest that you click around, turn some knobs, and not only listen but also look while you listen to what you are doing. It will help you better understand the fundamentals of how an EQ works. Ultimately, the way something sounds is the most important thing, but learning how an EQ works and understanding its parameters is a vital part of engineering and can have a huge effect on your how your recordings turn out.

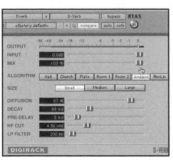

EVERYBODY NEEDS THEIR OWN SPACE

Oftentimes when an artist is recording a track, they not only need the backing track to inspire them, but also need to have a good headphone mix and an inspiring sound setup. They may ask you to put some effects on their voice to vibe them up. The most common request in my experience is "Can you put a little reverb on my voice or guitar, etc…?" This lets the artist loosen up a bit and not feel so naked against the backing tracks. To get a good take out of them, it is wise not to have them smothered in effects, so that you both can still discern "pitchy-ness." This mainly applies if you are the one producing the track, too.

Wet/Dry

When applying reverb to a track, you do not want to insert the reverb plug-in directly on the audio track you are recording, the way you would for a dynamic effect. Instead, use an aux send, which is a copy of the dry signal from the audio track, to send the source to an aux input track that has its input set to receive the send copy. Then blend the two sounds together, which will give you a wet/dry mix.

For this example, you need to go to your "E gtr" track, click on the A send, and send it down bus 1–2. When the fader appears, set it to unity gain (0 dB). Then create two new stereo aux inputs and name them Reverb and Delay. Make sure that the reverb aux's input is set to receive on bus 1–2. On the reverb aux track, click on the insert and select the multichannel plug-in option, and then select the reverb category, choose D-Verb, and then play the track and you will see the aux track receiving input. When you do, set the fader at the desired wet/dry ratio.

D-Verb is another Digidesign plug in that comes with all Pro Tools systems. Once it opens, I suggest clicking around on the plug-in to get familiar with the parameters, and then choose what is appropriate for your or the artist's taste.

If for some reason you are not receiving any signal at the aux inputs, make sure you double-check the outputs of the sends and verify that you are using the correct inputs on the aux input.

If there is still no signal, click directly on the aux send of the dry channel, and you will see the send fader. Make sure that this is not set at the off position, which is the default setting. To quickly put any fader at Unity Gain, I suggest using the keyboard shortcut Option + click on the fader.

Remember, a large percentage of the plug-ins you have will come with factory presets that can be used as a good starting point if you don't have an exact sound in mind. These factory presets usually showcase what about them is unique or perhaps what the manufacturer deems their nicest settings for common applications for that particular effect. This is not cheating. Feel free to audition many factory presets and just tweak them to your own taste. You can also save your settings once you get a setting you like, and then build your own library of user presets to use as new starting points. D-Verb doesn't come with factory settings per se, but the user interface is simple to use and self-explanatory with regard to the algorithms and size options.

A SMOOTH OPERATOR

Now that you've recorded and overdubbed some parts and used everything required in a recording or production session, it is time to learn some editing and navigation features that will help you bring your production to the next level. They are basic Pro Tools concepts but are functional and commonly used. These basic editing techniques are power tools that are mandatory for any level of Pro Tools operator who wants to become "A Smooth Operator."

BASIC BUT ESSENTIAL
EDITING TECHNIQUES

There are a few key elements that are of great help when you are learning to edit in Pro Tools. Number 1, it is important to have a good visual understanding of what you are looking at in the Edit window, and that information was broken down for you in chapter 3.

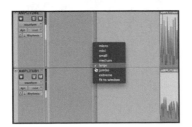

Since Pro Tools version 7.*x* (the past two years or so), more and more new view functions have been added that will quickly become favorites if they aren't already. Notice at the very bottom, in the track name area, there is a very thin line that represents the division between the tracks. If you hover the cursor over the line in between the track names, regardless of the currently selected tool, you will see an icon that is a plus sign with Up and Down Arrows attached. If you hold down the Command key and click-and-drag vertically when you see that symbol, you can resize the track height to any size, not just one of the preselected sizes.

The newer versions of Pro Tools (7.4 and above) also come with two new track views, and they are Fit To Window and Micro. You can select these view sizes by clicking on the arrow just to the right of the track view selector. If you click on the track ruler on an audio or an aux input track, you can select the size. Or if you hold down the Control key and click on the track ruler on a MIDI or an instrument track, you can change the track size.

As you now know by now, you also have access to many useful functions of the tracks, such as Rename, Duplicate, Make Inactive, and so on, thanks to the new right-click features added in recent versions of Pro Tools.

As you finish this chapter, please make sure that you have all of the following simple edit commands in your power tips tool belt also. Use the Grabber tool to highlight a region, and the keyboard shortcut Command + D to duplicate the selection. You can also repeat a highlighted selection by going to the Edit window and selecting Repeat or using the keyboard shortcut Option + R. If you choose this option, a dialog box will appear and require you to type in the number of times you would like the selection to be repeated.

Remember that you can always highlight a region by double-clicking with the Selector tool. If you would like to repeat a particular selection that isn't yet its own region, you can turn your selection into a region by going to the Region menu and selecting Capture…, or you can use the keyboard shortcut Command + R. When the dialog box appears, you will have to give the new region a name.

If you only capture the region, it will appear in your regions list and you will need to select it with the Grabber tool and drop it into the desired track display spot. However, if you use the Separate region function from the Edit menu or the keyboard shortcut Command + E, it will create a region from the specified selection by separating it from the left and right portions of the main whole file.

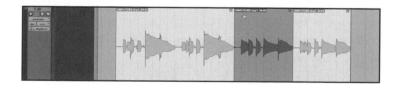

Separating the region is much more convenient, because now you can use the Grabber tool to select the separated region, and then use the keyboard shortcut Option + click-and-drag to quickly make a copy of your separated region. Notice the outline of the region as you move it along the timeline; doing so allows you to visually confirm where it is that you are about to drop the copy of the region.

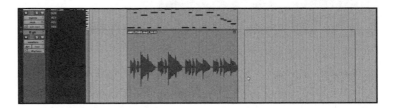

After you have your copy in the timeline, you can go back and put the whole file back to its original form by highlighting over the two separation points and choosing to Heal Separation from the Edit menu or by using the keyboard shortcut Command + H.

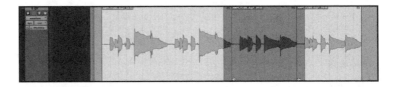

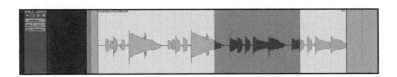

Now that you've recorded MIDI data and want to move regions around to build your production, you should understand that the tools used for editing audio apply to MIDI as well. To use audio-type editing on a MIDI or instrument track, go to the track view selector on the desired MIDI track in the Edit window and select the regions view, and then you are able to edit the region just like any other audio track. There are many other powerful new ways to edit MIDI data in Pro Tools 8, and we will go over many of them in the upcoming chapters of this book.

At this point, you should have at least four MIDI tracks with recorded parts and two audio tracks with recorded parts with dynamic processing and time-based effects applied to them. Now you just need to finish this exercise by using some of the editing tools that were mentioned above. Since there is a 4-bar loop used as the theme for the "Armed and Ready" session, I would like you to trim up any parts that may be longer than four bars. All you should see in the Edit window is six tracks that are exactly four bars long.

Assuming you have all six parts at exactly four bars each, make a 4-bar selection on all six parts and use the Repeat function to repeat one time (Option + R).

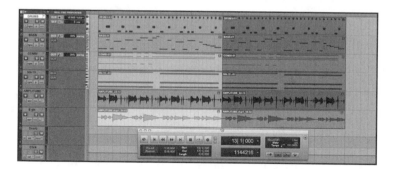

Then make a perfect 8-bar selection of all six parts and use the Duplicate function (Command + D).

Last, but not least, select the last four bars of all six parts, then use the cut command (Command + X). This should leave you with 12 bars of music starting at measure 9, ready to for a nice neutral mix. Obviously, we could have simply repeated the 4-bar region three times; however, I just wanted to go through some basic commands as an exercise.

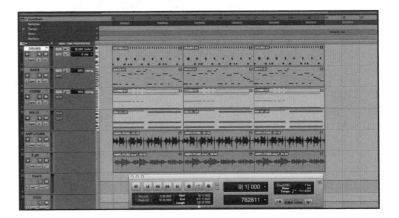

A NEUTRAL MIX

As we have gone through this chapter, I'm sure there have been times when you have been adjusting your faders and maybe moving the pan positioning of the various instruments. A nice thing about Pro Tools is that you can mix your track as it is being created. What we would like to set up for now is a nice, neutral mix. This means that nothing is louder than everything else, all parts can be distinctly heard in your mix, and the overall effects balance isn't out of whack. With any luck, your ideas are starting to sound like music. If you haven't already done so, I suggest that you save your session after you are done recording all of your basic parts and you are happy with the overall content. Once your session is safely saved, go to the File menu again, select the Save As feature, and name the session "Mini Mix 1." Using this feature allows you to start your preproduction mix session from scratch and still have your original session settings to go back to if you desire. Once the session is resaved and given a new name, you can verify this by looking at the top of the Mix or the Edit window, and you will see the new session name.

Now you can bring down all of the faders and bring up a new mix. I like to use the All feature in the mix groups list on the lower left of the Mix window. Once this is selected, you bring all of the faders down at the same time and start to remix the session by bringing the faders up one at a time. When the faders are all down, turn off the All Group function.

For this mix, pay closer attention to all of the elements in the production. Make sure that every instrument has a home, not only in volume level, but also exactly where you would like it to sit in the stereo field. Do this using the pan sliders on any given channel in the Mix window. When creating your mix using the faders and pan sliders, you will notice that both of them move in preset increments. If you would like to have total control over the placement of these functions, simply hold the Control key on your QWERTY keyboard while adjusting a fader or pan slider. You will notice the increments are much smaller and precise. If for some reason you would like to start over and "zero" your settings, hold down the Option key and click on the fader or pan slider, and they will snap to either Unity Gain for the fader or zero for the pan slider. I will cover many other mixing techniques in the mixing chapter of this book. For now, just use the basics and pay close attention to the panning, volume, and wet/dry relationship on your aux tracks. Small things make big differences when mixing, so take a little time and try to get a nice neutral mix.

DUPLICATING TRACKS

Now that you have a nice mix going, try adding one more electric-guitar part to your production and put one more tool into your audio toolbox.

Instead of using the New Track feature and setting it up all over again, just duplicate the whole channel strip and all of its settings to put your idea down while it's fresh. To make this happen quickly, highlight the desired track name, then use the Track window and select the Duplicate option; alternatively, you can use the keyboard shortcut Option + Shift + D. When the dialog box appears, you have the option of selecting only the elements you would like to be duplicated. For this example, I've chosen to duplicate the track only one time, uncheck Active Playlist, check the Alternate Playlists option, and keep everything else.

This allows you to quickly create a new track that already has the Amplitube and EQ III plug-in selected. Your send configuration is still sending to the reverb, and there is no audio cluttering up the track view window. Before you record the new electric-guitar part, rename it (otherwise it will just show it as a dup track.) Finally, change the plug-in settings around or pick a different preset and record a new part over the middle four bars of the "Mini-Mix 1" session. When you are done recording your new part, save your work; you'll continue to build on your session in the next chapter.

FINAL THOUGHTS

I suggest that you reread anything you are not clear on. Remember, watching the QuickTime tutorials that relate to each chapter makes understanding what you've read a lot easier.

Always take a few minutes to see if you can answer the Pro Tools Tune-up questions at the end of each chapter, and make sure that you review the Keyboard Shortcuts and User Tips Summary. If you know all of the end-of-chapter material, then you are on your way to being a Pro Tools user with real chops.

POWER TIPS SUMMARY FOR CHAPTER 5

1. QuickPunch is probably the most convenient and most commonly used mode for recording in Pro Tools. Also, when you use QuickPunch mode, recording starts as soon as the transport starts, and not when the punch-in was executed. So even if you forget to punch in on a track until the very end of the take, as long as you punch in for a few seconds before you stop the transport, you can use the Trimmer tool to trim the region all the way back to the point at which the transport was set into motion.

2. You can toggle through the four different record modes quickly by holding down the Command key and clicking on the Record button on the transport. The various modes are indicated by the different icons that appear on the transport's Record button.

3. Input is always active in Input Only Monitoring mode, regardless of the status of the transport. It is convenient to use input-only monitoring when you are setting your input level to Pro Tools or when an artist wants to practice along with the track before they record. Also, remember to use Auto Input Monitoring mode when doing overdubs. This ensures that the artist will hear what is recorded on the track up until the point that the new punch-in material is recorded.

4. When using a send to create an independent headphone mix, it is important that you send the mix to prefader so that the artist does not hear any changes to the fader volume, panning, mutes, or solos you may be doing during a take.

5. In Grid mode, to insert the play-head cursor in the timeline without using the mouse, you can use the sequence = + *measure number* from the numeric keypad to move the cursor where you want it. You can also tap into the main counters and the start, stop, and length time by using only the numeric keypad. Say you want to create an 8-bar loop at measure 17. You would simply use the following keyboard shortcut: / + 17 + / + / + 8 + Enter (all from the numeric keypad).

6. You will usually want to use the MIDI Merge function when entering MIDI data to create or build drum loops or whenever you want to keep layering new parts on top of each other. If MIDI Merge is not selected, every time the section loops, the recorder will record over what you just played into the sequencer. You can quickly turn this function on and off by using the number 9 on the numeric keypad.

7. The addition of Real-Time Properties is a great option that allows you audition quantizing of MIDI parts nondestructively. You can turn Real-Time Properties on and off quickly by using the keyboard shortcut Option + 4. If you like the Real-Time Properties parameters that you set up, you can write them permanently on the track by selecting the part you would like to write, and then going to the Track menu and selecting the write Real-Time Properties option.

8. When you would like to have precise control over a fader, a slider, or any parameter in Pro Tools that moves in preset increments, you can hold down the Control key, and Pro Tools knows to adjust the selected parameter by the smallest amount it can.

9. You can quickly duplicate an entire channel strip with plug-ins, sends, input and output settings, and even the playlists and region material by highlighting the desired channel and using the keyboard shortcut Option + Shift + D.

10. If you would like to create a region anywhere along the timeline that is within the whole file, simply select the desired area and use the keyboard shortcut Command + E to use the Separate Region function. To make the file whole again, highlight over the separation points and use the keyboard shortcut Command + H to execute the Heal Separation function. Both of these functions can be found in the Edit menu.

KEYBOARD SHORTCUT SUMMARY FOR CHAPTER 5

Try to memorize as many of these commands as quickly as you can. Knowing the menus is important too, but knowing the shortcuts saves you time and is a real convenience once you get used to them.

KEYBOARD SHORTCUT	FUNCTION
7 numeric keypad	Toggles transport Metronome on/off
8 numeric keypad	Toggles transport Count Off on/off
9 numeric keypad	Toggles transport MIDI Merge on/off
Option + 4 numeric keypad	Toggles Real-Time Properties on/off
Option + click faders and pans	Sets parameter to Unity Gain (global command)
Option + Shift + L	Toggles Loop Playback on/off
Option + Shift + D	Duplicates selected track (entire channel)
Option + K	Toggles monitoring modes
Option + R	Repeat selection function dialog
Option + click-and-drag w/ Grabber	Makes a copy of the selected region
Command + Shift + P	Toggles QuickPunch record mode on/off
Command + K	Toggles Pre-roll and Post-roll on/off
Command + D	Duplicates selected region
Command + R	Captures a region
Command + E	Separates a region
Command + H	Heals separation
Control + Click on track ruler	Changes track height

PRO TOOLS TUNE-UP
FOR CHAPTER 5

1. List the four modes for recording.

   a. _____

   b. _____

   c. _____

   d. _____

2. You can access the different modes of recording by going to the _____ menu and selecting one of the four. A quicker way is to hold down the Control key and click on the Record button in the transport.

3. _____ is primarily used when you would like to record multiple takes in quick succession. Each audio take is automatically placed on the playlist of the record-enabled track and makes it easy to use the matching start time takes list feature.

4. QuickPunch is probably the most commonly used recording mode in Pro Tools, and it can be quickly turned on and off with the number _____ in the numeric keypad.

5. There are several ways to punch in and punch out of a record-enabled track in Pro Tools, including using the keyboard shortcuts F12, Command + Spacebar, and the number _____ on in the numeric keypad.

6. The Pre-roll/Post-roll function is very important, because it allows artists to hear some of the music before they are actually punched in and recorded. Some artists have a particular preference; however, two to four bars are usually sufficient. The quickest way to turn this function on and off is to use the keyboard shortcut _____.

7. The Input Only Monitoring and Audio Input Monitoring features are important during the recording process. You can toggle the status of this feature on and off by using the keyboard shortcut _____.

8. To create track groups, you need to select all tracks you would like to include in the group, and then use the keyboard shortcut _____ + _____.

9. A good headphone mix can be a key part of inspiring the artist to give a good performance. When sending an independent headphone mix, you must remember to send the mix to _____ so the artist will not hear any changes you make to your control-room mix.

10. To create a click track, go to the _____ menu and select Create Click Track.

11. After creating a click track, make sure that the _____ is selected in the transport, or you will not hear the click.

12. Using real-time properties is a valuable tool when recording and premixing your recordings. There are five options to features to choose from, and they are _____, change duration, delay, velocity, and transpose.

13. Recording an audio track is similar to recording a MIDI or an instrument track. The main difference lies with where the source is originating. MIDI is generated from a controller or is input manually with edit tools or your computer keyboard. Live audio requires an _____ with digital-to-analog converters, so that the audio can be digitized and played back or manipulated by the computer.

14. When recording an audio track and you cannot see any signal getting to the input in Pro Tools, ake sure _____ monitoring is turned on and that you are connected to and properly set up on your audio interface.

15. Amplitube is a guitar-amp emulator that comes bundled with many Mbox configurations. When selecting it from your inserts, choose the _____ category from the plug-in list.

16. Most plug-in manufacturers have _____ built into their product to "showcase" how they were designed to sound and can oftentimes be found in the Librarian menu near the upper left of the plug-in.

17. Dynamic processing is used to change the amplitude of a sound in various ways. Common dynamic processors include equalization, _____, and gate/expansion.

18. Dynamic processing is typically applied directly on the track by using one of the five _____ on the channel strip.

19. Reverb, delay, chorus, phasers, flangers, pitch transposition, and so on, are effects that are considered by most as _____ effects.

20. Contrary to dynamics processing, time-based effects are not typically applied directly to the track. Most time-based effects are set up on an _____ track, and sent via busing from the dry channel to achieve an easy way to blend the wet/dry balance between the two tracks.

21. The Edit Window view sizes most recently added to Pro Tools were the _____ and Micro track size selection.

22. The _____ feature is often used to save the progress of a session in order to conveniently revisit it later.

Making Room for Your VIP's

6

VIRTUAL INSTRUMENT PLUG-INS

Up to this point, you have done a system check, making sure that everything in Pro Tools is working and that your controllers are functioning properly. You have "ignited" your Pro Tools system by implementing Xpand, Reason Adapted, and Amplitube into your session. You created a 4-bar loop and used a few basic editing techniques to trim up the regions and lengthen your loop to 12 bars. By now, you should have the concept of recording audio and MIDI, as well as some basic editing skills in your toolbox. In this chapter, you will be introduced to a few more virtual instruments to refine your basic loop session so that it starts to sound like a real project and not just an exercise. You will learn to use memory locations to easily identify sections and navigate the timeline and create view markers that give you instant access to easy-on-the-eye Edit window setups for commonly used work-flow methods. You will also learn about internal submixing, buses, and using AudioSuite plug-ins to save on CPU usage. Applying these techniques will allow you to move forward with the example sessions and add more virtual instrument tracks without taxing your CPU beyond its capacity.

I'll continue to develop and expand on concepts as they occur in the production of a music session. I urge you to follow along with your own sessions, watch the QuickTime tutorials associated with the various chapters, and go over the Power Tips Tune-up questions at the end of the chapter. Many times, the QuickTime tutorials will clear up any questions you may have about what you have read, and the Tune-up questions will help you review the most important information in the chapter.

ENERGY CONSERVATION

In the upcoming section of this book, you will learn how to conserve your system's resources to maximize your computer's potential. Since all computers have different technical specifications, you will need to know when it is time to apply conservation techniques. Viewing your system usage meters will show you what you have left in your CPU gas tank.

System Usage Meters

As you continue to add elements to your session, you may notice, that your CPU system usage meter starts to light up. This lets you know that your CPU is getting low on resources. If you haven't been paying attention to the system usage meter, you should start now. Remember, you can find it under the Window menu in the toolbar. Newer computers with fast processors will increase the performance of Pro Tools quite a bit, but even if you have a fast computer, your creativity will most likely outgrow your computer's CPU speed, forcing you to find ways of conserving your resources.

Submixing is used for various applications, but one of its primary functions on a Pro Tools LE or M-Powered system is to bus the output of your instrument tracks to the input of new audio tracks so that you can record the processing to the new audio track. This allows you to make the instrument tracks inactive, thereby taking the strain off your computer's processor. When working on a host-based application such as Pro Tools LE or M-Powered, you are bogging down your system with every plug-in you use, regardless of whether it's a virtual instrument plug-in, a time-based processor, or a dynamic processor plug-in; they all use the CPU power on your computer. At some point you will want to use the following techniques to get the most out of your computer.

Bouncing Instrument and Aux Tracks to Audio Tracks

As you to continue to add new elements to this project, you may need to start replenishing some of your CPU power. You can do this by submixing many tracks down to two tracks (commonly referred to as "stems" mixes) or creating new tracks for each individual part and busing the outputs of the fully processed audio track to the inputs of a new empty track. Doing so allows you to make the processed track inactive and cut back on your resources. Recording the processed tracks individually will give you more control over them during the mixing stage of your project. You will also learn to use AudioSuite processing on your tracks that are using dynamic, or modeling-type, plug-ins as another way of freeing up CPU resources. Using a combination of these methods usually works well.

Begin by opening the "Mini Mix 1" session. Once the session has opened up, go to the File menu and select the Save As option. Name the session "Conservation."

Once you verify that your "Conservation" session was renamed properly, you can start taking note of how many instrument or auxiliary tracks need to be recorded to audio tracks. Your session should have at least, two Xpand tracks and two Reason tracks, so create four new stereo audio tracks. At this point, things can start getting a little bit messy and hard to organize visually, so go to the tracks list and hide everything except the four instruments tracks of Reason and Xpand and the four new stereo audio tracks you created for them.

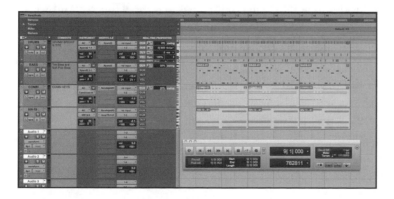

Once the new tracks are created and organized, it is time to use the input and output sections of the channel strips to record your new processed audio parts. On the first two Xpand tracks, set the outputs to bus 11–12 and bus 13–14 by clicking on the Output selector boxes. On the next two Reason tracks, set the outputs to bus 15–16 and bus 17–18. Then, one at a time, select each new stereo audio track and put them next to each instrument part you are going to record onto them. Set the input buses of the new audio tracks to correspond with the output buses you have selected for the Xpand and Reason tracks.

Next, record enable the new stereo audio tracks and press Play in Pro Tools, and you should hear the audio sounds through each of the new audio tracks. If you don't hear the instruments, make sure that you have the Auto Input feature selected either by looking in the Track menu, using the keyboard shortcut Option + K, or checking the indicator on the main transport, next to the record button. If you still do not hear them, check your routing again. Once you hear or see the audio tracks being played through the new audio tracks, be sure that you name the new audio tracks properly (Xpand print and Reason Print), and then record them. As they are being recorded, you will see the overviews being calculated in the Edit window unless you are in QuickPunch mode. When in QuickPunch mode, you will not be able to see the overviews being calculated in real time.

Once they have been recorded, highlight each one of the Xpand and Reason plug-in tracks and make them inactive. Remember, you can make a track inactive several ways, but the quickest way is to make sure that all of the track names are highlighted, and then right-click on the track name and choose Hide And Make Inactive. If you don't have your computer set up to use the right-click functions, you can go to the Track menu and make the tracks inactive from there or simply hold down the control key and click on the highlighted track name and select it from there. Making the tracks inactive allows you to keep all of your channel settings so you can get back to them if you need to, and turns them off so they are not using any of your computer's resources. Since you have recorded the plug-in sounds onto audio tracks, it is as though you still have the MIDI or instrument tracks turned on in the session. Hiding them after they are made inactive simply provides you with more Mix and Edit window real estate.

From RTAS to AudioSuite

In addition to using buses to submix and record your instrument tracks and any other tracks that are using CPU-intensive plug-ins, there is yet another way to maximize your CPU usage. As was mentioned in chapter 3, there is a menu item named AudioSuite. As you know, when you are using an assortment of plug-ins on various channels, each plug-in used taps into your computer's CPU. However, most of the time, you can apply the same plug-ins directly to the track by using the AudioSuite feature for each plug-in you have on a channel. To do this, you must first click on the plug-in you have instantiated on the track. When it opens, you can go to the drop-down Settings menu located just to the left of the Librarian menu in the upper-left side of the plug-in. When the list appears, you select the Copy Settings option.

Now you can close the plug-in that is on the channel, open the AudioSuite menu, and select the same plug-in that you copied the settings for. You will notice that most of the plug-ins you have installed on your system will show up in the AudioSuite menu. When the AudioSuite plug-in appears, go to the Settings menu once again, and choose Paste Settings. You will notice that all of the parameters of the plug-in will change to the settings that were copied from your RTAS plug-in settings. Once the settings have been pasted, you must select or highlight the track or portion of the track that you would like to "print" the AudioSuite settings to. After the track or chosen region has been selected, choose the

Process option. The key thing to realize here is that you have three options for processing the track. They are Create Continuous File, Create Individual Files, or Overwrite Files.

If you have any regions that have yet to be crossfaded, creating a continuous file would be a bad choice because the clicks and pops from the region separations would be printed onto the file or "track" as one continuous file. Therefore, if you have unedited regions that still require crossfades, you should select Create Individual Files, so you can apply the appropriate crossfades later. The final choice would be to overwrite files. This should be used only if you are absolutely certain you want to apply the plug-in settings you have. There is no going back to the original file if you choose the Overwrite Files option. Also, keep in mind that when you use the AudioSuite feature, you lose the option of trimming your processed regions. Once they are processed, they are each considered to be their own whole file.

Another important thing to remember when using this method of saving your resources is to make sure you process your audio tracks in the order that they are being processed in the channel. In other words, if your channel's insert order is Compression, EQ, and then Gate, you should use the AudioSuite processing in the same order. Also, once you are through processing the audio, be sure to make the plug-ins inactive on each track. If you don't, you will hear the processing twice and not only will it sound differently than you had intended but, because the plug-ins are still instantiated, you won't be freeing up any system resources. To make a plug-in inactive you can either right-click on it and choose Make Inactive or use the keyboard shortcut Command + Option and click on it. Use this method on the two audio tracks that have the Amplitube and EQ plug-ins in them. Sometimes it is nice to just apply the AudioSuite process to the plug-in that is using the most CPU power.

EASY ON THE EYE

Once you have optimized your session and refilled your CPU's gas tank, you should start arranging your session so it is easy to work with and look at. An organized session that is visually pleasing really helps the creative work flow. The "guests" we are preparing for in this chapter include Strike and Velvet from the Digidesign AIR (Advanced Instrument Research) group box set. We will also be using other third-party software from Native Instrument's Komplete 5 bundle and some of the new plug-ins that come bundled with Pro Tools 8.

As you can probably imagine, any Pro Tools session can grow fast, so being organized and cleaned up for the new elements is key. I mentioned that you should start arranging things in a logical order. To clarify, there are typical ways to set up session arrangements, but nothing is set in stone. How to arrange things logically will vary from person to person and session to session. The idea is to arrange your session in a way that makes you comfortable, in a way that you can do anything you are asked to do or that makes it easier for you to navigate your session more efficiently. In this book, I will always suggest ways of doing things. If you are following along with the sessions, please arrange things the way I have requested for the examples. Doing so will make it easier for you to understand and follow the theme of this book. When you are working on your own, feel free to do as you wish; just have a method and refine it. Do not be sloppy and unorganized—that is the point here. Over the next few pages, you will learn how to group tracks, color-code them, and create custom markers not

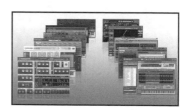

only for timeline events, but also for Show, Hide, and Zoom views as well. This is where things really start becoming fun, because now we can customize things in ways that until a couple of years ago were only "on the wish list." Once we are done organizing the session and are prepared for our guests to arrive, you will wonder how you ever did things any other way.

Grouping Faders in the Mix and Edit Windows

Once a session begins to take shape and it contains several similar parts, it's a good idea to start creating groups. Groups are convenient to use when you're making volume changes to multiple instruments that together already have a nice balance. Groups are equally useful when you're making edits across many or all of the tracks in your session.

Let's start out by grouping the plug-in categories. Select both Xpand Tracks, go to the Track menu, and select Group; alternatively, you can use the keyboard shortcut Command + G. This will bring up the Group dialog box. Here, you can enter the name of the group, choose the group type, see a list of tracks that are available for grouping, and make other organizational changes. In one of the earlier versions of Pro Tools 7, the grouping options started to include four banks with 26 groups available in each bank, and you were given the ability to choose which grouping options you would like to use, including Send Mutes and Send Levels, and which ones are linked within the group. For our session, we will just apply traditional group features. When the dialog box is open, name the group "Xpand," keep the type of group in the default

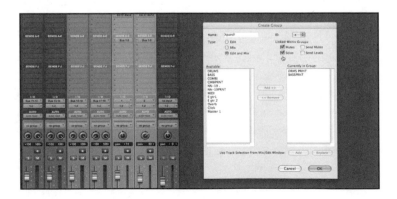

Edit and Mix selection an ID assignment of bank "A," and select only the Mutes and Solos to be linked within the group.

Apply the same technique to the Reason and Amplitube tracks. When you are done, you will notice the letters of the group IDs in the lower section of each channel just above the pan knobs.

Now that your tracks are grouped, you will be able to make volume changes, edits, solos, and mutes on a group level. This often comes in handy; however, sometimes you still need to have control over a certain channel within the group. To regain individual control, you can Suspend All Groups by clicking on the Mix Group's drop-down menu on the lower-left side of the Mix or the Edit windows, or you can use the keyboard shortcut Command + Shift + G. This will temporarily deactivate the groups, allowing you to make the changes you wish. Suspend All Groups is indicated by the Mix and Edit Group views being grayed out.

When you only need to make independent level changes, you can do so quickly by holding down the Control key while changing the fader level. This way you don't have to suspend the groups at all and you can keep your workflow going smoothly. At some point, you may want to separate your mix and edit groups when you are creating the groups. You'll know when it is time to separate your them after you've been working with the above basic grouping features and techniques for a while.

Color Coordination

Now that your tracks are grouped, you can assign colors to your session. This provides you with a nice way to identify all of your different track types, track groups, or any combination of the two. Pro Tools 8 offers a brand-new color palette to work with and a more convenient way to adjust the hue of the color-coding on your channel strips when the Apply To Channel Strip option is enabled. You can also apply colors to channel strips in the Mix and Edit windows. Let's start by highlighting the names of two Xpand tracks. (You'll have to follow along on your computer monitor to see the colors.) Then click on the thin, rectangular color-selector box located at the top and bottom of the channel strip. When the color palette appears, you can change the color of the tracks by making a selection. You can select which part of

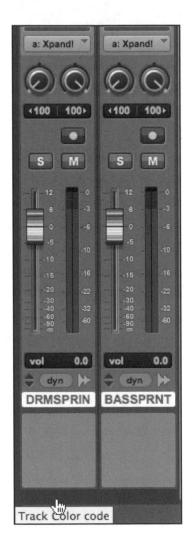

Track Color code

the track receives the color features by selecting them from the Apply To Selected option box.

For example, to apply color to the channel strip, make sure that the channel names are highlighted, bring up the color palette, and choose to apply the color in the tracks. Notice that the whole channel strip in the Mix window has changed the Xpand group to the color that was selected. Now, from the Edit window, triple-click and select the whole group of Xpand tracks in the Track Display area. When the tracks are selected, choose the option Apply To Selected → Regions In Tracks. Notice how the waveforms or overviews in the Track Display change to the color you selected.

You can use the other color selections too, but for now, just color the tracks and the regions in Tracks. You can use any color scheme you wish, or you can follow the book by applying red to the Xpand tracks, a shade of orange to the Reason tracks, yellow to Amplitube, blue to Click, and gray to the Master. When you are through color-coding your session, use the Save As feature and name this session "Color-Coded." Here is an example of what your session should look like in both the Edit and the Mix windows.

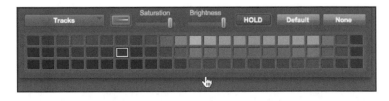

Cleaning Up the Audio Bin/Regions List

You should get into the habit of removing all unused regions from the Regions List. This leaves only the regions that are used in the Track Display area and keeps your session clean and organized.

However, simple mistakes can have a destructive effect on your session, so please follow along closely. Before moving on, save your session again, but this time name it "Clean Up." This is just another precautionary measure to make sure that you can get back to where you started if necessary. To clean up the Regions List, go to the Regions List drop-down menu and choose Select, and then Unused.

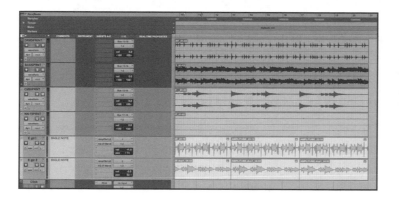

Notice that all of the unused regions become highlighted in your Regions List.

Next, from the Regions List drop-down menu, select Clear.

When the dialog box comes up, you will have a few options. This is where it is extremely important that you make the correct choice. If you select Remove, the unused regions will be removed from your Regions List for this session only. If, however, you choose Delete, the regions will be permanently deleted from your hard drive. Be sure to remove and not delete the unused regions. You should use the Delete option only when you are absolutely certain that you will never need the selected regions or files again.

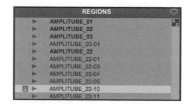

To do this much more quickly, you can use the keyboard shortcut Shift + Command + U to select the unused regions, and then Shift + Command + B to clear selected regions.

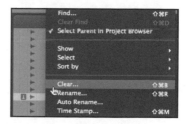

Notice the results in the Regions List. The only tracks in the list are the same as the tracks being used in session.

AIRING OUT YOUR SYSTEM

Digidesign's Advanced Instrument Research (AIR) group was created because of the demand from Pro Tools users who wanted high-quality virtual instruments that not only sounded great, but also were completely compatible with Pro Tools and were easy to use. AIR products are designed specifically for Pro Tools, with no other host-based application consideration, which allows them to integrate seamlessly with Pro Tools. Since these virtual instruments are developed for a single host platform, they aren't subject to the functionality, user-interface, performance limitations, and compromises that are often required when developing products for multiple host platforms. Pro Tools 8 now comes with the AIR Creative Collection plug-ins. These new plug-ins are great to get your productions going without having to use any third-party software. The instruments include a nice drum-programming plug-in named Boom, a tonewheel organ instrument named DB-33, a great piano plug-in called Mini Grand, a very rich-sounding analog synth plug-in named Vacuum, and last but not least the Structure Free sampler, which has been available for a while now.

In the next section of this book, we will go over some of the software included in Digidesign's Virtual Instrument Box Set. If you do not have these plug-ins, you should still read this next section and watch the associated QuickTime clips that are included. Most of the basic principles demonstrated in the QuickTime clips for this section of the book apply to all of the

AIR plug-ins, including the new Creative Collection plug-ins. Having an awareness of what is available is very important, and it will help inspire you to keep pushing your own limits. You can get an idea of just how good the AIR plug-ins sound with the new instruments that come with Pro Tools 8; however, this particular box set features the ultimate in sound quality, feature innovation, performance, and musical playability. If you are looking for some incredible-sounding virtual instruments to add to your new Creative Collection, then getting the AIR Virtual Instrument Box Set is something to seriously consider.

STRIKING GOLD WITH DIGIDESIGN'S ULTIMATE DRUM TRACK PRODUCTION PLUG-IN

Now it's finally time to get things movin' and groovin' with Digidesign AIR group's Strike plug-in. We have all waited a long time for a good drum machine type of plug-in that integrates easily with Pro Tools. There are plenty of nice drum programs out there and lots of great samplers with several ways to sequence and build professional-sounding drum tracks, but Strike puts all those elements together in one user-friendly plug-in that is 100 percent compatible with Pro Tools.

Strike uses five high-definition drum kits that have up to 12 instruments in each kit, and it has as many as nine different playing styles per instrument. The preset drum patterns are based on real recordings and have an incredible human element to them. The interface is simple to use and pleasing to the eye. The control you have is endless. Not only can you create your own unique drum patterns, but you can also easily edit the preexisting ones with the Style Editor. Strike also allows you absolute control over literally every aspect of the drum performance, in real time and through automation. There is a built-in mixing console that allows you to have control over the microphone placement, the direct and ambient sounds of the kit, and the inserts for dynamic and time-based effects. It even has individual channel outputs so that you can run them through a professional analog console or simply use your favorite plug-ins on the individual Strike sounds. It would be impossible to cover everything about Strike within the context of this book, so I will give you a brief overview of how to quickly breathe some new life into your preproduction ideas. Strike instantly adds a human element to the programming of drum parts. It will be up to you to take it to the next level.

THERE IS CREATIVITY IN THE AIR

Okay, assuming that you are following along and have your "Clean Up" session open, do one more Save As and name your new session "AIR." Then create three more stereo instrument tracks and name them "Strike," "Velvet 1," and "Velvet 2." Color-code the tracks and the regions in the tracks a nice shade of green.

On the Strike track, go to the insert and select Instrument, and then choose Strike.

When the plug-in appears, you can see right away that it is an intuitive interface. On its left-hand side there is a browser column, which contains four main folders: Settings, Styles, Kits, and Mixes. There are preset and user settings available for creating and saving your custom settings in each main folder. Click on the Settings folder and open the Preset Settings folder. You will see a long list of different styles from which to choose. To audition one of them, click on the Speaker icon that is just to the right of the styles names.

For the example in the book, I am using the LAFunk 115 preset. If you have been following along with the examples, I suggest you use one that fits the music in your session.

To load the kit, double-click on it and you will see Strike loading the selected kit below the Keyboard section at the bottom of the plug-in.

Once the kit has loaded, you can use the mouse to click on the white keys in the middle of the Keyboard section, and instantly hear a loop play. Once you find the kit that you like, you can go back to the Styles folder and select a different style, and still keep the sound of the kit you originally picked. If you look closely toward the bottom of the plug-in, you will see that there are six octaves in the Keyboard section. The first octave is located all the way to the left and is made up of yellow buttons, which are used to pause certain instruments and keep them from playing. While the loop plays, pressing button 1 will stop the kick from playing. Button 2 stops the snare, 3 stops the hi-hats, 4 stops the ride, and so on. This is cool if you find a good preset loop groove, but let's say the kick pattern just isn't right. When you pause the kick from playing in the loop, you can go over to the blue keys at octaves 4 and 5, find the kick drum, and play in your own kick pattern. The white keys are zoned in three octaves in the middle of the keyboard. These zones provide you with various grooves and fills. All of the white keys in the first zone play verse-style grooves, and the black keys play intro fills. The second zone is for bridge-section grooves and transitional fills. The third zone is for chorus grooves and outro fills. Just remember that the white keys are grooves and the black keys are fills.

Before you go any deeper into Strike, take a few minutes to play around with the keys and get a feel for "playing" Strike as an instrument. If you have a MIDI controller, you will notice that everything should be lined up with your keyboard perfectly. How many octaves your controller has will determine the number of zones you will be able to access at one time. I am using the M-Audio Axiom 49 and it works perfectly with Strike. When you are comfortable switching from pattern to pattern, start your Pro Tools session and play along with your own tracks. You may want to mute the original Xpand drum loop that we recorded earlier and let Strike become the only drum track in the session, or you can leave the loop on and layer your drum parts. Either way, you'll notice how Strike automatically locks to the tempo of your tracks and instantly makes your session sound as though a real drummer is playing to your music.

Before you record your new drum part, highlight the 12 bars of music you recorded earlier, and use the repeat command (Option + R) to repeat all of the parts one more time so that you have 24 bars total. This will keep you on pace if you are following along with the examples in the book. Once you have 24 bars of music, it is time to record your new drum part using Strike. First, put your cursor at measure 8 in Pro Tools. Show the click track from your track list and make it active again. Set the preroll to 1 bar and record enable the Strike track. The goal is to start by recording a 1-bar drum fill into your music track. Then play different loops and fills along with your music track, and end it with an outro drum-fill loop. Again, looking at the corresponding QuickTime tutorial will clear up any questions you have about the exercises.

Once you have your drum parts recorded, you can go over some of the other amazing features in Strike. As you play back and listen to your new drum part, look at the Control section of the plug-in. It is divided into three subsections: Style, Kit, and Mix. In the center of the Control section, you will see a Drum Kit icon playing back your programmed parts and accurately reflecting the instruments being hit. Just to the left and right of the Virtual Kit are two sliders. The Intensity slider controls the level of the overall drum kit, allowing you to control the dynamics of your part. The Complexity slider allows you to determine how complex your chosen drum loops will be. You can move these sliders with the mouse in real time as your track plays back, giving you the ability to conduct Strike. If you have a MIDI controller, the Complexity and Intensity sliders are automatically assigned to the mod wheel and pitch-bend controllers. In addition, if you loop a section with the MIDI Merge function on, you can press Record and record your style and complexity parameters without writing over the programmed loops.

Style

The Style section of the plug-in allows you to adjust the timing and dynamic behavior of Strike. Using the Hit Variance parameter allows you to control how loudly and softly each instrument in Strike is triggered with each hit in the selected loop that is playing. Turning the Hit Variance all the way to the left makes every sound, equal in velocity or volume, as if it were an older drum machine with no human element. If you turn it to the right, you will hear the velocity of the drum hits vary, giving your loop a humanlike quality. The timing control determines how tight or natural the quantizing of the loop is. The Feel parameter lets you choose whether you want the looped drums to be laid back or on top of the beat. One really nice feature is the Jam button. There are five selections to choose from, and each one plays your loops back slightly differently every time. The Style section of the Control area in Strike lets you produce realistic drum performances that are unlike any other program out there.

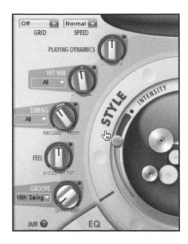

Kit

The Kit area in Strike allows you to adjust nuances of the drum kit as a whole or on select instruments within the kit. The tuning knob changes the overall tuning of the entire kit. The Timbre Shift knob allows you to change the character of the kit's sound without having to readjust the individual instruments' levels. Moving the knob to the right produces a harder timber at a lower volume, and turning it to the left produces a softer timbre at a higher volume. You can also adjust nuances of the snare, hi-hat, and ride cymbals instantly from the Kit section of the Control area.

Mix

The Mix section is amazing. You have control over the high and low frequency of the kit with the EQ section and the amount of compression of the kit in the Dynamics section. In the middle of the Mix section, you can choose the blend of close mics to overhead and room mics. There is even a talkback microphone knob that allows you to blend in the overly compressed and dirty characteristics of a common mono talkback mic.

NOT ENOUGH FOR YA?

As if there isn't enough control in the Main Control area, you can use the buttons at the bottom of the Browser area to get in there and fine-tune each section of the Main Control area at an instrument level. If you want to get even deeper into the features of Strike, you can click on the Edit Style button just under the Style button and see a nicely laid out grid view of each of the patterns you have programmed. You can make changes in real time, such as changing the placement of the individual notes in the loop, the velocity of any instrument, and even the instrument itself.

Once you are completely satisfied with Strike parts, you can save your settings by selecting the Save Mix button. Once you click

on the Save Mix button, you will need to create a new folder and name your mix settings so that you can recall them anytime by using the Import Settings from the Settings menu just to the left of the Librarian menu.

Please watch the QuickTime tutorial for using the Strike plug-in; it may help you understand some of these features more clearly.

VELVET

Digidesign's new Velvet plug-in is just as its name implies: its sounds are smooth as silk, and the playability is just as nice. Velvet re-creates the sounds of four classic stage pianos, which are all based on selected mint-condition, original electromagnetic pianos. The plug-in has models of three Fender Rhodes pianos (the Mark I, Mark II, and Suitcase) and the distinct sounds of the Wurlitzer A200 piano. The way you can program in the mechanical keyboard noises you would hear if you actually sat down at one of the original vintage instruments is amazing. You can adjust the timbre, the velocity curve, and the dynamic range separately, allowing you to define the sounds of various electric keyboards you've been listening to on the radio for decades.

I'm not a keyboard player, but I can play a few chords, and this plug-in makes me want to start taking piano lessons again. If you would like to get your hands on some killer vintage-keyboard sounds but without having to lug around the heavy, costly, and hard-to-maintain originals, Velvet would be an inspiring addition to your collection of virtual instruments.

OPEN UP THE SUITCASE

Using the Velvet plug-in is as easy on the eye and as straightforward as it can get. Just insert the plug-in on an instrument track, and you are ready to go. To continue with the examples in the book, insert the Velvet plug-in on the Velvet 1 track. When the plug-in opens up, you will immediately see how simple the interface is. Digidesign has definitely gone out of its way to make things easier visually than ever before. There are three basic sections: Piano Front Panel, Setup, and Preamp/EQ/FX.

The Piano Front Panel

This section is located in the lower-third section of the plug-in and gives you a visual representation of a piano keyboard that has 73 keys. You will also find the basic parameters such as the Model Selector, Master Volume, Tremolo controls, Rate and Depth knobs, and at the lower left of the plug-in, the Keyboard Extension Switch.

Clicking on the Down Arrow in the Model Selector area is how you select from the four keyboard models. The volume knob should be self-explanatory. You can turn the tremolo status on and select whether it is a stereo or mono tremolo effect. The Rate knob determines the speed of the effect, and the Depth knob determines the amount of tremolo effect you want added to the signal. If you right-click on the Tremolo on/off switch, you can decide whether you would like the tremolo to occur before or after the effects controls.

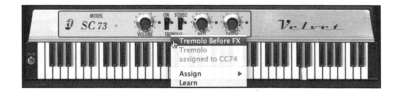

Setup Section

The Setup section is where you select the amount of waveform data that is loaded into RAM and set up the "personality" of the model you are using. The Pickup Level allows you to choose how much signal is being sent to the virtual line out. When recording vintage keyboards, it is common to take the line out directly to the mixer or amplifier to be miked up. The Pickup Level re-creates this gain-staging scenario.

The Mechanics feature is one of the things that make Velvet so unique. This parameter allows you to re-create the sound of the keys being pressed, as heard by the player. You can also select whether or not you would like to re-create the sounds of an instrument with its lid open or closed. The Key Off selection determines how you would like to hear the sounds of the keys being released. Use the knob to increase or decrease the level of this effect. If you choose the Staccato switch, it plays the release sounds more quickly. Try right-clicking on the Key Off switch, and you can select to hear the sounds of the sustain pedal. Digidesign has even gone so far as to allow you to choose the condition of the piano. The Condition knob simulates sounds that range from a mint-condition vintage instrument to one that is in need of some major maintenance. These features make Velvet unique, because it is the first plug-in that enables you to use these mechanical elements to add to the realism of the selected model.

Using the Memory Selector allows you to control the amount of strain put on your computer's CPU. The Eco setting is the smallest load size, but it limits the range of expression that is available. XXL is the biggest load size and provides maximum expression range, but it uses up your system resources much faster. The Mid selection is a good balance between the two settings. However, you can always "print" the sounds once they are recorded, just as you did for the Reason and Xpand tracks. Having the ability to print your tracks is a good alternative to using a smaller load size and sacrificing the incredible range of expression obtainable in Velvet.

Another nice feature is the Fine Tune knob. This allows you to pitch the entire keyboard up or down a maximum of two semitones, giving you the ability to assign a pitch-wheel controller to a vintage instrument. To finish off the Setup section, there are Velocity and Timbre functions as well. The four Velocity Curve sliders allow you to adjust Velvet's velocity sensitivity from no velocity response to a wide range of dynamic range. The Timbre knob allows you to adjust from a soft timbre for mellow sounds to a hard timbre for bright sounds. Using this in combination with the Velocity Response parameters allows you to achieve a wide range of timbral responses.

Preamp, EQ, and FX Section

This third and final section of Velvet provides you with a Comp knob for adjusting the amount of soft-knee compression that is applied to the sound. To bring out the attack of the keys, turn the knob to the left. To boost the sustain, turn the knob to the right. The Tube Drive adds harmonics and compression and emulates a tube preamp that reacts dynamically to the input level.

The 3-band EQ section provides fixed Bass and Treble tone-control knobs and a parametric Mid band knob to shape Velvet's fundamental sound. To round out this section, there are five categories of classic vintage effects. You can select one effect from each category to manipulate the various parameters within each effect. The effects you have available are Distortion, Wah, Modulation, Cabinet, and Delay. You can use any combination of these effects or turn them all off globally by de-selecting the FX box. All of the effects are after the Setup and Preamp/EQ section, with its outputs being directly routed to the Master Volume knob in the Piano Front panel. You can use the right-click feature on the Mode selector switch in the Wah category to place the Wah effect before the Fuzz effect if you wish.

MIDI CONTROLLER MAPPING

All of the AIR group plug-ins allow you to MIDI map almost every parameter available within their plug-ins collection plug-ins. This makes assigning the parameters to a MIDI controller that has various sliders, pitch and mod wheels, knobs, transport, and trigger pads as easy as can be. To assign the parameters, right-click or Control + click on the parameter, and you will see a few options. Select the Learn option from the drop-down menu, and then move the desired control on your MIDI controller. The parameter is automatically assigned to that control. To unassign the parameters, right-click or Control + click on the parameter and select Forget from the drop-down menu, and the assignment is forgotten.

THE AFTER PARTY

As you can see, both Strike and Velvet from the AIR group's collection of virtual instruments adds elements that go a step beyond what most other virtual instruments bring to a session. The sounds are amazing, the realism is unmatched, and the functionality with Pro Tools is seamless. The plug-in interfaces are laid out beautifully, provide a great deal of inspiration, and make your MIDI programming sessions almost effortless. If you can afford to add the AIR box set to your collection, it will add a breath of fresh "air" to your sessions. In the next couple of chapters, we will touch on some other great third-party plug-ins that will raise your awareness level and let you see what's out there in the world of virtual instruments. If you are following along with the examples in this book, you need to simply record two new parts to your session. I used the Fender Rhodes MK I and the Wurlitzer A200 in the examples so that you can hear the difference between the two types of sounds. Feel free to add as many new parts to your session as you wish. Use the instruments and sounds that inspire you the most. However, if you add the same number of parts to your session, staying with the theme of this book will be much easier.

MEMORY LOCATIONS

Using memory locations to their full potential takes patience, understanding, and a lot of practice. The more you apply the various memory location techniques described in this book, the more organized and efficient you will become as a Pro Tools user. There are so many features in Pro Tools that it is sometimes difficult to determine what to work on to improve your operator skills. Knowing how to use memory locations pays off almost immediately, so take some time and practice using them as much as possible.

Memory Location Preferences

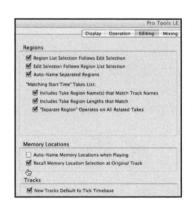

Using memory locations is valuable in a number of ways. Let's get started with them by setting up the preferences for their settings. Open the Preferences option from the Setup menu, and choose the Editing tab. When the dialog box appears, choose the Recall Memory Locations Selection At Original Track and leave Auto-Name Memory Location When Playing unchecked.

Memory Locations with Time Properties

As you listen to the track, you can create memory locations that correspond with the timeline. This makes it easy to see the different sections of a song when you have the Markers Ruler view selected and allows you to quickly create loops or navigate to different sections. To add timeline markers to your session, press the Enter key on your numeric keypad as the track plays. With the Auto-Name function turned off, you can name the memory location on the fly. Try to make this a fun challenge, as if it were a game. It will help you get faster at entering and naming several time-based memory locations in a session. If you set your session to Grid mode before you start creating markers, your markers will snap to the grid exactly where you want them to be, and they become very easy to use.

Marker Navigation

You can recall the Memory Locations window from the Window menu, or you can use the keyboard shortcut Command + 5.

It is possible to create a new marker from the drop-down menu located on the upper-right side of the Memory Locations window (using this option isn't very practical, but several other options in this menu are).

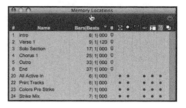

Memory locations are referred to as "markers," and you need to be aware of how to create and delete them. As you add markers to your session, you will notice that the Memory Locations window becomes a list that gives you access to your marker selections instantly. You will also notice that the markers will appear in the Ruler view if the Markers view is selected in the Edit window. You can click on these markers at any time from either the New Memory Locations window or the Marker ruler, and the selection will move to the beginning of the marker.

When you create markers, each one is given a number that can be seen just to the left of its name in the New Memory Locations window. You can add another important tool to your Power Tools tool belt when you learn to navigate the markers like this. From the numeric keypad select the decimal point, then the number of the desired marker, and then the decimal point again. This will take the play head to the beginning of your marker.

You can create loop selections by choosing one marker using the technique described above, holding down the Shift key, and then selecting any other marker from the list. This will set the playback markers in the timeline ruler to reflect the marker selections you have made. Playback markers are indicated by the blue Up and Down Arrows on the Timeline ruler just above the Track Display.

In order to loop your selection, make sure that the Loop Playback feature is turned on. To loop any selection, you can press the number 4 in the numeric keypad, use the keyboard shortcut Command + Shift + L, or hit the Control key and click on the Play button in the transport. The blue Loop Arrow will verify that the loop function has been selected.

Deleting a Marker

To delete a marker, highlight it in the New Memory Locations window and select Delete "name of selected marker" from the drop-down menu in the upper-right corner.

You can also use the Ruler view to click on the marker and drag it down into the Track Display area until it turns into a trash can; then let it go to delete it. You can also hold down the Option key on your keyboard, and click on the marker in the Markers Ruler view to delete it. Last but not least, you can use the selector to highlight as many makers as you would like in the Markers Ruler view, and then press the Delete key on your QWERTY keyboard.

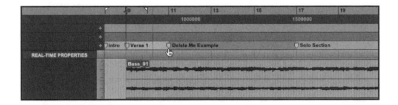

Using Memory Locations for Mix and Edit Views

One of the more powerful features of the memory location function is being able to save custom screen-view setups. This feature is extremely useful in every aspect of working in Pro Tools. Creating view markers has been around for years, and finally they seem to be pushing their way into the skill set of many Pro Tools engineers. They can be used for editing, recording, or mixing. To create these types of memory locations, create a new marker with the Enter key. When the Memory Location dialog box appears, select the None option from the Time Properties area. This is how these markers differ from the common timeline markers. Choosing None means that the memory location you are about to save does not refer to any time values. The way you use these memory locations is determined by the general properties you assign to them. Notice that you have several general properties to choose from. There is a place for you to name and number your view settings in order to stay organized. I suggest that when you are creating view-settings markers that you name them specifically and assign them higher number values than your timeline markers so that your Memory Location window stays neat and easy to navigate. The general properties you select will vary depending on why you are creating this particular view setting. You can also make notes in the Comments box to remind yourself of anything regarding that particular marker.

FINISHING UP STRONG

If you are following along with the exercises in this book, you will be creating both timeline markers and view-settings markers in the next set of instructions. Please make sure that you apply these ideas to your session. It is always nice to be aware of the many things you can do in Pro Tools, but sometimes you may not know when to use them or how they would assist you in your own session. If you take the time to go through this particular exercise, you will use the techniques you are about to learn in almost every Pro Tools session you ever work on.

Assuming that you still have your AIR session open and have recorded your Strike part, and that you have added two Velvet tracks, you should have plenty of material in your session to organize. If you don't have the Strike or Velvet plug-ins and you have been trying to follow along, you can use, as a substitution, the Strike and Velvet tracks with the Boom and DB-33 plug-ins that come bundled with the Pro Tools 8 Creative Collection. Then, take a quick inventory of everything in your session and make sure that your list matches the following list before going through this exercise.

Mix Window Track List Checklist

There are 16 tracks total:

2 hidden Xpand Stereo Instrument tracks
2 hidden Reason Stereo Instrument tracks
2 Xpand printed Stereo Audio tracks
2 Reason printed Stereo Audio tracks
2 Amplitube or miked Mono Audio guitar tracks
1 Strike Stereo Instrument track (or 1 Boom track)
2 Velvet Stereo Instrument tracks (or 2 DB-33 tracks)
1 Reverb Stereo Auxiliary track
1 Stereo Master fader
1 Click Mono Auxiliary track

Edit Window Checklist

1 bar of drum intro
24 bars of music
4 bars of outro music

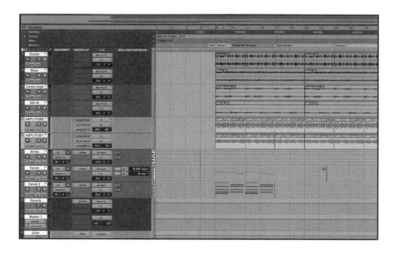

ON YOUR MARK, GET SET, GO!

Play your session from measure 7, and make sure that the click track is playing. Your first goal is to create six markers. Use the keyboard shortcut Command + 3 to bring up the Big Counter window. Your Main Counter window should be set to Bars|Beats; this way, the Big Counter will give you measure numbers to help you visually keep track of where you are in the session.

Marker List

Measure 8   — Intro
Measure 9   — Verse 1
Measure 17 — Solo Section
Measure 25 — Chorus 1
Measure 33 — Outro
Measure 36 — End

View Markers Exercise

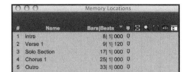

Once you are finished creating the timeline markers, you can start making your view markers. This should give you great ideas about how to organize your future sessions. The first view marker you create will show all of your currently active tracks in your session. Before you start, highlight all of the track names and hold down Shift + Option while selecting the Fit To Window track size. This should make all tracks take up the entire Edit window. Now, close the Regions List by clicking on the Double Arrows toward the bottom right of the Track Display area. Then, make a selection from measure 6 to measure 38, and click on Option + F. This will center the selection and allow you to see the whole timeline from the intro to the end markers. Click on the Enter key and select the Time Properties to Selection. Number the marker "19," and name it "All Active In." Select Zoom Settings, Track Show/Hide, Track Heights, and Group Enables. Finish creating the next two markers, with these specifications. Go through the following nine steps exactly as they are written, and you will be fine.

View Markers List

1. Hide and make inactive all tracks from the Edit window.

2. Make sure that nothing is in your Mix or your Edit window.

3. Use the Enter key to create a new marker.

4. Name it "All Inactive."

5. Number the memory location "20."

6. Set Time Properties to None. Choose Zoom Settings, Track Show/Hide, Track Heights, and Group Enables from the General Properties and then press Enter.

7. Show the four Xpand and Reason tracks and their corresponding audio "print" tracks, and make them active by a method of your choice.

8. Size all tracks to Fit To Window.

9. Use the same options as in the previous example, but name it "Print Tracks" and number it "21."

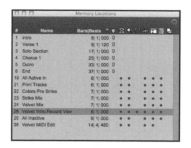

Once you set your timeline and view markers, I suggest you practice some of the marker navigation techniques as described earlier in this chapter.

FINAL THOUGHTS

We have covered a lot of material in this chapter, so take your time with it. Digest it, use it, and practice the methods you've learned about in this book thus far. The more you read over this chapter and the others and apply the concepts to your work flow, the more the gray areas that you've had in your Pro Tools skill set will start to darken—and before you know it, everything will be as simple as black and white. Speed is a by-product of accuracy, so try to do things deliberately and concisely. Use the keyboard shortcuts whenever possible; the more you use them, them quicker you will become.

POWER TIPS SUMMARY FOR CHAPTER 6

1. Printing your instrument-track outputs by busing them to an audio track and then making the track inactive is a common method of saving your computer's resources. Applying AudioSuite plug-in processing directly to the track is another good way to free up CPU power.

2. Making sure that you are not in QuickPunch mode when busing and recording your instrument tracks to new audio tracks will allow you to see the overviews being calculated in real time.

3. To quickly hide and make inactive several tracks at a time, highlight the desired track names, and then use the right-click feature to choose the option Hide And Make Inactive.

4. When using AudioSuite processing to save CPU resources, make sure to process the plug-ins in the order that they appear on the inserts. Doing so will assure that your insert signal flow is re-created just as it is in the channel inserts, and that the track will therefore sound the same.

5. Pro Tools 8 allows 104 group possibilities. You can customize which features are active in the group, including the send mutes and the send levels. Also remember that when groups are active and you would like to adjust the position of one fader within the active group, you can hold down the Control key and freely adjust any fader's output level without applying the volume change to all of the faders in the group.

6. When customizing the channel strip with the color palette, you can adjust the opacity of the color on the track by holding down all three modifier keys (Command + Option + Control), clicking on the color from the color palette, and then moving the mouse up and down.

7. When cleaning up the Regions List you can always use the Regions List drop-down menu; however, if you use the keyboard shortcut Shift + Command + U, that will select the unused regions. Using the keyboard shortcut Shift + Command + B will remove the selected regions from the list.

8. When using Strike, you can mute individual instruments from the loop that is playing by using the yellow 1–12 buttons on the left-hand side of the Keyboard section. Once the desired instruments are muted, you can use the blue

buttons located on the far right of the Keyboard section to add your own pattern for the instrument you muted. You can assign any of the blue buttons to a sound in Strike by right-clicking on a blue button and selecting the desired sound from the pop up list. Also, using the Jam button from the Style area of the interfaces makes subtle changes to the loop as it plays, creating a very humanized performance.

9. When using Velvet, you can access some very cool features by using the right-click features. From the piano front panel, you can choose whether you would like the tremolo effect to occur before or after the master FX section by right-clicking on the tremolo switch. From the Setup section, right-clicking on the Key Off switch allows you the option of hearing the on/off sounds of the sustain pedal if you are using a sustain pedal. Also, right-clicking on the Mode selector switch in the Wah category allows you to place the Wah effect before or after the Fuzz effect.

10. If you set Pro Tools to Grid mode when entering markers, this makes the markers snap to the grid as you enter them, allowing accurate timeline navigation. You can navigate the markers by using the numeric keyboard command (decimal + marker number + decimal). If you would like to loop a particular section of the song, you can choose one marker number, hold Shift, then select the second marker; this makes a selection from the first entry to the second entry. Next, either use the keyboard shortcut (Command + Shift + L) or Control + click on the Play button in the transport to activate the Loop Playback function.

KEYBOARD SHORTCUT
SUMMARY FOR CHAPTER 6

Try to memorize as many of these commands as quickly as you can. Knowing the menus is important too, but knowing the shortcuts saves you time and are a real convenience once you get used to using them.

KEYBOARD SHORTCUT	FUNCTION
Enter	Creates Marker When Transport is Playing
. (decimal) + location number (numeric keypad) + .	Access Specific Marker Numbers
Option + Click	On Marker in Marker Ruler View to Delete Marker
Option + F	Centers Select in Edit window
Command + Control + Click	On a Plug-in To Make Inactive or Re-activate
Command + 3	Shows Big Counter
Command + 5	Shows Memory Location window
Command + G	Creates Group
Command + Shift + G	Suspends Groups
Cmd + Opt + Ctrl + Click + Mouse Up or Down	Adjusts Opacity of Colors on the Channel Strip
Command + Shift + U	Selects Unused Regions from the Region List
Command + Shift + B	Clears Selected Regions from the Region List
Command + Shift + L	Loops Playback
Control + Click	On Play Button In Transport to Loop Playback

PRO TOOLS TUNE-UP FOR CHAPTER 6

1. The system usage meter is used to see how much CPU power your computer is using for the current session. It can be accessed from the _____ menu.

2. Submixing, busing instrument track outputs, and applying _____ processing is used to take the strain off the CPU and allow more RTAS effects to be applied to the channel strip.

3. When using AudioSuite processing, it is very import to
    _____ before you try to
    process the track, otherwise the track will not be processed.

4. The three choices for processing an audio track with
    AudioSuite plug-ins are to create continuous files, create
    _____ files, and overwrite files.

5. The quickest way to hide and make tracks inactive is to high-
    light the desired tracks and then, _____
    on the track name, and select the Hide And Make Inactive
    option.

6. To make any plug-in inactive on the insert, you can
    right-click on the plug-in itself or you can hold down the
    _____ + _____ keys, and then click on the
    plug-in.

7. The main difference between bypassing a plug-in and
    making a plug-in inactive is that when the plug-in is made
    inactive, it no longer uses _____.

8. To create fader groups, you need to select all tracks you
    would like to include in the group, and then use the keyboard
    shortcut _____ + _____.

9. To control one fader in an active group, hold down the
    Control key and move the fader independently. To suspend
    all of the faders in a group quickly, use the keyboard shortcut
    _____ + _____ + _____.

10. To color-code your session, go to the Windows menu and
    select the _____, and then select
    the desired apply to selected option.

11. To clear and remove information from the Regions List, use
    the Regions List drop-down menu and choose the Select
    Unused, and then choose Clear Selected. After choosing
    the Clear Selected option, you will be given the option to
    _____ or _____. Making the
    wrong choice is very destructive.

12. When using the Strike plug-in, you can access all of the kits and loops from the browser's Settings folder. To preview the various loops and kits, click on the Speaker icon located just to the left of the preset name. If you would like to load that particular kit or loop, simply _____ on the desired loop name.

13. Once the desired Strike kit is loaded, you can use the mouse or a MIDI controller to play the loops, grooves, and individual instruments. With the mouse, you can use the buttons in the Keyboard section located at the bottom of the screen. Strike's loops and fills can be played using the white buttons at the bottom of the GUI buttons that are placed in a keyboard style method in the Keyboard section. They are spaced out over three octaves using three separate zones. The white buttons that resemble a standard keyboard configuration are specifically for _____, while the black keys buttons that resemble a standard keyboard configuration are programmed for _____.

14. The white and black buttons that resemble a standard keyboard configuration cover three octaves of keyboard section at the bottom of Strike's main page and are considered to be zones 2, 3, and 4. The yellow buttons assigned to the first zone allow you to _____ individual instruments of the loop or fill that is playing. If you would like to add individual instruments to the loop or fill, you can use the _____ buttons assigned to zones 5 and 6.

15. Strike has four sections on the main page of its interface. They are the Browser, _____, _____, and _____ sections. The parameters on the main page are overall global settings that apply to the entire kit. However, you can make specific changes on an instrument level by using the Kit, Style, and Mix buttons located at the bottom of the browser.

16. The _____ is used to change individual instrument sounds, rhythmic placement, velocity, and things you would like to edit.

17. Velvet re-creates the sounds of four legendary electro-magnetic stage pianos. The four keyboards it emulates are the Fender Rhodes MK I, MK II, and Suitcase 73, and the distinct sounds of the _____ A200.

18. Velvet's main interface consists of three sections and gives you total control of Velvet's parameters. They are the Piano Front Panel, _____, and the preamp, EQ, and FX section.

19. One major benefit of using the AIR virtual instruments is that MIDI mapping is easy. Mapping a MIDI controller's knobs, trigger pads, and sliders is achieved by right-clicking on the parameter you want mapped, choosing the _____option, and then moving the controller's knob or slider or tapping on the trigger pad you would like to use to control the parameter.

20. To set the preferences for the memory locations, go to the Setup menu and choose the Preferences option. When the Preferences dialog box appears, click on the _____ tab and choose the options you prefer.

21. Standard memory locations are also known as "markers." These markers allow you to quickly see and easily navigate to different sections of the song. Markers can be viewed from the Memory Locations window. To view the Memory Location window, go to the Windows menu and choose Memory Locations or use the keyboard shortcut _____.

22. There are several ways to delete a marker. You can highlight it in the Memory Location window, and then choose Delete "name of selected marker" from the drop-down menu. You can highlight a marker or several markers from the Markers Ruler view and press Delete, or you can hold down the _____ key and click on the marker in the Markers Ruler view.

23. To create a memory location, press the _____ key.

24. If you would like to create a marker for custom view settings that do not reference the timeline, press Enter to create a new marker. When the New Memory Location dialog box appears, make sure that the Time Properties are set to either _____ or _____, and then choose the general properties that you would like to be stored with your memory location. When you click on the marker from the New Memory Location window, it will not take you to a place in the timeline, but it will show the general properties you have stored.

25. To center a highlighted selection in the Edit window, use the keyboard shortcut _____.

Editor's Choice

7

By now, you should be starting to realize that there are endless possibilities when working with Pro Tools software. Once you understand the basics of digital recording and how to set up your system for optimal performance with your properly installed software, plug-ins, and peripherals, your sessions should become a more creative environment to work within. In the previous chapter, I discussed more virtual instruments and how to use them, bouncing tracks, printing effects, ways to organize your sessions, and several more convenient keyboard shortcuts. In this chapter, we will go over many incredibly useful editing and organization methods that are considered advanced by some, but essential to most. We will learn about some of the new plug-ins that come bundled with Pro Tools 8, and continue to discover some of the brand-new features inside Digidesign's powerful new software.

HISTORY IN THE MAKING

For many years, Pro Tools has been known to be an amazing audio-editing program that provides a great way to mix in the box if you have a Pro Tools TDM (Time-Division Multiplexing) or HD system. Unfortunately, for the average hobbyist or recording enthusiast, an entry-level price tag of around $10,000 is still not within the average user's budget. However, in 1999

Digidesign introduced the Digi 001 interface and LE (limited edition) software, which finally allowed the consumer to taste what professional audio recording, editing, and mixing was all about. The 001 was awesome. It had a built-in MIDI I/O, 24-track playback ability, RTAS plug-in capability, and most importantly, an identical set of its unparalleled editing tools—all for less than $1,000. Nothing could even come close to touching it, and it set a new standard for the "pro-sumer" line of products that were saturating the market at the time.

Over the past decade, the Pro Tools LE line of products has grown into the powerhouse it was always meant to be. It is now three generations strong and is still the trendsetting "one to beat" in the standalone audio/MIDI interface and software package market. With Pro Tools 8 software and the 003 control-surface LE system leading the way, Digidesign is still making major improvements that help the products stay ahead of the curve on the professional and consumer level.

Since personal computers have become so much faster, stronger, and more affordable, the need for time-division multiplexing has become less of a prerequisite for audio programs to achieve professional results. These technological advancements have allowed many companies to introduce powerful and respectable host-based recording and editing software, virtual instruments, and plug-ins. With this in mind, Digidesign has had to take its industry-standard software and hardware combination to a new level. Digidesign has been perceptive enough to listen to its loyal users, pay close attention to its competition, and adopt some great ideas from them.

In the final chapters of this book, I will cover tools that have been deeply embedded into Digidesign's software for years, along with the many great improvements that the manufacturer has made to them. It is important to not only learn about the "latest and greatest" advanced techniques that Pro Tools has to offer, but also to be aware of some of the history behind how these things came to light. It is wise to have an awareness of something's history, because that knowledge will almost always give you a better understanding of what is happening with it currently and what is likely to happen with it in the future.

CUSTOM SESSION PREPARATION USING TEMPLATES

Creating custom templates or using the Pro Tools new Quick Start creative templates gives you a logical way of setting up different work flows that make things easy for you. Creating your own custom templates provides a certain amount of comfort when you are working in Pro Tools under a number of various circumstances. Whether you are a songwriter, a musician, an engineer, or a one-man band, you can have the perfect session laid out for you ahead of time, and then recall it at a moment's notice. This means that when the creativity fairy waves her magic wand, you can simply open up a Pro Tools template session that will be ready to let technology help rather than hinder you. Imagine being able to sit down with a friend, a colleague, a client, or even by yourself and having various types of sessions already set up to your own specifications, so you can start creating with very little hassle. They can be set up for small but quick and efficient songwriting sessions or for any size, type, or style of session that your particular system or your creativity allows. Pro Tools 8 comes with several session templates to help inspire your creativity.

If you have been following along with the examples in this book, you should have an average-size session that has been saved at various stages of production. Along the way, you learned how to use quite a few features in Pro Tools. We started out with an Xpand drum track and bass track, and then added two stereo Reason tracks, and two mono audio tracks for harmonic plug-ins or live audio tracks. We applied dynamic and time-based plug-ins to the audio tracks. To round things out, we created a Strike track and two Velvet tracks. We also learned how to color-code the session and make custom view settings with memory locations. We set up our main counter, subcounter, grid value, nudge values, and the main transport settings. Let's use some of the same things to set up a custom template. This time, we'll do it all at once and then fine-tune the session with some other user tips we have learned so far in this book. Maybe, we'll even add some more new things along the way.

If you can do all of these steps without referring back to the previous sections of the book, you are doing really well. If this list gets a bit difficult to follow, go back and review these topics to complete this exercise.

Template and Review Exercise: 20 Steps

1. From the File menu, create a new blank session and set up the desired options.

2. Create the following new tracks: seven stereo instrument tracks, three stereo audio, four mono audio, one mono aux input, two stereo aux input, and one stereo master fader.

3. Organize the tracks and name them in the following way:

a.	1 Stereo Instrument	Strike	Drums
b.	1 Stereo Audio	Rex/Wav	Loops
c.	1 Stereo Instrument	Boom	Percussion
d.	1 Mono Audio	Bass Guitar	Bass
e.	1 Stereo Instrument	Reason	Bass
f.	1 Stereo Instrument	Xpand (2)	Arpeggiated Synth Bass
g.	1 Stereo Instrument	Massive	Fat Bass Double
h.	1 Stereo Instrument	Velvet	Electric Keys
i.	1 Stereo Instrument	Mini Grand	Acoustic Piano
j.	1 Stereo Instrument	Hybrid	Arp Synth
k.	1 Stereo Audio	Guitar Rig	Clean Electric Guitar

l.	1 Stereo Audio	Eleven LE	Dirty Electric Guitar
m.	2 Mono Audio	Real amp	Solo Guitar close/far
n.	1 Mono Audio	Acoustic Guitar	
o.	2 Stereo Aux	Plug-in FX	Reverbs, Delays
p.	1 Stereo Master Fader		
q.	1 Mono Aux	Click	Cowbell 1 No Accent

4. Color-code them for Drums, Percussion, Bass, Keys, Piano, Guitar, Click, FX, and Master Fader.

5. Use the list to instantiate all listed plug-ins and make sure they are working. If you do not have all of the plug-ins, use something similar from the new Creative Collection while following along with this exercise.

6. Set up Reason for independent Rewire outputs and direct MIDI to Pro Tools.

7. Create an audio track next to each plug-in for printing to conserve resources. Also, make them inactive and hide them.

8. Create groups according to color code.

9. Create custom view markers to see each group of instruments and tracks independently and one for all tracks. Select the view setting Fit To Window for each new view marker you create.

10. Select Grid mode, set the grid value and the nudge value to 16th notes.

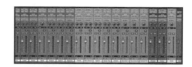

11. Set the main counter to Bars|Beats and the subcounter to Min:Secs.

12. Set the pre- and postroll to 1 bar.

13. Expand the transport.

14. Set up the click track to play during record and playback. Make the sound of the click a Cowbell 1, and Option-click

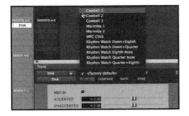

on the sliders or move them all the way to the right for no accent.

15. Set up the playback engine to accommodate a session of this size.

16. Set up for input-only monitoring.

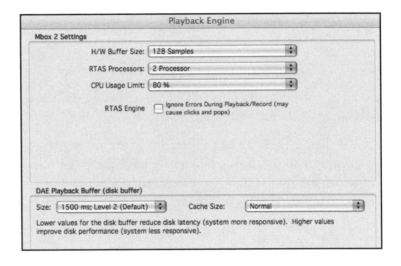

17. Choose the Save As Template option in the File menu.

18. Select Add Category from the Category drop-down menu and name your new category "My Custom Templates."

19. Name your template "Power Tools Example" and press OK. (Notice you can choose a different location to save your templates, but if you assign them to a custom folder, your templates will not show up in the Quick Start menu.)

20. Now, double-check to see if your template was saved properly by opening a new session from the File menu. Click on the Create Session From Template drop-down menu and select My Custom Templates, then select Power Tools Example, and click on OK. You will be asked where you would like to save your new session and what you would like to name it.

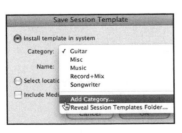

You have just created a session template that you can open any time you are ready to create in Pro Tools. The beautiful part about this is that not only are you ready to create with everything set up but, when you open the session you are also forced to name it and select where to save it. This ensures that you will not

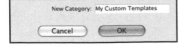

overwrite the basic template, therefore always leaving you with a clean session every time you open your template.

Importing Session Data

Importing session data is a great feature that has been around for some time now. Although the features are slightly different between the HD and the LE systems, using this feature is handy and effective in many circumstances. It allows you to import one or multiple tracks of any type from any session you have access to on your computer. Suppose you have a Pro Tools session open and you know that there is a guitar track from another session with a certain chain of plug-ins on it that you really like. You decide you want to use the same sounds in your current session, but you don't quite remember what those settings are. Here is how you can recall them.

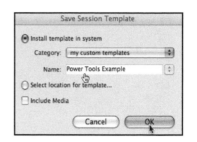

Go to the Track menu, choose the Import option, and then select Import Session Data. When the dialog box appears, navigate to the session and double-click on the Session icon. You can also use the keyboard shortcut Option + Shift + I.

You will see the Import Session Data page appear.

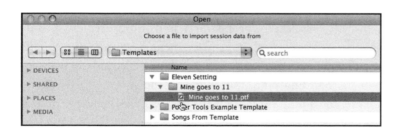

From here, you will need to make some choices. The most important things to know for this common situation are the source tracks and destination information and the settings options when importing.

The source track comes from the list of tracks contained in the session from which you are trying to import data. In this case, select the desired track as your source track, set the destination to New Track, and leave all of the import options unchecked. Sometimes you might want to take a look at your sampling-rate conversion options. If the settings that have inspired you are in a session having a different sampling rate than your current session, select the Apply SRC option, select the source sampling rate and the conversion quality that the destination session requires, and then select OK. Pro Tools HD systems have even more detailed options that are very cool, but you can achieve the same results in Pro Tools LE for this particular situation.

Once you've chosen your options, click on OK and the track selected for import will appear in your current session, exactly as it was in the session from which you imported it.

The last thing to do is get rid of any audio that the import session data function put into your region list. Most of the time, you'll want only the channel strip information, not the audio, from the other session. Remove the region from the list using a similar method to the one you used to clean up your session in the previous chapter. Find the region that was imported as session data, highlight it, and use the keyboard shortcut command Shift + Command + B. Select Remove. Remember that if you select Delete, you will lose the audio for your other session, and it will be erased off the hard drive completely. (Use extreme caution when doing this type of session-file management, because because if you don't, it is very simple to click too quickly, make a mistake, and lose files forever.)

Now you can select the proper input and output settings, record-enable the track, strum your instrument, and enjoy the sounds just as you remember them. Imagine how great this will be when you are recording a multiple-song CD and you want to keep the sounds consistent throughout the project. This feature is perfect for that scenario.

ADVANCED TOOLS FOR EDITING

Next up are the Pro Tools Keyboard Focus options. Getting these Digidesign quick keys under your fingers can really set you apart from the average hobbyist. It can be a slow and tedious process to get these quick keys under your command, but try to use them as often as possible. You'll be glad you did when you notice yourself whizzing around your session like a professional Pro Tools editor.

Keyboard Commands Focus

Pro Tools has a nice feature that allows you to execute shortcut commands with a single key on the QWERTY keyboard. I have already touched on a few of these keyboard shortcuts in previous chapters, but some of them were global computer commands; Keyboard Commands Focus shortcuts are exclusive to Pro Tools software. There are three Keyboard Focus modes, and you can enable only one at a time. When you enable one of them, the previous one becomes disabled. Keyboard Focus modes are indicated by the small square box with an "A–Z" on it. In Pro Tools 8, the Keyboard Commands Focus button has been moved to the upper-right-hand corner of the Track Display window in the Edit window.

Here is a brief summary of what each of them does.

COMMANDS FOCUS

This Focus mode provides a variety of single-key shortcuts for editing and playing. If it is turned off, you can still use the same commands by holding down the Control key before selecting the desired key.

REGIONS LIST FOCUS

This Focus mode allows you to locate a particular region from the Regions List by typing in the first few letters of the region's name.

GROUPS LIST FOCUS

This Focus mode allows you to quickly select the desired group by typing the group ID letter in either the Mix or the Edit window.

Important Keyboard Commands Focus Shortcuts for Editing and Navigation

NAVIGATION AND PLAYBACK

P = Move Edit selection up
; = Move Edit selection down
L = Tab cursor back
' = Tab cursor forward
[= Plays Edit selection
] = Plays Edit selection and includes Pre- and Post-roll

EDITING

A = Trim start to insertion
S = Trim end to insertion
D = Fade in to insertion
G = Fade out from insertion
N = Toggles Timeline Insertion Follows Playback option on and off
R = Zoom out
T = Zoom in

MORE TOOLS FOR PRO TOOLS
Tab to Transient

When you enable the Tab To Transient feature in Pro Tools, you can navigate the selected audio track by pressing the Tab key. This will automatically navigate to transients in an audio waveform and place the cursor just before the detected transient peak. Pro Tools 7.4 introduced new enhanced-resolution transient-detection algorithms for the best and most reliable transient detection.

To use Tab To Transient, you must first turn it on by clicking on the Tab To Transient icon just above the Bars|Beat ruler. Now, using the Selector tool, drop the cursor just before the start of where you would like to make a selection, and press the Tab key repeatedly until you find the desired start point. You can hold the Shift key and add to your selection by continuing to press the Tab key. If you need to move to the previous transient, you can use the keyboard shortcut Option + Tab. To move the end point of your selection to the previous transient, use the keyboard shortcut Option + Shift + Tab.

You can also turn the Tab To Transient function on and off by using the keyboard shortcut Command + Option + Tab. Remember, if Tab To Transient is not turned on, the same tab features will apply to the regions on the track.

Region Mute

When working with multiple regions on a track (or even if it is a whole file in which you want to selectively mute certain parts of the track), you can mute and unmute the individual regions by using the keyboard shortcut Command + M.

This mutes the region and leaves it in the timeline, but it is grayed out and is not audible. Sometimes this method is used for comping tracks; it also serves as a good visual aide.

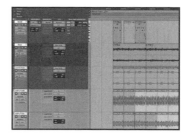

Region Lock

This feature locks the regions in place so they cannot be edited or moved unless they are unlocked. To lock or unlock a region, use the keyboard shortcut Command + L.

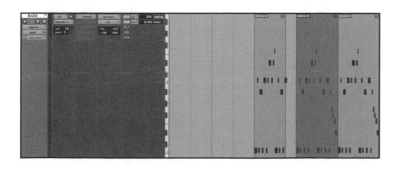

Snap to Insertion Point

If you would like to move a region to a specific place along the timeline, you can use Spot mode. Click on the region you would like to move, and then type the desired start time. Next, click on OK, and the region will move to the entered start time.

However, sometimes it might be quicker to drop the insertion cursor at the desired spot, and then make sure you change over to Slip mode. While holding down the Control key, use the Grabber tool and click on the region you would like to move to the insertion point. Holding down the Option key before you press Control-click on the region makes a copy of the region and snaps the copy to the insertion point.

ADVANCED TRANSPORT NAVIGATION

The Dynamic Transport feature was originally added to Pro Tools in version 7.3. It can be a bit confusing if you have never used it or don't know when or why to use it. The main purpose of the Dynamic Transport is to speed up your work flow in general, but especially while you are editing, auditioning loops, and recording overall. If you are already an above-average Pro Tools operator, you can sometimes feel as though you don't need to learn new ways to do what you already do well. Learning how to use the Dynamic Transport may take a minute and frustrate you, but it's worth taking a little extra time to work this feature out. It's pretty cool.

Before you dive in and learn how to use the Dynamic Transport, let's go over various transport, timeline, and insertion-selection playback options. These features may be familiar to you, but these functions still tend to baffle some people. Besides, it's really easy to get used to working the way your computer happens to be set up. Then you inadvertently change something, or maybe someone uses your computer and sets things up differently and doesn't put it back the way they found it, and you are lost on your own computer. These things are very common, so do yourself a favor and dedicate the following scenarios to memory as quickly as possible. A good understanding of the following facts will do wonders for your navigation and work-flow skills.

Timeline Insertion/Play Start Marker Follows Playback

To turn the Timeline Insertion/Play Start Marker Follows Playback feature on and off, go to the Setup menu and choose Preferences. Then select the Operations tab, and you will notice that Timeline Insertion/Play Start Marker Follows Playback is the first transport option available. Pro Tools 8 has added the ability to conveniently turn this option on and off from the toolbar. You can also turn this feature off and on by using the keyboard shortcut Control + N.

Choosing this option makes the timeline insertion cursor follow along while the track is playing, and when the transport is stopped, the cursor stays exactly where it stopped. Therefore, when you play the track again, you have to make sure you have selected where you want playback to start. Otherwise, the transport will play back from where it left off. Think of it like using a standard tape deck when it is turned on. When you stop the transport, you have to rewind to hear the tape play back from the start. If this feature is turned off and you press Playback, Pro Tools starts playback from your most recent selection's start time.

Link Edit And Timeline Selection

To turn this feature on and off, use the Options menu and select Link Edit And Timeline Selection, or you can click on the Up or Down arrows that are just below the Zoomer tool.

Choosing this option allows you to listen to playback from wherever you drop the cursor, make a selection, or start or restart the transport. If you leave the Link Edit And Timeline Selection option off, you must make a selection in the timeline or use the transport functions to rewind or fast-forward to playback from different places in the timeline. You cannot just drop the cursor anywhere in the timeline and play the track from there. This feature can prove to be frustrating if the Link Edit And Timeline Selection option is not selected and you aren't aware of its functionality.

Dynamic Transport

To turn on the Dynamic Transport, go to the Options menu and select Dynamic Transport. You can also use the keyboard shortcut Command + Control + P. You'll notice that as soon as the Dynamic Transport is activated, your timeline gets wider and the Link Edit And Timeline feature is turned off. Another thing to be sure of is that the Loop Playback feature has been turned on. You can confirm this by checking to see if the green arrow around the Play button appears in the transport. To use the Dynamic Transport, simply make a selection in the new timeline. In addition to your selection becoming highlighted, a new Play Start Marker will appear. This allows you to start playback from anywhere in the timeline without losing your selection. If you place Play Start Marker within your selection, your track will loop from the selection start time once it gets to the end, and it will keep cycling until you move the Play Start Marker again or stop the transport. You can also move the Dynamic Transport up and down the timeline and keep the same selection, and you can even use the Play Start Marker as a way to allow some preroll for recording without using the Pre-roll and Post-roll options.

Since the Dynamic Transport automatically turns off the Link Edit And Timeline Selection, you have the possibility of using two completely independent playback selections. This is nice if you are working with loops or are editing on the fly. To make this work flow extremely convenient, set your Pro Tools preferences so that there have separate start and stop keys. To do this, simply select the Setup menu, choose Preferences, then go to the Options tab and select Use Separate Play And Stop keys.

Using Separate Play and Stop Keys

If you are using the Dynamic Transport function, you have the ability to listen to two separate playback selections. To have total control over navigating your transport and edit selections, turn this selection on by going to Preferences, under Operations. When this option is turned on, you can make a selection from the Dynamic Transport and start playback by pressing the Enter key on the numeric keypad. If you make a secondary edit selection, you can use the Play Edit Selection key, which is the left bracket ([) on the keyboard. Finally, use the 0 (zero) key on the numeric keypad to stop the transport. The secondary edit selection is identified by the yellow line that has a single yellow dot to both the left and the right of it.

If you noticed, you did not use the Spacebar to start or stop the transport. This is because when using the Dynamic Transport and a second edit selection, you could very well be using the new Workspace and Project Browser features to have the Spacebar audition your loops. I will be touching on this subject again before this chapter is over.

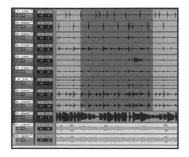

EDITING MULTIPLE AUDIO TRACKS WITH GROUPS ENABLED

Having all of your tracks grouped when doing multitrack edits is important, especially when editing drums. Editing all parts of a group ensures that your tracks stay in time with each other with each edit you make. If you are editing a source that was captured using multiple microphones, it is even more important to edit as a group, so that the phase relationship of all the instruments within the drum group stay in check.

CREATING REGION GROUPS

A region group is any combination of audio and MIDI regions that are gathered together in a selection and then tied together as one big region. A region group has many features and is very easy to edit once it reaches its destination. Region groups are used for arranging multiple tracks and "flying" them to different places along the timeline using Snap To Insertion editing techniques. A separate Region Group folder is generated with the first region group selected, and a file with the extension ".rgrp" is created for each new group that is created.

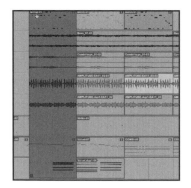

To create a region group, use the Tab To Transient function to find the correct edit point, and then use the Shift + Tab feature to determine the desired length of your region for grouping. Now, while still holding down the Shift key, use the Selector tool to select all of the tracks you would like to be a part of the group, and then select the Group option from the Region menu; alternatively, you can use the keyboard shortcut Command + Option + G. You can ungroup the region by selecting Ungroup from the Region menu, or you can use the keyboard shortcut Command + Option + U. If you are creating a region group and some of the tracks have fades applied to Elastic Audio tracks, you will have to consolidate the tracks before you can commit them to a group. Once the tracks are turned into a region, you can move them freely along the timeline just as you would with any single region.

COMPING IN PRO TOOLS 8

One of the most exciting things added to the editing features in Pro Tools 8 is the new comping feature using multiple playlists. The concept of comping playlists has been around for years, and there have been various methods used to gather the best takes of an artist's overdubbed performances and compiling them into one "perfect" take. Since the new version of the comping feature has been added to Pro Tools, there is no reason to consider using any other method. This new way of working with comping tracks is easy, smart, and intuitive. Once again, Digidesign, through Pro Tools, shows that it has been paying attention to its competitors and putting its own spin on how things should be done. These methods may seem similar to other programs, but the bottom line is that it is now being done in Pro Tools—the best audio-editing software on the planet.

One Perfect Take

Start by going to the Operation Preferences and selecting the Automatically Create New Playlists When Loop Recording option under the Record tab. This ensures that when you are using Loop Record, multiple playlists will be recorded and will be ready for comping when it comes time to edit.

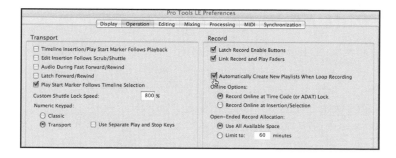

Next, once the parts have been recorded in Loop Record, you can change the Track view to Playlists instead of Waveform. This will drop down a list showing all of the takes. You can arrange them in any order by clicking-and-dragging any of the tracks and moving them to the desired position. Once you are organized,

you must create a new playlist by clicking on the Up and Down Arrows just to the right of the of the track name. Name your new playlist "PT 8 vox comp" if you are following along in this exercise.

Once the new playlist is created, you can solo any of the alternate playlists and audition the various performances. When you decide which take of the first line of the first verse you like the best, highlight the selection and then go to the Edit menu and select Copy Selection To Main Playlist option. This will move the selection to the main playlist. Next, select the best take of the second line, and this time use the Up Arrow just to the right of the alternate track name; alternatively, you can use the keyboard shortcut Control + Option + V to fly the next take up to the main playlist.

Finish choosing the best remaining takes for the rest of the first verse. When you are done, you will see that all of the best takes from the various performances will be compiled into one magnificent main playlist.

When you are finished, close the playlists by using the keyboard shortcut Command + Control-click, or click on the Track view indicator and set it back to Waveform. It's as simple as that.

ZOOMING IN ON CROSSFADES

During this chapter, we have learned how to use multiple takes to make one great take by making a compilation of the best takes on one new playlist track. This means that you have regions in your playlist that do not represent how they were originally recorded. In general, when you start to edit, arrange, and do other various editing tasks, there is a good chance that when the track is playing over the crossing point where the regions butt up against each other, you will hear a little click or pop. This is common and easy to fix.

To quickly fix these crossing points between regions, you use something called a crossfade, or a spot where the first region quickly fades out as the next region quickly fades in. Crossfading is an audio-editing technique that should be used all the time when there are separated regions that butt up against one another. Since the "fade is quicker than the ear," using this technique usually eliminates any pops and clicks that occur at the region crossings. To do a basic crossfade, use the Selector tool to highlight a selection that includes the crossing point of two regions. Once selected, go to the Edit window, choose Fades from the menu, and select Create. The dialog box will appear, and you can select the type of fade settings you would like to use.

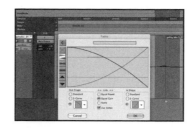

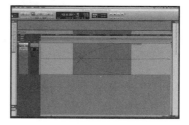

Using crossfades is so common when working with audio that if you happen to have a particular fade setting that you like to use all the time, you can create a preference for it. To do this, go to the Setup menu and select Preferences. From the Preferences dialog box, select the Editing tab. In the Fades box, notice that there are several options to choose from. Make sure the Preserve Fades when Editing option is checked. A QuickPunch crossfade length of about 7 ms is fine for most situations. You can select the individual slope of both the Fade In and Fade Out and select the exact settings of your preferred default Crossfade that will occur with every QuickPunch or batch fade automatically.

This is a great feature. You can even set the crossfade settings for REX files that we will be importing in some of the QuickTime tutorials. We will talk about setting this fade preference when the time comes.

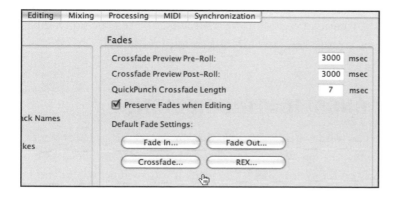

If you would like to make multiple crossfades after doing several edits or punch-ins, you can use the Selector tool and triple-click on the regions to select all regions on the track; then use the keyboard shortcut Command + F, and the Batch Fades dialog box will appear. Set the crossfade time selection and select OK, and you will create as many fades as are required by the track.

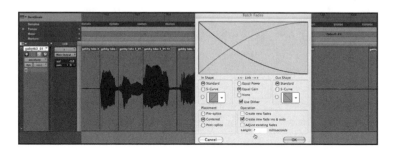

One last thing to realize about fades is that the SmartTool gives you access to all of the above-mentioned fades. If you are using the SmartTool, go to the upper-right or upper-left side of the region and hover until you see a small box icon. When you see this icon, click-and-drag on it horizontally to select and create a fade-in or a fade-out with a length determined by the length of the horizontal drag you've performed. You can also quickly create crossfades by navigating the SmartTool to hover over the region crossing, toward the bottom of the region, and the box will appear again. When you click-and-drag this time, you are creating the length of the crossfade that will be performed. As you can see, there are many ways to set up your fade functions in Pro Tools, and you should take advantage of them. Feel free to try creative ways of using crossfades. You may be surprised at how creative you can be with a simple crossfade.

CONSOLIDATING REGIONS

Once you have done several edits on a track or group of tracks, there are a few ways these edits affect your session. First, it's not easy on the eye the way it was when it was a whole file. Second, if there are too many edits on several tracks, your hard drive may not be able to access the little chunks of audio regions quickly enough to play through densely edited parts. If you consolidate the track, you will not only get a better visual perspective on the track, but you will also achieve better overall system performance.

One crucial tip is to always create a duplicate track in the playlist so that you still have a copy of the original edited track. Once you consolidate the track, you can no longer trim regions or redo crossfades that still click and pop or that you didn't have time to check thoroughly after you first created them. To make a duplicate of a track in the playlist, click on the Up and Down Arrows next to the track name in the Edit window, and select Duplicate. Consolidate the selection using the keyboard shortcut Option + Shift +3.

IT'S ABOUT TIME

It is always important that musicians play "in time." I have every drummer I ever record play to a click track if at all possible. Sometimes a drummer's, or any musician's, timing becomes less accurate when they feel the pressure of playing to a click track. If this happens but the band has a good overall feel, you can still let them record their music, and then go in and manually identify the beat so you can quantize with Elastic Audio or use Beat Detective later in the production. This allows you to play a click to them instead of them playing to the click. The key is to be able to know how to execute this function. If you are considering becoming a professional Pro Tools operator, you will be expected to know how to do this.

Identify the Beat

Identify Beat is an awesome tool to use when you have an audio part that was created without a click. Or maybe it was played to a click but you don't know the tempo, and you would like to produce tracks around it and use your Grid mode editing techniques or Beat Detective.

Let's say you recorded a drummer who played to a click that was from a drum machine that he brought in. The tempo wasn't noted at the time of the session, because you didn't realize that you would want to produce the track and create MIDI parts around it later on.

Open the session that has the tracks (but no set bpm information). Play the track, and as it is playing, you must capture a 2-to-4-measure selection and let Pro Tools calculate the average tempo for the selected length. To quickly capture four bars, make sure you are in Slip mode, play the track, and as you are tapping along in time, use the Up and Down Arrows to set your in and out points. When you select the Down Arrow while a track is playing, Pro Tools remembers this location. When you select the Up Arrow at the end of four measures, Pro Tools will highlight a selection based on when you pushed the Down Arrow and when you pushed the Up Arrow. Once you have a 4-bar selection, Control-click on the transport and put Pro Tools into Loop Playback mode. Listen to the four bars and make sure that you have a tight loop. To make sure you have a perfect 2-bar loop of the drum part, use the Zoom tool and get up close to your in point. While holding down the Shift key, use the Selector tool to click-and-drag the selection to the onset of the downbeat transient of the part. To quickly do the same thing to the end point, click on the Right Arrow one time to go to the end of the selection, and then apply the same Shift + click-and-drag technique to select exactly four measures according to your drummer's feel.

Once you are confident that you have the selection you need, make sure that you turn on the Conductor located in the transport. Now go to the Event menu and select the Identify Beat option. You can also use the keyboard shortcut Command + I. When the Add Bar|Beat Markers dialog box comes up, select location start and end times that are exactly four bars apart, and then select OK. Pro Tools does the math, and you get an exact bpm based on how your drummer played the part.

If you look at the Conductor again, it will have an accurate number for the tempo. This number will determine the tempo you will use when quantizing your drums. At this point, you have two options. You can either keep repeating the process until you have tempo-mapped the whole song based on your drummer's performance or use this number to use Beat Detective or Elastic audio to quantize the performance to one specific tempo for the whole song. If you tempo-map the entire song, you can simply create a click track, and it will follow the tempo map you created and you are good to go.

Beat Detective

Beat Detective was added to Pro Tools several years ago but was not yet available when I was first starting out as a Pro Tools operator. Back in the day, if you wanted to edit drum parts to make them tighter, you had to spend hours upon hours editing one song to achieve "acceptable" results. When Digidesign introduced Beat Detective, the plug-in simplified the drum-editing process and allowed the entire drum kit to be edited at least ten times faster than if you were editing it manually. For the most part, it automated what professional engineers would spend hours doing. When it was introduced, Beat Detective was, in my opinion, great in theory but not as accurate as doing things manually. Over the years, however, the plug-in has been revised repeatedly and has had a number of new features added, making it a powerful editing tool if you take the time to learn and use it properly. With features such as extracting tempo from audio, creating DigiGrooves, Region Separations, Edit Smoothing, or Region Conform functions, Beat Detective is a great editing tool to have in your Pro Tools toolbox. There is still no magic button to edit drums, but Beat Detective sure can save you a lot of time and allow you to do some amazing things.

Using Beat Detective can be a challenge, even for the above-average Pro Tools operator. In this section of the book, I will start by giving a brief explanation of the plug-in's features, and then finish up with what I feel is the most effective way of using it for editing a full drum kit and conforming, or quantizing, the drums. Pro Tools LE supports only stereo Beat Detective, unless you have the Music Production Toolkit upgrade.

Since the addition of Elastic Audio in Pro Tools version 7.4, some users may wonder why one would want to use Beat Detective if you can use Elastic Audio to do the same thing without any upgrades. The short version of the long answer is that Beat Detective is great for conforming audio to a custom grid using professional editing techniques. Elastic Audio is a plug-in that quantizes audio by using Time Compression and Expansion (TCE) algorithms. Some amazing TCE algorithms were added in Pro Tools 7.4, and I'm sure they will continue to improve sonically with each new Pro Tools release. Keep in mind, however, that regardless of how much the TCE algorithms improve, there will be a sonic compromise. Another big difference between Beat Detective and Elastic Audio is, even though Elastic Audio allows you to use groove templates, it doesn't extract custom groove templates for you like Beat Detective does.

If you read and understand Beat Detective the way it is taught in this book, using and understanding Elastic Audio will be painless, and even easier. This is why I am explaining Beat Detective first. After you understand both plug-ins, you can apply quantizing techniques using Beat Detective and Elastic Audio, and then audition the differences for yourself. Out of the box, Elastic Audio can be easier to use and is certainly an instant-gratification type of plug-in, but it may not be the right tool for the job in every scenario. Having both options at your disposal is definitely nice, and it's clear that Elastic Audio is the superchild offspring of Beat Detective and great TCE algorithms. This option will quickly become one of your favorite creative editing tools.

INSPECTING THE DETECTIVE

Beat Detective is divided into three sections: they are operation, selection, and detection. The controls in each of the sections vary, depending on which operation mode is being used.

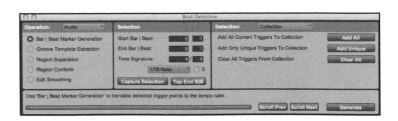

Operation Menu Section

The Operation section is where you find the Operation pop-up menu. This section allows you to choose whether you would like to analyze audio or MIDI information.

BAR|BEAT MARKER GENERATION

This selection creates Bar|Beat markers according to the transients detected in the audio selection.

GROOVE TEMPLATE EXTRACTION

This selection is used for extracting the feel and dynamics of the selection and saves this information to the Groove clipboard to be used in the current session, or the settings can be saved to create your own personal DigiGroove template library. You can apply these settings to other instruments to make the entire track have the same groove. Pro Tools comes with several DigiGrooves. We will cover how to use custom and preset grooves later in this chapter.

REGION SEPARATION

This is used for audio only. It creates new regions based on the transients in the selected audio and trigger pads used in the Detection section of Beat Detective.

REGION CONFORM

This selection is used for audio only and conforms, or quantizes, the selection to the current tempo map and to a groove template.

EDIT SMOOTHING

This selection is used for audio only, and it fills the gaps between regions after they have been conformed. If you desire, you can choose to have automatic crossfades inserted as well.

Selection

This section is used to define the audio or MIDI selection that will be analyzed. This section of the Beat Detective window provides the tools required to define and capture the time signature, swing, or subdivision content of your selection, and the selection range. In order to achieve the best possible results with a high degree of accuracy, make sure that your selection starts exactly on the attack of the first beat and does not contain any meter or tempo changes.

Detection

This section allows two modes of detection and gathering of beat triggers. How you use this section is of great importance. If you want to be a real "Beat Detective," know why you are choosing each mode of Detection.

NORMAL AND COLLECTION

These are the main Detection selections.

ANALYSIS

When Pro Tools 7.4 was released, there were three choices for transient analysis instead of just two. Since this was a subtle addition and possibly overlooked by many, you will notice the extra transient analysis option in Pro Tools 8. We will learn about what the difference is between the three choices in the next section.

HIGH EMPHASIS

This option is designed for analyzing high-frequency, inharmonic material while avoiding low-frequency material.

LOW EMPHASIS

This option was designed to analyze inharmonic material with low frequencies, such as bass guitar or kick drum.

ENHANCED RESOLUTION

This option was added to Pro Tools version 7.4 and was designed to produce the best results for the widest variety of audio material.

USING BEAT DETECTIVE

The exercise below should be repeated until you understand what is actually going on. You must learn to be able to see and describe to yourself how Beat Detective is working in Collection mode. Pay close attention each time you reanalyze each track individually, and notice how only new beat triggers are added to the "collection bank." Take it slow, be precise, and be patient. If you understand this method of transient-detection analysis, you will have a better understanding of how Elastic Audio uses Event and Warp markers. They are very similar in the detection area for transients.

Timing Is Everything

To get straight to the point, Beat Detective was designed for editing drums. It can do a few things very well, but let's start with what it was designed to do. There is no doubt that using Collective Beat Detection is the way to go when you want to optimize the way beat triggers are collected, by gathering them with separate analysis and giving them different detection settings on each track. This is the only way to analyze and create beat triggers on one track, and then apply them to another track. This method yields the best results without having to edit or delete a bunch of false triggers that occur when using normal Detection mode. It takes more time, but the result is worth it.

A Collection Mode Exercise

Collection mode allows you analyze all tracks independently and add, remove, and edit trigger points. Moreover, it lets you add only the unique triggers onto the Main clipboard from each independently analyzed track. So, first make an edit group of your drums and name the group. You always want to apply Beat Detective to the entire drum group to avoid phase issues. Also, sometimes you can apply Beat Detective to the entire song, but it is highly suggested that you do things in sections of 4 to 16 bars. Let's start by selecting a perfect 4-bar loop. Make sure that you have a tight loop before continuing. Then open Beat Detective from the Event window or use the keyboard shortcut Option +

8. When the Beat Detective dialog box appears, start by making sure you are in Region Separation mode.

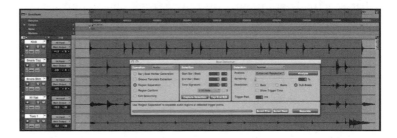

In the Selection box, press Capture Selection. The Start Bar and End Bar boxes will have captured the same measure numbers as your loop selection. Most of the time, a note value of 16th notes is fine. If the beat you are working with is a swing groove, you can select the triplet option (indicated by the number 3, just to the left of the note-value box). In the Detection section, set the resolution option to Sub-beats.

Now turn your groups off (Option + Shift + G), and then select only the Kick track. Click on the Analyze tab, and use the Sensitivity slider to adjust how much sensitivity is being applied to the transient-detection function.

Once you do this, make sure that you see all of the kicks being detected. If a couple of extra transients are detected that are not kicks, use the Grabber to Option-click on the undesired triggers to remove then from the selection. Use the Option + F command to recenter the selection, and make sure that you have all of the triggers you need and that you have deselected the ones you do not need. From the Detection section, click on the pop-up menu, choose Collection mode, and then select Add All.

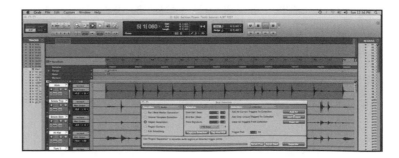

Once you are done, do the same thing for the Snare track. Put the Detection selection back into Normal mode, analyze the snare track, bring the sensitivity slider all the way down, and then bring it back up until you have all of the snares being triggered. Set your Detection mode back to Collection, and this time you will choose Add Unique. This adds only the unique triggers instead of erasing all previous triggers and adding just the new triggers.

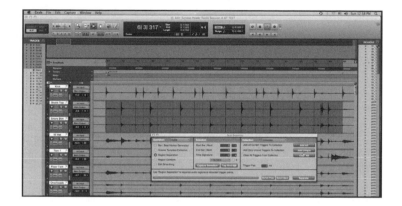

Repeat these steps until all of the instruments you would like to add to your Collection Detection are chosen. If you analyze your toms or overheads and are picking up way too many triggers, you can use something called Promote Triggers. This feature allows you to Command-click on each trigger, and it promotes triggers manually. Now, when you bring the sensitivity slider down, you can bring it up to as little as 1 percent and Beat Detective will put beat triggers on only the promoted triggers. Once all of your desired instruments have been added to your Collection mode bank, turn your group back on. Zoom out and resize so you can see that all of the triggers have been placed on an individual basis for each track and independently collected for a more specific analysis of the entire drum track.

Once you are sure all instruments have been added to your Collection mode bank, with Region Separation on and Collection mode selected, choose the Separate function located at the bottom right-hand side of the Beat Detective box; this separates all of the beat triggers.

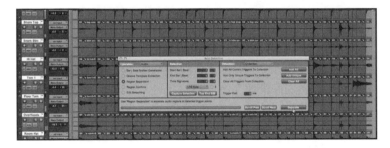

Once all regions are separated, choose the Region Conform option from the Operation box. This is where your regions become quantized. In the Conform section, you can select Strength to set how close to the grid you would like your quantize to be. For example, if you choose 50 percent, then things will be quantized half way to what is exactly perfect. One hundred percent quantizes things perfectly and really tightens things up. The Exclude Within function quantizes only things that are out of time by a certain amount, and you can choose the Swing option if your track has a swing feel. Now select Conform and watch as all of the regions conform to where they should be. If things move dramatically, then something probably went wrong. The regions should move by only a little bit.

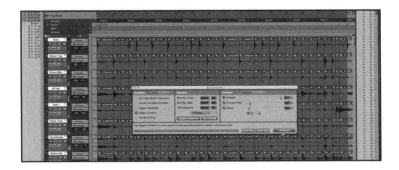

Once everything has been conformed, choose the Edit Smoothing option and set it to Fill and Crossfade. A Crossfade length of about 3 to 6 ms is plenty. Finally, choose the Smooth function, and you will notice that any gaps that were created by the conforming operation have been filled in and crossfades applied across all region separations. This usually gets rid of any unwanted clicks or pops caused by the edits of Beat Detective.

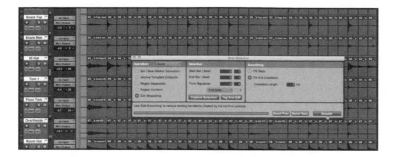

Time to Make a DigiGroove Template

If you really like the groove that the drummer or any particular instrument has, you can use the Groove Template Extraction option to save the fine-timing nuances of its rhythmic performance. This can then be saved to the Groove clipboard or saved to disk as a DigiGroove template. When creating DigiGroove templates, Beat Detective also analyzes the dynamics of a performance. If the selection is a MIDI performance, MIDI Velocity data is saved from the MIDI track, and accents and peak levels in audio data are incorporated into the Groove template as Velocity data. This is very cool if you want to apply the dynamics of an audio track performance to your MIDI tracks, allowing them to share the same dynamic feel.

The key to a good groove extraction is to make sure that all of your beat triggers are accurate, so that all of them can be applied to the template and accurately save the integrity of the original groove. To make a DigiGroove template, you must generate all of your beat triggers the same way you did in Collection mode. Be sure not to conform once the beat triggers are made, because once the tracks are conformed they are quantized, and the timing of the groove has been altered. However, if you like the feel and the timing is close to dead-on, then you can do the groove after you conform; but if you are fixing very small, subtle timing issues, adjust your Strength and Exclude Within options so that some of the original timing of the groove will be extracted with the DigiGroove template.

Once beat triggers are selected, choose Groove Extraction Template mode. Use the Selection options to define or capture the selection and configure the Detection options so the selection's peak transients are accurately detected as described just before the Groove Extraction time-out. Click on Extract, and either save it to your Groove clipboard to use immediately with the current session or select the Save To Disk option so you can use this DigiGroove anytime you would like to. Make sure that you save it in your Grooves folder, located in the Pro Tools folder inside the Digidesign folder in your Applications folder. Groove templates that are stored elsewhere will not be available in either Groove Quantize or Beat Detective.

EDITING MIDI

The best part about editing MIDI with Pro Tools is that you use the same tools you use for editing the audio. Some of the features are slightly different, but at least you don't have to learn how to use a new set of tools. Most MIDI editing functions are intuitive if you are already familiar with audio editing in Pro Tools, so the learning curve is fast. Pro Tools 8 has added some very powerful MIDI editing features that make Pro Tools even easier to work with than it was in the past, not to mention that it has more power than ever before.

In this next section, we'll go over the essential MIDI editing techniques that will get you through just about any MIDI situation. I'll start with the fundamentals that have been around for a while, and then touch on some of the new features that were added in Pro Tools 8. A whole chapter could be dedicated to MIDI alone, and maybe there will be a more advanced edition of this book that will go into greater detail on editing MIDI, but this brief overview of the essentials will work fine in most scenarios.

Notes View Editing

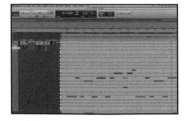

When you create an instrument or MIDI track, its default view is Notes. This is indicated in the Track View Indicator. When you enter MIDI data, you will see small chunks of data on the track. Each small chunk of data represents two things: the duration of the note, and the actual note that was played or entered.

We have already talked about using Real-Time Properties to do an overall nondestructive form of editing for feel and quantizing. In many cases, simply using the Real-Time Properties will get your MIDI tracks just the way you want them. However, sometimes you may want to dig in a little deeper and be more precise with your editing. Keep in mind that since you already know what all of the standard editing tools do, you will find editing in Pro Tools quite simple.

If you use the Grabber tool, you can click on each one of the MIDI notes and hear the note play back to you. If you look at the main counter at the top of the Edit window, you will see a little MIDI and speaker icon just to the right of the Start and End indicators. This toggles the MIDI note's sound off and on while editing.

You can use the Grabber to move the note along the timeline to change its time placement, or you can move it up and down to change its pitch. If you would like to change the length of the note, use the Trimmer tool and click-and-drag the desired note to make it longer or shorter. The movement of the note will be determined by the mode that you are working in. If you would like all notes to snap to the grid values when editing, select Grid mode. If you would like to change the grid value without clicking on the drop-down menu, you can use the keyboard shortcut Control + Option + (or −) to make the grid value bigger or smaller. For a more human feel, select Slip mode and vary the lengths of the individual notes. If you find that there are wrong notes in your track, you can easily delete them by clicking on them to highlight them and then pressing the Delete key. If you would like to add notes, you can use the Pencil tool to draw in notes wherever you like.

The length of the note will be determined by the grid value, or it can be trimmed in Slip mode to a specific length.

Another way to manipulate the MIDI notes on the track is to use the Grabber tool to "rubber band" the desired notes and edit as you wish. For example, say you play a 4-bar phrase but then realize that you should have laid out on the last bar: you can use the Grabber tool to click-and-drag around the group of notes on the fourth bar; then, once they are selected, simply delete them.

When selecting multiple notes using this method, you can use the Trimmer tool to apply trimming to all of the selected notes in the group. You can also apply Velocity changes to all of the grouped notes or even individual notes. This is done in the Velocity view.

Velocity View Editing

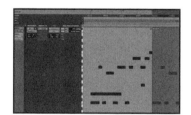

If you would like to edit the Velocity of individual notes or even a group of notes, this is achieved by using the Track View Selector and the Velocity view. For example, let's say you play a piano part and everything is fine except that the bass line is kind of weak. You can switch to the Velocity view and use the rubber-band method to select only the bass line.

Notice that only the bass line notes are selected and are indicated by the white diamonds at the top of each Velocity stem. To lower or raise the Velocity value, use your Trimmer tool to click-and-drag up or down anywhere in the area of the selected notes until the desired volume is achieved. You can also use the Grabber tool in this view to select and change an individual note's Velocity.

Regions View Editing

When you change your MIDI tracks to Regions view, they are treated the same way audio regions are treated. You can use any audio-editing techniques you are accustomed to for quick and easy MIDI editing. This includes, copy, paste, duplicate, repeats, nudge, trim, region separation, region lock, region mutes, and any other navigation methods you enjoy using for audio.

Pro Tools 8's New MIDI Editor

In the previous section of MIDI editing, we went over the standard techniques needed to confidently edit MIDI in Pro Tools, and we did it all from the standard view in the Edit window. For years Pro Tools has been a simple, easy-to-use, two-window format that was very easy on the eye. There wasn't a lot of clutter, and you could get to everything you needed from one of these two windows. Pro Tools 8 is still this way. Although you can achieve just about anything you need to from the two basic windows, Digidesign finally gave in and added a third window to its highly acclaimed software. This is the new MIDI Editor window.

When you are in the Edit window, select Regions as the MIDI track view, and double-click on the MIDI region or use the keyboard shortcut Control + = to open up the new MIDI Editor window. You can always do the same thing by using the Windows menu and selecting the MIDI Editor option. Once the MIDI editor opens, you will see a giant version of your selected MIDI track in the new MIDI Editor. If it does not open and use all of your window's real estate, click on the little red plus sign in the top-left corner of the window, and fit the MIDI Editor to the window.

If you take a close look at this window, you will see that it is a standard Edit window, but this new window shows only MIDI information. Everything else about it is the same as the regular Edit window. You have a Track List that shows which MIDI parts are being displayed in the main window, a Groups List for quick access to any MIDI tracks that are grouped together, an additional set of your standard editing tools (including the Smart tool, Key Focus on and off, Grid selector, Target), and just about everything else you can imagine. You can even customize the view of your toolbar to make this new window comfortable to work in.

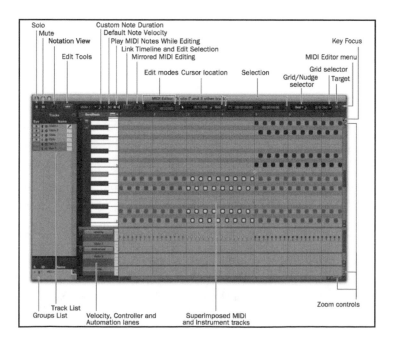

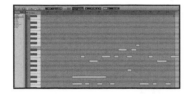

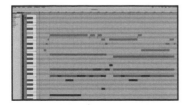

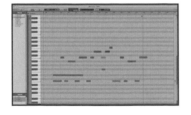

The default view for the MIDI Editor will show the Notes view, so you can quickly start editing in the way I described above. You can not only edit MIDI from this window, but you can also record your MIDI parts directly into the MIDI Editor. Another convenient feature of this window is that when you select multiple MIDI tracks from the Tracks List, the MIDI notes of the various instruments are superimposed over one another, with different colors indicating the different instruments. You will see in the example below that the red colors in the window indicate the bass line, the orange colors represent the NN-19 keyboard part, and the aqua color represents the Velvet melody line.

Even with multiple instruments selected in the MIDI Editor, you can add notes to or delete them from the instrument of your choice by making sure that you have them targeted in the Tracks List. To target a particular instrument, click on the right-hand side of the instrument's name and you will see a small pencil appear, indicating which track is targeted for editing.

Remember to add notes. You can play them in, or you can draw them in with the Pencil tool. You can choose the Velocity at which the new notes are written by changing the Velocity input values from the box of numbers just to the left of the Play MIDI Notes When Editing icon in the toolbar area. You can also mute notes by rubber-banding them and using the keyboard shortcut Command + M, or you can even split the notes by using the new keyboard command Control + Shift-click on the MIDI note you would like to split.

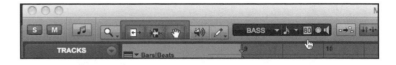

Another powerful new feature gives you the ability to split this new MIDI Editor window into scalable halves. This view shows you the Notes view on the top half, and you can open up new lanes on the bottom half to show MIDI Velocity, Controller data, and even Automation data. To do this, hover the cursor at the bottom of the MIDI Editor, and you will see a double-headed arrow icon appear. Double-click on it, and the window will split in half; it can then be resized to accommodate your desired sizes.

Just to the left of the new lane, you will see a plus and minus toggle that allows you to add or take away new lanes. In the example, I have created three new lanes that show Velocity, MIDI panning, and mod wheel data. As you can see, this is incredibly powerful and highly intuitive. This view allows you to see and edit multiple parameters, all without changing windows. For people who use MIDI a lot, this is a major addition with Pro Tools 8. Many MIDI users did not like Pro Tools because the convenience factor just wasn't there yet. With the addition of the new MIDI Editor, even the harshest critics of Pro Tools will have to applaud these new features.

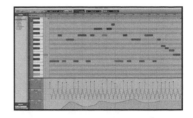

SCORE EDITOR WINDOW

Yes, that's right—yet another window has been added to Pro Tools 8. This time, it is the Score Editor window. This much-welcomed window allows you to edit and even print your scored arrangements with no problem at all. To view the Score Editor, click on the icon that has two small musical notes on it in the toolbar area of the MIDI Editor. You will see that whichever tracks are selected in the Tracks List will show up as music notation.

If you choose, you can edit directly from the Score Editor using the same editing tools that you used in the MIDI Editor. Pro Tools makes learning the Score Editor painless. You will find that when you are clicking around in the Score Editor, it will seem as though you already know how to use it. For instance, using the Trimmer tool on a musical note allows you to change its duration. The Grabber tool works as a note selector. Once the desired notes are selected, they are highlighted in blue and can be deleted, moved, and transposed. Use the standard Pencil tool to insert, select, move, or delete notes. If you use the Free Hand Pencil tool, you can draw notes of varying duration depending on your Default Note Velocity settings. The Line Pencil tool lets you draw multiple notes of the same pitch and duration. The Triangle Pencil tool lets you draw in a series of notes on a single

pitch, and their Velocities will oscillate between the defined Default Note Velocity and the 127 in a triangle pattern. You can lock your notes to the grid and use the Nudge functions just the way you do when you are editing anything else in Pro Tools. The Score Editor even adds rests as necessary, so you don't have to worry about having the right amount of beats per measure. It's automatic. Listed below are some of the things you will need to be able to find quickly. Try to dedicate these things to memory as quickly as possible, and you will be scoring music as though you had been doing it for years.

Custom Note Duration

From the Custom Note Duration selector you can choose the desired note value. You can choose the Follow Grid option if you want the Custom Note Duration to use the selected Grid value. You can also select dotted notes or triplets if you would like your Custom Note Duration to use those note values.

Default Note Duration Selection

Select the default Velocity for any notes you are inserting into your score by changing the values to numbers ranging from 0 to 127.

Link Timeline and Edit Selection

Turning this option on allows you to link the timeline with your sheet music by way of your cursor selection. Having this option on allows you to play your music from wherever you drop your cursor in the Score Editor.

Scrolling Options

Navigate to the Toolbar drop-down menu and select Scrolling. This allows you to scroll in one of four ways.

Main Score Editor

This option can be selected by going to the Window menu and selecting the Score Editor option, or you can use the keyboard shortcut Control + Option + =. Your score will appear with a title, the composer, measure numbers, and instrument names. The instruments that appear in notation are determined by what is selected in the Tracks menu. The following example shows the Bass and the Melody tracks.

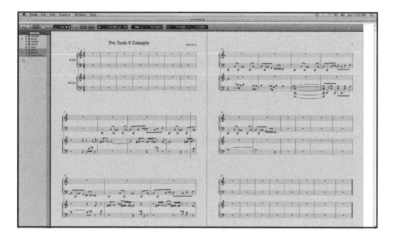

Score Setup

The Score Setup is activated if you double-click on the title of the arrangement. From here, you can customize your arrangement however you see fit. The options are all self-explanatory.

Print Score

Once you are finished with your arrangement and you would like to print your final product, go to the File menu and choose the Print Score option. From there you can select your standard

printer setup options, print your arrangements, and hand the copies out to the musicians playing your music or send the arrangement off for copyright registration.

FINAL THOUGHTS

This chapter has covered many of the standard techniques used for editing with Pro Tools software. You can see that there are often several ways to do the same thing when using Pro Tools. Here, I have given you the most essential elements and the most efficient methods of operation, and you should incorporate them into your skill set as soon as possible. It is nearly impossible to cover every aspect of editing with Pro Tools software in such a small amount of space, but if you dedicate these techniques to memory, you will get much better, much faster. The same thing applies to the new MIDI and Score Editors; not every new feature could be covered here because these were major additions to the Pro Tools software, and the information on the MIDI and Score Editors could fill its own book if we really got down to the details of the program. However, memorizing the many things included in this chapter will have you well on your way to becoming a Pro Tools 8 power user.

POWER TIPS SUMMARY FOR CHAPTER 7

1. Creating templates is a logical way of setting up different work-flow scenarios that make sense to you. It provides a certain amount of comfort under various circumstances when you are working with Pro Tools. You can create a folder that has several custom templates with various types of sessions to choose from that are already completely set up when you are ready to start creating. It is a real time-saver.

2. Importing session data is a great feature that has been around for years, but many are unaware of its relevance. Using this feature is handy and effective in many circumstances. For instance, it allows you to import a track or multiple tracks

of any type from any session that you have access to on your computer.

3. Eight essential Keyboard Focus commands for navigation and playback are the following:

    P = Move edit selection up
    ; = Move edit selection down
    L = Tab cursor back
    ' = Tab cursor forward
    [= Plays edit selection
    ] = Plays edit selection and includes Pre- and Post-roll

4. Six essential Keyboard Focus commands for editing are the following:

    A = Trim Start to Insertion
    S = Trim End to Insertion
    D = Fade in to Insertion
    G = Fade out from Insertion
    N = Toggles Timeline Insertion Follows Playback
           option on and off
    E = Zoom toggle feature
    R = Zoom out
    T = Zoom in

5. You can turn the Tab To Transient function on and off by using the keyboard shortcut Command + Option + Tab.

6. To quickly move regions around the timeline, drop the insertion cursor at the desired spot, and then make sure you change over to Slip mode. Then, while holding Control, use the Grabber tool to click on the region you would like to move to the insertion point. Holding down the Option key before you Control-click makes a copy of the region and snaps the copy to the insertion point. If you use the keyboard shortcut Command + Control and then click on the region, that snaps the region's end point to the insertion point.

7. If you are using the Dynamic Transport function, you have to ability to listen back to two separate playback selections. To have total access over navigating your transport and edit selections, you should turn this selection on. It is located in the Preferences section, under Operations. When this option

is turned on, you can make a selection from the Dynamic Transport and start playback using the Enter key from the numeric keypad. If you make a secondary edit selection, you can use the Play Edit Selection key, which is the left bracket on the keyboard; furthermore, you can use the 0 key from the numeric keypad to stop the transport. Setting up your transport functions this way also allows you to use the Spacebar to audition audio files from the Workspace browser, giving you the ability to choose three different audio audition modes at any given time—a very powerful user tip.

8. If you have a particular fade setting that you like to use all the time, you can create a preference for it. To do this, go to the Setup menu and select Preferences. From the Preferences dialog box, select the Editing tab. In the Fades box, notice that there are several options from which to choose. Make sure that the Preserve Fades When Editing option is checked.

9. Using the SmartTool gives you access to all available fades. When using the SmartTool, go to the upper-right or upper-left side of the region and hover until you see a small box icon. When you see this icon, click-and-drag horizontally to select and create a fade-in or fade-out with a length determined by the length of the horizontal drag you've performed. You can also quickly create crossfades by hovering the SmartTool over the region crossing toward the bottom of the region, and the box will appear again. When you click-and-drag this time, you are creating the length of the crossfade that will be performed.

10. Using Collective mode in Beat Detective is the best way to optimize how beat triggers are collected, by gathering them with separate analysis and using different detection settings for each individual track. This is the only way to analyze and create beat triggers on one track and then apply them to another track. This method yields the best results without having to edit or delete a bunch of false triggers that occur when using Normal Detection mode. It takes more time, but the result is worth it.

KEYBOARD SHORTCUT SUMMARY FOR CHAPTER 7

Try to memorize as many of these commands as quickly as you can. Knowing the menus is important, too, but knowing the shortcuts will save you time and be a real convenience once you get used to them.

KEYBOARD SHORTCUT	FUNCTION
Option + F	Centers Selection in Track Display Area
Option + Shift + 3	Consolidates Selection
Option + Shift + I	Imports Session Data
Option + Tab	Moves Selection to Previous Transient
Option + Shift + Tab	Moves Selection End Point to Previous Transient
Option + Command + Tab	Toggles Tab to Transient On and Off
Option + 8	Turns on Beat Detective
Command + I w/Selection	Shows Identify Beat Dialog box
Command + L	Region Lock
Command + M	Region Mute
Control + Command = P	Toggles Dynamic Transport On and Off
Command + Option + G	Creates Region Group
Command + Option + U	Unlocks Region Group
Command + Click on Playlist Audio File	Shows alt. takes for matching take's start-time function
Command + Shift + W	Closes Pro Tools session w/o quitting Pro Tools

PRO TOOLS TUNE-UP FOR CHAPTER 7

1. To close a Pro Tools session without closing the Pro Tools application, use the keyboard command _____.

2. To quickly recall all settings for a particular track from another session, you can use the Import _____ _____.

3. There are three modes for Keyboard Focus. They are Commands Keyboard Focus, Region List Keyboard Focus, and _____.

4. The Timeline Insertion/Play Start Marker Follows Playback option is turned on and off from the Operations tab below Preferences. When it is turned on, Pro Tools, transport functions just like a _____, meaning playback will start from where the transport was stopped.

5. The _____ allows you to listen to playback from wherever you drop the cursor anytime that a selection is made, even if the transport is in motion. Also, when making an edit selection, the timeline playback markers mirror the edit selection.

6. When selecting the Dynamic Transport, it automatically turns off the Link Edit And Timeline Selection, and it engages the _____ feature.

7. Using the Dynamic Transport in conjunction with using Separate Play and Stop Keys allow the possibility of _____ selection options. Your choices are to listen to the Dynamic Transport selection or separate edit selection.

8. To group several types of tracks at one time, for easy arrangement in Pro Tools, you can use the _____ option by pressing the keyboard shortcut Command + Option + G.

9. To ungroup the region groups, you can deselect it from the Regions menu, or you can use the keyboard shortcut _____.

10. When using Loop Record to record several takes while performing overdubs, you can use a great feature called _____ to create one compilation of the best takes from the multiple playlists.

11. Consolidating a region after making several edits allows your system to respond better and is a little easier on the eye. The important thing to remember when consolidating your selection is to make a _____, so you can go back and use the Trimmer tool or any other editing tools to manipulate the original regions in the playlist. To quickly consolidate a region, you can either use the keyboard shortcut Option + Shift + 3 or find it in the Edit menu.

12. Using the _____ option allows you to create a custom tempo map for the song if the artist did not record to a click track or if it has several tempo changes within the song. To identify the tempo properly, you must make sure that you have an accurate loop selected so the Identify Beat can give you a perfectly calculated tempo for the selection.

13. _____ is used primarily for editing drums and conforming or "quantizing" the drum performance. However, you can also extract the "feel" or "groove" of a drummer's performance by using the Groove Template Extraction feature.

14. When using the _____ feature, you can use your DigiGroove Template on other tracks in your session, including MIDI performances, to give the overall session the same feel as your drummer.

15. When applying DigiGrooves to MIDI performances, the accents and peak levels from the audio track's beat triggers are analyzed and converted to Velocity values on a MIDI track on a linear scale. A signal level at 0 dBfs equals a MIDI Velocity of 127, a level at −6 dBfs has a Velocity of 64, and so on. The most important thing about extracting a great DigiGroove Template is to make sure that all beat triggers are gathered accurately. Capturing beat triggers in Normal mode achieves acceptable results, but using _____ generates the best results when using the Groove Template Extraction feature.

16. The five operations that Beat Detective uses are _____, Groove Template Extraction, Region Separation, Region Conform, and Edit Smoothing.

17. The _____ operation is what Beat Detective uses to conform, or quantize, audio.

18. To get rid of all of the unwanted clicks and pops in the tracks after using the Region Conform operation, use the _____ feature in Beat Detective. You should also use the Fill and Crossfade option, with a 3 to 5 ms crossfade when smoothing your edits.

19. Although Elastic Audio is also able to quantize audio, it uses TCE to warp the performance to a grid. Beat Detective is an automated _____ application that keeps the integrity of the audio file. For this reason, Beat Detective should be your first choice when quantizing drums, even it takes a little bit longer.

20. Beat Detective's Detection section has three modes of analysis. They are high emphasis (which is best for analyzing high-frequency audio), low emphasis (best for analyzing low-frequency audio), and _____ (designed to produce the best results for the widest variety of audio material).

Elastic Is Fantastic

ELASTIC AUDIO

Elastic Audio is a powerful new feature introduced in Pro Tools with version 7.4 that allows audio to be treated as if it were MIDI. It uses high-resolution transient-detection algorithms and real-time TCE algorithms to analyze all transients within the track. There are four new algorithms used to detect different types of transients within a complex waveform. The various settings are designed to help analyze different instrument types. Sung notes, drum parts, chords played by guitar, and so on, are all different types of complex waveforms that are better analyzed by using different transient-detection algorithms. Once the analysis is complete, event markers are placed on the track and act as control points for warping the audio.

Elastic Audio allows you to automatically quantize audio to tighten up a performance with the click of a button. You can also realign a note manually to the grid or freely along the timeline using a modifier key before you drag it. Using tick-based tracks allows Elastic Audio tracks to automatically warp the audio to conform to the tempo of your session or change the entire session to a different tempo. There are two basic track types in Pro Tools: tick based and sample based. The difference between them is that a tick-based track can conform to the Conductor's tempo, so if you change the tempo of the session, the Elastic

Audio track changes to match the tempo. A sample-based track does not conform to tempo and will not move from its unique sample location, and the bars and beats will change around it. When you analyze a track, event markers based on the transients detected are placed on the track. Most of the time, you will not need to use the Analysis view unless erroneous event markers were added or you need to add event markers for transients that weren't detected. (This is similar to how Beat Detective works.) Using Warp view allows you to dig in and manipulate the warp markers manually. You can fix timing issues on an individual event basis because you have the ability to add and delete Warp markers as needed. If you make big changes in tempo, the TCE function may add some strange audio anomalies that can be compensated for by using the Elastic Audio plug-ins. These are not the typical insert-type plug-ins used on the channel strip, and they are available only in the Edit window. Adjustable plug-in parameters, if any, can be manipulated from the Elastic Audio Plug-ins window and cannot be automated.

Elastic Audio Track Controls

There are three new audio track controls for Elastic Audio, and they can be accessed only from the Edit window.

PLUG-IN SELECTOR

This selects the Elastic Audio Plug-in for Elastic Audio processing, and it is used to choose real-time or rendered processing. This pop-up menu is also where you can disable Elastic Audio features on a track.

PLUG-IN BUTTON

This button displays the name of the selected Elastic Audio plug-in, and clicking on this button opens the Elastic Audio plug-in associated with the track.

REAL-TIME OR RENDERED-PROCESSING INDICATOR

This indicator lets you quickly determine if a track's processing is in real time, or if the indicator is rendered. If it is lit up, then the processing is being done in real time. When the indicator is dimmed, the processing has been rendered.

ENABLING ELASTIC AUDIO

Making a standard audio track an Elastic Audio track is simple. You can either create a new audio track or use an existing one. First, select the track's Elastic Audio Plug-in selector and select the proper algorithm that is best suited for your track's content. Here are your choices for audio analysis.

Elastic Audio Analysis

Listed below are Elastic Audio Analysis types that are currently available for Pro Tools 8. Each of them is used for various reasons. Understanding which algorithm works best for which application will allow you to fully utilize Elastic Audio.

POLYPHONIC

For complex loops and multi-instrument mixes, the Polyphonic algorithm is your best choice. It is the all-purpose algorithm and is best suited for a wide range of material. It is the default algorithm for auditioning from the Digibase browser or the Region List.

RHYTHMIC

If your source material has clearly defined attack transients, Rhythmic is the choice to make. It's the best selection for drum content.

MONOPHONIC

The Monophonic plug-in is best suited for monophonic material and when maintaining formant relationships is crucial. This is the best choice to use for vocals or for instruments with single-note melody lines, such as with bass lines or guitar solos. The Monophonic plug-in analyzes peak transients and pitch to provide the best quality TCE. It takes longer to analyze with the Monophonic algorithm, but the results are worth the wait.

VARISPEED

This algorithm links time and pitch changes for nice tapelike speed-changing effects.

X-FORM

This algorithm is only for rendered audio and cannot process in real time the way the others algorithms do. However, using X-form provides the highest quality time compression and expansion for audio-loop, music-production, and sound-design applications.

ELASTIC AUDIO PLUG-INS AND WINDOW CONTROLS

When you convert an audio track to an Elastic Audio track, the track is analyzed by its relative plug-in. It is kind of like an AudioSuite plug-in that isn't applied to an insert point but is nondestructive, unlike AudioSuite plug-ins. Each Elastic Audio type has an associated plug-in with either a couple of parameters or sometimes no parameter to adjust. Although there are only a few parameters to work with, each one is specifically tailored to optimize the type of Elastic Audio track selected. To open the associated plug-in on an Elastic Audio track, click on the Elastic Audio Plug-in button, and the plug-in will appear.

Polyphonic Plug-in

The Polyphonic plug-in has two selections from which to choose. If you select the Follow control, this creates an envelope follower that mimics the original acoustics of the audio being stretched. Click on it to turn it on or off. The other parameter to adjust is the Analysis window size for TCE processing. I'd love to say there is more to it, but you simply have to adjust this parameter until it sounds the best for your particular application. It is suggested you use smaller window sizes for percussive tracks (20 ms or less) and larger window times for legato instruments (60 ms or more).

Rhythmic Plug-in

This plug-in is usually applied to tracks with clearly defined attack transients—primarily drums and percussion. You can adjust the Decay Rate parameter to determine how much of the decay from a transient is heard in the processed audio. If there are gaps created between transients during processing, these gaps are automatically filled in with audio. Sometimes this gap-filling audio is not a desired sound, so using a shorter decay time allows you to fade out the processed audio before the gap-filling audio is heard. If you are feeling creative, use a long decay time and enjoy the madness.

Monophonic Plug-in

This plug-in has no options.

Varispeed Plug-in

This plug-in has no options.

X-Form Plug-in

This plug-in has two options from which to choose. The quality choices are Low and Maximum. Maximum yields the best results but takes the longest time. Sometimes the Low option will do the job. This should be determined on a track-by-track basis.

ELASTIC AUDIO TRACK VIEWS

When Pro Tools analyzes audio with one of its various algorithms, it puts Event markers and Warp markers on the Elastic Audio tracks, and they can be observed and manipulated from two different window views: Analysis view and Warp view. Both views are allowed only on Elastic Audio tracks. To select either view, use the Track view pop-up menu, and choose either Analysis or Warp.

Analysis View Editing

Analysis view allows you to see all of the Event markers that were placed on the track. You can also add, move, and delete Event markers. Pro Tools analysis usually detects all of the transient events in an audio file, but sometimes it can miss a few or add in some extra events when analyzing certain types of material. Legato instruments and instruments that do not have clearly defined attack transients are often the victims of erroneous Event markers. You can add, delete, and move Event markers by using any of the editing tools. I find the Grabber tool to be the most convenient. To add an Event marker with the Grabber tool, Control-click on the area where you would like to add the Event marker. To move a marker with the Grabber tool, click-and-drag it to the desired position. To delete a marker with the Grabber, Option-click on it.

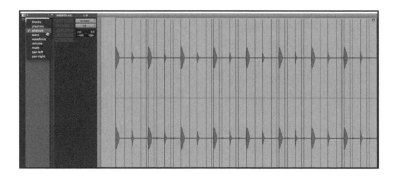

Warp View Editing

In Warp view, you can see three types of markers: Event markers, Warp markers, and Tempo Event–generated markers.

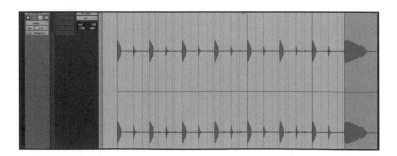

Event markers appear as thin gray lines that do not fully extend to the top and bottom of the track. If there are Warp markers present in the region, they can be moved horizontally with the Grabber tool to apply different types of warping. You cannot add, delete, or move event markers in Warp view; that must be done from Analysis view. Warp markers appear as thick black lines with a triangle at their base. These markers serve as anchors for the audio at different points along the timeline. This allows you to stretch or constrict audio over a specific time value. You can move (without warping), add, or delete Warp markers only in the Warp view. There are a few ways to add Warp markers to achieve various types of warping; there is Telescopic Warp, Accordion Warp, Range Warp, and Region Warp. Here are descriptions of each type. The QuickTime tutorial gives an example of each, so be sure to check it out.

TELESCOPIC WARP

Telescopic Warp can be applied to sample and tick-based tracks either before or after a Warp marker, as long as no other Warp marker precedes or follows it. You can be creative with Telescopic Warp, but one of its more practical uses is to adjust audio files so that they match the current session tempo. This is how it is done.

Here is a 4-bar drum loop. Notice that it does not match the session tempo and is nearly five bars in length. Using the Pencil tool, add one Warp marker to the downbeat of bar 1. It should be the only Warp marker in the loop.

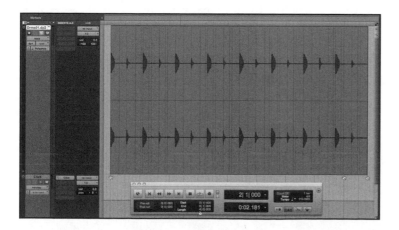

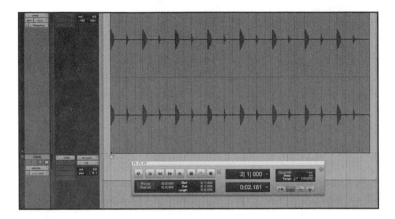

The hand that is pointing at the Event marker represents the first snare transient. Notice that it is not exactly on count 2 of bar 1; rather, it is just to the right of it.

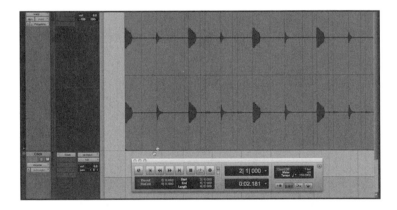

Use the Grabber tool to move that Event marker to snap to count 2 of bar 1. Once you move it, it should look like this.

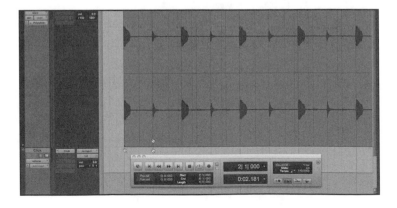

The result is a perfect 4-bar loop that has conformed to the tempo of the session.

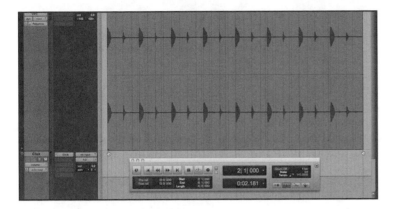

ACCORDION WARP

Accordion Warp allows you to expand or compress the audio equally on both sides of a fixed point. To get a better idea of how this works, apply one Warp marker to any region (preferably in the middle of the region) by double-clicking with your Grabber tool. The only Warp marker in the region should be the one you added. Use the Grabber tool to stretch or compress any of the Event markers before or after the Warp marker you created. This method is most practical when the downbeat of an audio file is in the middle of the region, but it changes the timing of the loop. The following pictures demonstrate a 2-bar loop stretched into four bars by moving the Event marker on count 3 of bar 10, to the downbeat of bar 11. The Accordion Warp feature stretches both sides of the Warp marker, and you end up with a 4-bar loop that is half the speed of the original.

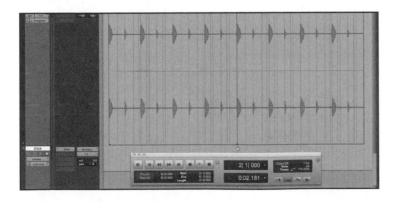

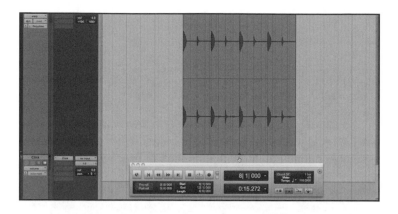

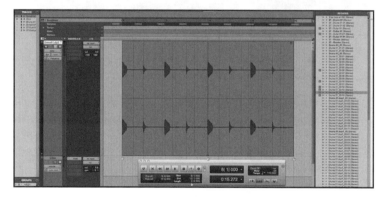

RANGE WARP

To apply Range Warp, there must be at least two Warp markers in the region. It applies Elastic Audio processing between two fixed points in a region. Add one Warp marker to the first marker that you would like to anchor to the timeline. Add the next Warp marker where you would like the end of the range to be anchored. Then use the Grabber tool to click-and-drag any Event marker in between the two Warp markers you have created. When you do this, a Warp marker will be added to the Event marker, and the audio is compressed or expanded on either side of the marker that was clicked-and-dragged. All other audio outside the two original Warp markers remains unaffected.

To apply individual Warp Range, press down the Shift key and click on an Event marker; that will add a Warp marker to the Event marker and to the two Event markers surrounding the addition. Click-and-drag the middle Warp marker to apply Elastic Audio processing.

To delete a Warp marker, hold down the Option key and click on the Warp marker you would like to remove. To delete a range of Warp markers, use the Selector tool to highlight the Warp markers you would like to remove, and then press the Delete key.

The following pictures show Range Warp being applied directly to an Event marker in between two existing Event markers.

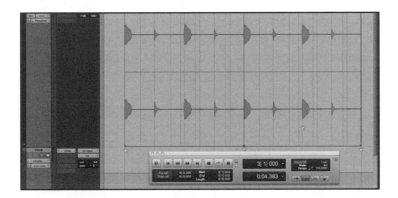

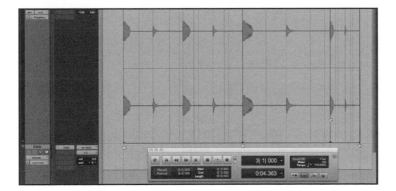

Moving the Warp marker to the right stretches the first half of bar 10, but everything after the new Warp marker is sped up to complete the loop cycle on time.

Event Confidence

When audio is being analyzed and converted to Elastic Audio, the transient events are detected and given Event markers. When analyzing different sources, the number of Event markers will differ. Audio with clearly defined peak transients are analyzed with the highest degree of confidence, and may contain more

Event markers than necessary. On the other hand, things such as strings and keyboard pads, with less defined transients, will be analyzed with a lower degree of confidence.

Therefore, if you are analyzing something like a synthesizer or violin part, you can filter out some of the false or unnecessary Event markers by lowering the Event Sensitivity from the Elastic Properties window. In Analysis view, you may notice that there aren't enough Event markers or that they should be in different places. That's okay because you can add, move, or take away individual Event markers and choose the necessary amount of Event Sensitivity. Decreasing or increasing the amount of Event markers with the correct amount of Event Sensitivity can result in better Elastic Audio processing. In the following graphic, notice that there are fewer Event markers added when setting the Event Sensitivity to 50 percent. When the Event Sensitivity is set to 90 percent, you will see that every transient is given its own Event marker.

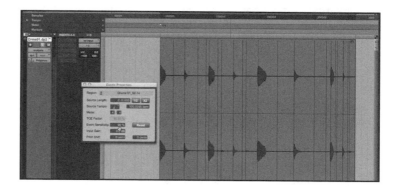

ELASTIC PROPERTIES

To open Elastic Properties for any given region, you can either go to the Region menu and select the Elastic Properties option or use the right-click function on your mouse to access it more quickly. This window contains information about Elastic Audio processing and analysis for one or more regions. There are options within this window that can quickly add to your creativity. Notice that there is a Source Length window. If you choose the "½" option, your track will speed up to twice its original time. If you select the "×2" option, your track will become twice as slow. These particular options apply only to tick-based tracks.

In addition to some of the creative features of this window, this is where you set the Event Sensitivity for Elastic Audio analysis. You can also adjust the input gain settings from here. Sometimes clipping occurs when you are time-compressing audio. If this occurs, it will be indicated in the associated real-time Elastic Audio plug-ins, and you can reduce the gain of the track before it is processed by lowering the Input Gain control. Pro Tools 8 has also added the Elastic Audio Region-Based Pitch Transposition feature. With this new feature, you can change the pitch of whole audio regions in semitones and up to four octaves. It is available only with the Polyphonic and Rhythmic Elastic Audio Algorithms and is part of the Elastic Properties tools.

To use this feature, make sure that the region you want to process is Elastic Audio enabled, and be sure to make an accurate selection. Then right-click on the selected region and choose Elastic Properties, then adjust the pitch in semitones and cents.

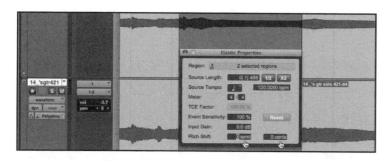

If you would like to transpose the pitch of an audio region in the Transpose window, use the Grabber tool and make sure the whole region is selected. Next, choose Event, Event Operation, and Transpose. From this window you can set the options as desired and enjoy.

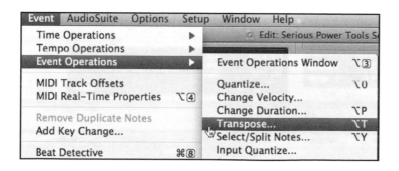

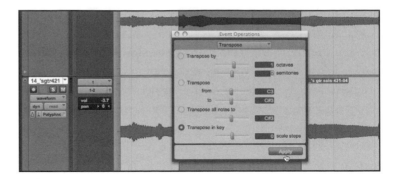

QUANTIZING ELASTIC AUDIO

Quantizing audio with Elastic Time is a very simple process, and there isn't much to write about it. The nice thing is that you can quantize individual and multiple tracks that are grouped at the same time. In the QuickTime tutorial, the example will be on quantizing a drum kit using multiple microphones. Here is how it is done. Highlight any track or group of tracks that you would like to quantize.

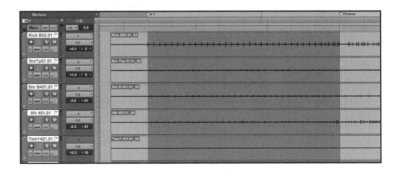

Then, from the Event menu, select the Event Operation option and choose Quantize, or use the keyboard shortcut Option + 0.

Where it says What To Quantize, the selection should be Elastic Audio Events. Set the Quantize grid to the desired value and change any of the note values or feel options that fit the audio that is being quantized, and then select Apply.

When you click on the Apply tab, you will see the selected audio slightly shift in the timeline. This indicates that the audio has been quantized.

If you have saved a Groove template or you would like to use a Preset Groove template, select the desired template in the Quantize grid drop-down menu and apply it.

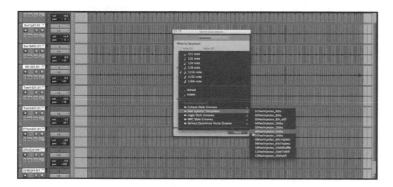

If you go to the Analysis view, you can add, remove, and arrange the Event markers as described earlier in this chapter. If you go to Warp view, you can add, remove, and arrange the Warp markers to make the desired adjustments.

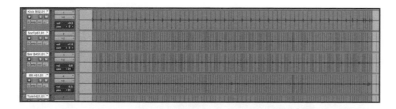

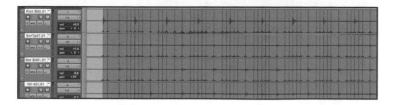

ELASTIC AUDIO TUTORIAL

The QuickTime tutorial will go over everything mentioned above. Sometimes it is easier to understand something if you get a visual demonstration of it after you have read about it. The tutorials that come with this book are great for this purpose.

THE THREE AMIGOS

The Workspace browser, Elastic Audio, and the Dynamic Transport have added some incredible flexibility to various work flows in Pro Tools. Each feature is powerful on its own, but when your system is set up to use all of them together, you will find yourself wondering how you used to work any other way.

Workspace—Elastic Audio—Dynamic Transport

Using the Workspace and Project browsers is easier than ever. With the addition of the Separate Play And Start Keys option, you'll notice that the added functionality with the Dynamic Transport and Elastic Audio features makes for a powerful trio. You can find the Workspace and Project browsers under the Window menu, or you can use the keyboard shortcut Option + ; to access the Workspace browser and Option + O for the Project browser.

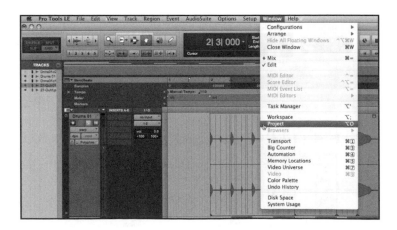

Here are some features that were added since Pro Tools version 7.4's Workspace browser. The Workspace browser gives you access to all of the hard drives that are mounted on your computer. The Project browser shows you all audio assets in your current project.

Just Browsing

Looking for loops and samples is simple. You can even browse and audition audio while your session is playing, and you can analyze the Elastic Properties of your audio files in advance. That allows you to hear your audio loops either at their own bpm or at the session's tempo while Pro Tools is playing. Listening to them at the session's tempo while Pro Tools is playing makes it much easier to hear how the loops will sounds against the track once they are added.

The new features in the Digibase browser are very nice. Conform To Tempo has been added to make real-time browsing and auditioning audio and loops a snap. The Conform To Tempo button is located at the top of the browser window, just to the left of the four algorithms used to audition your files. To turn it on, click on it and it will light up. When you audition your audio with Conform To Tempo off, the audio will play back at its original tempo. With it turned on, the audio will be analyzed with the Polyphonic algorithm, and it will play the audio at the speed of your current session. You can tell if your audio has been analyzed by the check mark in the far left column, and you can also see which sample-based tracks have been turned into tick-based tracks in the Kind column.

Another nice feature is that you can right-click on any folder in the browser and analyze all audio files in the folder in advance to help speed up your work flow.

By default, Auto Preview is selected, but to take full advantage of the functionality of Pro Tools 8, you can change this to Spacebar Toggles File Preview.

This is awesome because, if you remember when we set up to use Separate Play and Stop Keys, we were able to start the

Pro Tools session with the Enter key and stop it using the 0 key from the numeric keypad. Now that the Spacebar is left open, it can be used to preview loops in the browser. Pretty cool stuff.

Once you find the audio files you would like to use in your session, click-and-drag them into the Tracks List; they will automatically conform to tempo, and a new tick-based audio track will be created for them. Now you can apply any editing or Elastic Audio features you desire.

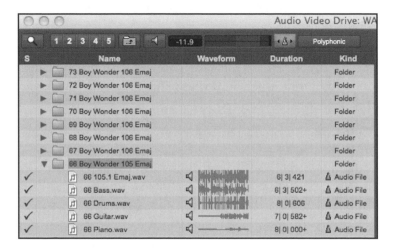

FINAL THOUGHTS

The Elastic Audio features are an amazing set of tools that take creativity to a new level. No software program on the market makes manipulating audio and creating professional productions with such ease and flexibility so attainable. With the introduction of Elastic Audio, Digidesign shows us once again why Pro Tools is the world leader in digital audio recording software. The best way to use this new technology is to get in there and try it out. I've included the essential elements about Elastic Audio that will enable you to use it easily and effectively. QuickTime tutorials and exercises accompany this chapter, so be sure to watch them.

POWER TIPS SUMMARY
FOR CHAPTER 8

1. After you analyze your audio tracks, most of the time you will not need to use the Analysis view unless erroneous Event markers were added or you need to add some Event markers for transients that weren't detected during analysis.

2. All Pro Tools versions after 7.4 include four new algorithms used to detect different types of transients within a complex waveform. The various settings are designed to help analyze different instrument types. Sung notes, drum parts, guitar chords, and so on, are all represented by different types of complex waveforms that are better analyzed by using different transient-detection algorithms. Once the analysis is complete, Event markers are placed on the track and are then used to act as anchors for warping the audio.

3. Using tick-based tracks allows Elastic Audio tracks to automatically warp the audio to conform to the tempo of your session or to change the entire session to a different tempo. To automatically make all new audio tracks tick based, go to the Editing tab and select New Tracks Default To Tick Timebase from the Track selection.

4. The X-Form algorithm is only for rendered audio and cannot process in real time the way the other algorithms can. However, using X-Form provides the highest quality time compression and expansion for audio-loop, music-production, and sound-design applications.

5. When using the Polyphonic plug-in, it is suggested to use smaller window sizes for percussive tracks (20 ms or less) and larger window times for legato instruments (60 ms or more).

6. When working in Analysis view, you can add an Event marker with the Grabber tool by simply Control-clicking on the area where you would like to add the Event marker. To move it with the Grabber tool, simply click-and-drag it to the desired position. To delete it with the Grabber tool, Option-click on it.

7. You cannot add, delete, or move Event markers in Warp view; that must be done from Analysis view. A Warp marker appears as a thick black line with a triangle at its base.

8. Decreasing or increasing the number of Event markers that are applied to a track can result in better Elastic Audio processing.

9. In addition to containing some of the creative features of Elastic Audio, the Elastic Properties window is also where you set the Event Sensitivity for Elastic Audio analysis.

10. To take full advantage of the functionality of Pro Tools 8's Workspace browser, you can change the Spacebar Toggles File Preview by right-clicking on the icon in the upper-left corner. Using this setup method is perfect when you are set up to use Separate Play and Stop Keys. This allows you to start the Pro Tools transport with the Enter key and stop it using the 0 key from the numeric keypad, while using the Spacebar to audition loops from the Workspace browser.

KEYBOARD SHORTCUT SUMMARY FOR CHAPTER 8

Try to memorize as many of these commands as quickly as you can. Knowing the menus is important too, but knowing the shortcuts saves you time and is a real convenience once you get used to using them.

KEYBOARD SHORTCUTS	FUNCTION
Option + 5	Brings up the Elastic Properties window
Option + 0 (zero)	Selects Quantize function from Event Operations
Option + ;	Shows the Workspace browser
Option + O	Shows the Project browser
Option + J	Brings the browsers to the front of the window
Option + Shift + J	Sends the browsers to the back of the window

Separate Play and Stop Keys Function	
Enter (numeric keypad)	Starts playback
0 (numeric keypad)	Stops Playback
. (decimal point) + Enter	Adds Memory Location
[(left bracket)	Plays Edit Selection
Control + Option + P	Turns on the Dynamic Transport
With Grabber Tool	
Option-click Event marker	Deletes Event marker in Analysis view
Control-clicking on an Event marker	Adds Event marker in Analysis view
Shift-click event marker in Range Warp	Adds a Warp marker and two Warp markers

PRO TOOLS TUNE-UP
FOR CHAPTER 8

1. Elastic Audio uses four high-resolution transient-detection algorithms for processing audio files. They are Polyphonic, Monophonic, Rhythmic, and _____.

2. In order for Elastic Audio tracks to conform to the session tempo, they have to be _____ -based tracks.

3. The Real-Time or Rendered Processing Indicator light lets you know the status of each Elastic Audio track. If the indicator light is on, that means the Elastic Audio track is in _____ mode.

4. There are two new track views available for Elastic Audio. They are Analysis and _____.

5. Event markers can be edited only when the track is in _____ view.

6. The three types of warping audio discussed in this book are Telescopic Warp, Range Warp, and _____ _____.

7. The Event Sensitivity for Elastic Audio analysis is selected from the _____ window.

8. To quantize with Elastic Audio, you must go to the Event menu, select the _____ option, and choose Quantize.

9. The _____ button is located at the top of the Workspace browser and just to the left of the four algorithms for processing Elastic Audio. Using this feature allows the audio in the Workspace browser to be auditioned in real time while playing at the session's tempo.

10. You can select the _____
_____ option by right-clicking on any file. This allows you to use the Spacebar to audition loops in the browser, the Enter key to start the Pro Tools Dynamic Transport, the left bracket to play Edit Selection, and the 0 (zero) key to stop playback.

11. The three most essential MIDI track views are the Notes view, the Velocity view, and the _____.

12. In Notes view, you can use the Grabber tool to click on a note to hear it, and if you click-and-drag on the note, you can change _____ by moving it up and down, or you can change its placement in the timeline by moving it left to right.

13. The timeline placement, duration, and trim values of MIDI notes while editing in Grid mode are determined by the grid value of the session. You can change the grid value by using the keyboard shortcut _____ to make the value higher or lower.

14. Trimming MIDI notes in Slip mode allows you to trim them freely along the timeline and adds a _____ _____ to a MIDI performance.

15. Anytime that more than one MIDI note is selected, any edits that are made to them are _____ to all of the notes that are selected.

16. When editing MIDI in Velocity view, notes that are selected for editing are indicated by a _____ _____ at the top of the Velocity stem.

17. To lower the Velocity of MIDI notes in Velocity view, you can click-and-drag on them with the Grabber tool, but another option would be to use the _____ to click anywhere in the selected area and click-and-drag up or down to trim the Velocity of the MIDI data.

18. When editing MIDI in _____, the MIDI regions are treated as though they are audio regions and can be edited in the same ways.

19. When working with MIDI, most quantizing, feel, and transposition features can be done using the _____ _____.

20. When using the Grabber tool to edit MIDI, the method for grabbing a range of MIDI notes is referred to as _____ the MIDI data. It is achieved by clicking-and-dragging the range of MIDI notes you would like to be part of the selection.

Mixing and Mastering Essentials

9

THE MAIN EVENT

It's finally that time. You have all of your parts finished. They are as good as they are going to be. All of the elements you wanted and needed were recorded, the editing is done, you have a nice-sounding rough mix, but now you want to take it to the next level. Everything you have recorded and edited up to this point should have been done in preparation for the mixing stage of production. Pro Tools is great in the way that you can mix and produce as you are creating the song and end up with something sounding close to finished. This process used to be called "preproduction." Theses days, the preproduction stage has been almost completely cut out of the equation because of how easily rough tracks can become final tracks. Unfortunately, this is the stage of production during which many people just add some equalization and limiting to the master fader, then say they are done with their mix. If you take mixing seriously, prepare your tracks to be mixed properly and start to perceive mixing as a specific stage of production; you will quickly realize why good mix engineers are paid so well. A good mix engineer has many things to think about when mixing a song. It is their job to make sure that all of the various instruments can be heard clearly and all of the frequencies in the mix are complementing each other and not fighting for space. A mix engineer can add elements of energy by using good dynamic processing and can add excitement by adding creative time-based effects.

Since mix engineers do get paid so well, it would be in your best interest to have your tracks fully edited and cleaned up before they are placed in the hands of the mix engineer. That will save you time and money in the long run. In this chapter, I will cover how to clean up your session and prepare it to be mixed. Even if you are doing the mixing yourself, you should take the time to set everything up as though you were preparing it for a professional mix engineer. You will notice improvements in the performance of your computer and the sound of your mix if you incorporate some of these simple suggestions into your production routine. Also included in this chapter are some mixing fundamentals regarding equalization, compression, and gating techniques that have been used by professionals for years.

SYSTEMS USAGE METERS

These meters indicate how much of your system's processing power is being used to process the audio that is being recorded, automated, mixed, and mastered. Now there are four system usage meters: PCI shows PCI bus activity; CPU (RTAS) shows how much computer processing power you have left for RTAS plug-ins; and CPU (Elastic) shows the remaining CPU power for Elastic Audio; and Disk, which indicates the amount of activity that is present on your hard disk.

You can make a few adjustments that won't have much of an impact on the way you work, but they will allow better processing efficiency. Here are just a few things to keep in mind when you are preparing to do your final mix. If your final tracks have a lot of edits and small independent regions, consolidate them so that Pro Tools doesn't have to work so hard to access the audio files on your drive. Always use the smallest component of a plug-in. For example, if you are using a 4-band EQ to filter out the low frequencies on the overhead microphones on a drum kit, try using a 1-band EQ instead, and only use the filters. This may not seem like a big deal, but when you apply this to several tracks with a few inserts on every channel, it can make a big difference. If you are using meters in your Sends view, turn them off by going to the Setup menu, selecting Preferences, choosing the

Display tab, and unchecking the option in the Meters section. Thinning automation will help too. The bottom line is to be resourceful. Make it a habit to use only what you need, and you will maximize the performance of your computer.

PLAYBACK ENGINE FOR MIXING

After you have gathered all of the audio that will be used for your production, you should have several stems of audio and perhaps several mono audio tracks, as well as aux inputs for your effects. There should be no instrument tracks or ReWire plug-ins being used in real time, taking up your CPU resources or causing unwanted latency.

Once you have everything set up properly, go to the Setup menu and select the Playback Engine option, and then apply the principles you learned in the earlier chapters of this book. Remember that choosing the correct settings for the job will make your session run much more efficiently.

PREMIX VISUAL SETUP

In the next several sections, I will go over even more ways to organize the visual aspect of your session. This will allow you to quickly go from one screen configuration to the next with very little effort. You'll also be able to access Mix and Edit window configurations of different sections of the song instantly. I will start with the Memory Locations feature.

Song Structure Memory

Before you start to mix, it is a good idea to set up all of the memory locations for the different sections contained in the song. This makes moving from section to section easy and allows you to make quick selections for looping or making Region Groups for particular sections of the song, giving you the ability to continuously audition certain sections and try different options. Make sure that these markers are snapped perfectly to the grid for optimal use. Also, remember to use the Keyboard Shortcuts for making memory location selections.

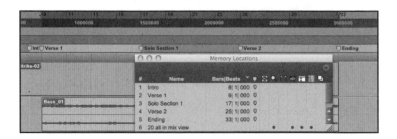

Mixer View Markers

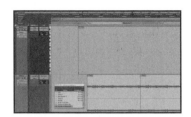

In previous chapters, we used memory locations for several reasons. In the mixing stage of your session, you should be listening to several sets of various combinations of instruments. For example, you may want to solo up the drums and bass every now and then to focus on how the kick drum and bass guitar sound together, or maybe you'll want to solo the acoustic guitars with the piano track to check your stereo image and volume blend between the two—the list goes on forever. As you find yourself auditioning your mix many different ways, take time to create markers that can recall the various Mix window instrument combinations you are using. You will save a lot of time when you can use the Memory Locations window to navigate the various Mix and Edit window views you have taken the time to create.

Window Configurations

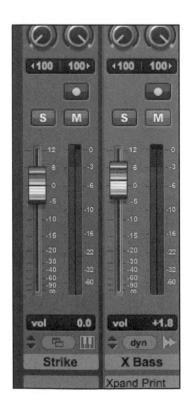

To continue a bit further on the subject of being organized during your mix, in Pro Tools, version 7.3, there was a new "logical" feature added to the Window menu called Configurations. This is a great feature that enables you to define exactly what you would like to see on the screen simply by storing it and using the new Window Configuration List. You can use the Window Configuration List in coordination with the Memory Locations window to go from edit views to mixing views with every floating window option you would like to see, with a click of the mouse. Once you have several window configurations stored, you can make them to part of your custom view marker locations by adding them to the General Properties settings selection when creating your view markers.

NEW WINDOW CONFIGURATION

Go to the Window menu and select Configurations, and then choose New Configuration.

When the dialog box appears, you can determine the way Pro Tools stores your window configurations. If you choose the Window Layout selection and the Include Edit, Mix, and Transport Display settings, Pro tools will save all of the floating windows on your screen as you see it when the new window configuration is created.

WINDOWS CONFIGURATION LIST

This feature is similar to the Memory Locations feature. You can view the Windows Configuration list by going to the Window menu, selecting Configurations, and then selecting it from the drop-down menu, or you can use the keyboard shortcut Command + Option + J. You can select any window configuration you have stored in your session by clicking on it directly in the Window Configuration list, or you can use the keyboard shortcut Period (·) + *the number of the window* + Asterisk (∗) on the numeric keypad. The current window configuration is indicated by a diamond icon just to the left of the window configuration number.

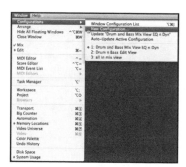

CUSTOM I/O SETTINGS

Creating custom input and output settings is great for the visual organization of your interface options. You can name them specific things that will speed up your workflow and keep you organized throughout any session, at any stage of production. For instance, if you have an interface that has eight inputs and eight outputs, you may be using them for various things such as outboard gear, headphone mixes, and so on; sometimes it can be easy to forget what you have connected where. Creating custom I/O settings

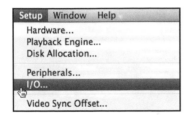

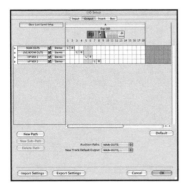

will make this problem go away. To create custom I/O settings, select the Setup menu and choose the I/O…option.

This will take you to the I/O Setup screen, and from there you can customize as you wish. You can modify what is already there, or you can delete everything and start from scratch.

Here is a typical I/O setup for a customized Digi 002 interface, with various options for inputs and outputs. To re-create this from scratch, go to the I/O Setup screen, click on the Input tab at the top of the screen, and select all by using the keyboard shortcut Command + A. Once everything is selected, press the Delete key or choose Delete Path from the screen. Once all paths are deleted, create custom inputs by choosing New Path. Select whether to have a stereo or mono path, and then click on the desired input number for the new path. Now do the same for the outputs.

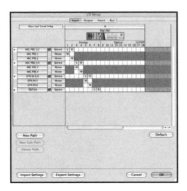

CUSTOM BUS SETTINGS

Customizing your bus settings is just as important and is done in the same way you set up your custom I/O. From the Setup menu, choose I/O and click the Bus tab. You can name up to 64 sends on an Pro Tools 8 LE system, giving you the ability to set up many useful custom bus names for various aux send functions. You will see how they are used and how helpful they can be from the examples in this chapter.

AUDIO TRACK CLEANUP FOR MIXING

Oftentimes the unglamorous task of cleaning up the final-mix tracks by using mute editing or cutting out all of the unwanted miscellaneous audio is overlooked because of its tedious nature. Patience and determination will pay dividends if you make sure that all of your mix tracks are perfectly edited and cleaned up for mixing. Pro Tools 8 has at least given us something new to look at while doing this kind of editing by introducing new waveform views.

ANOTHER NEW LOOK

As in the past, waveforms can still be displayed in positive and negative shapes around the zero-crossing, viewed as Rectified. The new views allow you to see your waveforms as calculated Peak or Power waveforms. The Peak waveform display is calculated based on the sample-by-sample peak level. This is the traditional Pro Tools view. Power view, on the other hand, is calculated according to the root-mean-square (RMS). This view is advantageous when zoomed out beyond the sample level. It can tell a better story about the characteristics of the audio than Peak view can and is often used when mastering. When playing with the new views, notice that you also have the option of viewing your audio set to Outlines. In addition to the standard waveform view, this setting will show an outline on the waveform. This is just a different look and is a personal preference. The graphics below show all of the View options available.

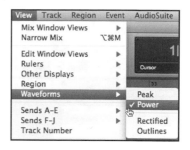

STRIP SILENCE

Strip Silence is a great feature for quickly editing out unwanted audio in a track, without having to manually cut every little unwanted section out. For instance, there may be microphone bleed of the headphone mix coming through the vocal track when the singer isn't singing, or maybe from the extra drum sounds that are picked up by the tom microphones. Pro Tools 8 offers Strip Silence threshold adjustments down to –96 dB, leaving the –48 dB resolution in the dust. This option is great for audio with low signal level or huge dynamic range. Using the Strip Silence feature is easy; here is how it works.

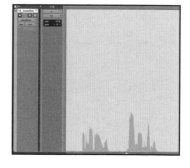

You can use your own material or, if you are using the supplied material, try using this feature on the tom tracks from the "Serious Questions" session. Start by highlighting the track from which you would like to edit out the background audio. Go to the Edit menu and select Strip Silence, or you can use the keyboard shortcut Command + U. When the Strip Silence dialog box appears, you will need to make choices in the following categories:

Strip Threshold

This parameter sets the amplitude threshold for the Strip Silence. The range is from −96 dB to 0 dB. Audio that falls below the set threshold is considered silence and is discarded. Audio above the threshold is kept and given new region names.

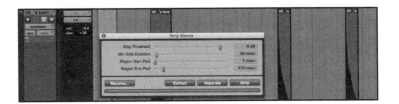

Minimum Strip Duration

This parameter sets how long the material below the threshold must last to be considered silence. This feature allows you to avoid several small regions that may be created within a section. When you actually use this feature, you will get a better visual perspective on it, and therefore a more thorough understanding of its function.

Region Start Pad

This parameter allows you to add a specific amount of time to the beginning of each new region that is created when using Strip Silence. It's good for preserving the subtle nuances of an instrument, such as a breath just before a vocal phrase or a finger slide before the strum of a guitar chord.

Region End Pad

This parameter does the same thing as the Region Start Pad, but it preserves the decay at the end of the region being created by Strip Silence.

Strip

This feature clears or "strips" the audio that has been defined as silence, but leaves the regions that have the audio on the track.

Extract

This parameter does the opposite of Strip, leaving on the parts that are considered or defined as silence. It's an ideal feature for generating room tone or ambience to be used elsewhere.

Rename

This feature allows you to rename the regions that are generated by the Strip Silence feature. If you choose this option, the Rename Selected Regions dialog box appears. Simply customize however you wish.

Separate

This selection separates the regions based on the boundaries that were detected by Strip Silence. It only separates them, and leaves all regions created, including defined silence, in the track.

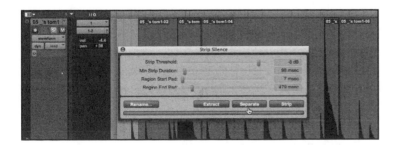

CONSOLIDATING TRACKS

Once you have stripped all of the silence from your tracks, made your final edits, and done appropriate track cleanup, you are usually left with multiple regions on all of the tracks in your session. In most cases, you would want to consolidate all of your regions that remain in your playlist and use them as your final mix tracks.

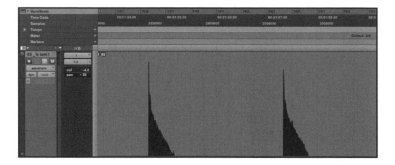

Consolidating the regions not only makes the overall look of the session cleaner, but it also helps performance. Having dense editing and too many individual regions makes it more difficult for Pro Tools to communicate with the hard drive that is storing your audio files. Another benefit of consolidating your final mix files is that it's easier to clean up the session and archive. Compacting files is another way to save your master backups and a little extra hard-drive space, but since it is destructive and hard-drive space isn't nearly that expensive anymore, I suggest doing the following.

Once all of your files are consolidated, use the cleanup methods you learned earlier in this book by selecting the All Group function from the Edit window and then triple-clicking on any track, and all of the consolidated tracks in your playlist or track display will become selected. Next, use the keyboard shortcut Command + Shift + U to select all of the unused regions in your Regions list, then press Command + Shift + B to remove the unused regions from the current session. Finally, go to the File menu and choose the Save Copy In option.

This allows you to make a copy of the "Final Mix" session data and all of its relevant audio files. When the dialog box appears, you have the option of choosing from Session File Format, Audio File Type, Bit Depth, and Fader Gain. You also can select specific Items To Copy. When backing up or creating your "Final Mix" session, I suggest you save all of the available items from the list—most importantly, choose All Audio Files; otherwise, none of the "Final Mix" audio files will be copied. Choose a safe destination for your new session to be copied. Name it accordingly, and then use your copy to do your final mix.

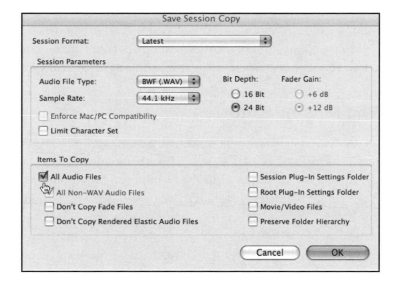

Go back to your session file that is still open, perform a Save As, and name the file "Final Mix Prep"; that way, you can still go back to the unconsolidated original session if you need.

THE FINAL MIX

Creating a final mix is sometimes the most challenging stage of preparing your music to be sent off for mastering. It is the process of combining multitrack recordings down to one or more channels. The most common is stereo; however, 5.1 surround sound is becoming quite popular. Pro Tools 8 offers upgrades that allow for surround-sound mixing, but for purposes of this book, we are going to stick to stereo mixing. During the final mixing process, all of the recorded sources, combined signals levels, frequency content, dynamic processing, and panoramic imaging and time-based effects are determined, and then manipulated to create an energy and overall mood for the mix, therefore giving it a more appealing sound for the listeners.

In this section, I will go over the essential mixing tools and terminology, along with a brief explanation of the purpose they serve. There will also be advanced tips about signal-routing techniques for dynamics and time-based effects, so you will be able to navigate your mix effortlessly and with confidence. Here is how to get your mixes ready to send to a mastering facility.

The Master Fader

In previous chapters, we have created a master fader in every session. The master fader is where all of the audio from the various tracks are "summed" to the main left and right outputs. It is not only a gathering place for all of the audio in your session, but it also serves as a "meter," or visual gauge, for the volume level of all of the summed audio. This allows you to make sure that you are not clipping the output. In my experience as an audio-engineering instructor, I usually see students putting compression or limiting on the master fader to boost the overall output of their mix. Sometimes they will even use both at the same time. That is a fine idea if you are doing a quick bounce to disk so you can hear your work for its musical content, but not the best choice if you are doing your final mix. When mixing, the goal is usually to mix and blend all the tracks of your session so that the individual instruments are heard clearly and they are spread nicely throughout the stereo field. This should be achieved without clipping the master fader. When you put a limiter on your master fader from either the onset of your mix or the point at which the master fader starts to clip, you're using a method that many professional mix engineers consider to be a lazy way of controlling dynamics. Instead of avoiding problems or just immediately using quick fixes, you should address these dynamic issues properly, and adjust your mix until you aren't clipping the outputs on the master fader without the need of a compressor or limiter to do the job for you. This is usually saved for the mastering process. Actually, it is pretty standard to try to leave approximately 3 dB of headroom on the master fader to leave room for the mastering engineer to manipulate the overall frequency curve and dynamics of the mix.

One of the biggest differences with contemporary mixes and mixes made prior to those mixes "in the box" is that there is little to no dynamic range. This is the result of mixes being overcompressed. Many people would say that the life has been squashed out of the mix. Nevertheless, this approach is used in a lot of contemporary music because everyone wants to have the loudest mix on the radio. Since responses to music and audio engineering are subjective, you can use whatever works for you. However, you should try mixing without compression on the master fader, and get the best mix you can that way. Of course, you would use compression on the individual faders, but try not to use master fader compression until it is time for the mastering process.

USING DYNAMIC PROCESSING ON A MIX

The use of dynamic processors during the mix process helps shape the over all tonal quality and allows total control over the dynamic range of each of the sources in your recording. For instance, if you are mixing a straightforward rock tune, you may want to make sure the kick, snare, bass guitar, and vocals are all consistent enough to drive the song. Using compressors and limiters during this process can help you achieve a particular energy that the song calls for. Overcompressing a signal will cause audio anomalies such as a "pumping" or "breathing" effect, so take your time when applying dynamic processing.

Equalization is very important as well. This type of dynamic processing allows you to have total control of the frequency content of the source. A major ingredient of a good mix is to consider — ahead of time — how every instrument's frequency content needs to be strategically manipulated so that it finds its own place to live in the overall mix. Applying EQ correctly will help ensure that all of the individual instruments in your mix are heard clearly without overpowering any other instrument.

Gating is another dynamic process used to help control excessive leakage of other instruments in the source track. For instance, it is common to hear a bit of music in the vocal track when the artist has had the headphones turned up so loudly during the recording process that it caused them bleed into the vocal microphone. Using a gate allows you to get rid of the unwanted headphone bleed on the track, and only let the recorded vocal be heard during playback of the track. I will cover how to use all of these processors in the next section of this book.

Equalization

Simply put, equalization (EQ) is the tonal control of the frequency content of an audio signal. It allows you to shape a signal's overall frequency curve without affecting its overall fundamental qualities. You can use EQ correctively and creatively, and knowing the basics of what EQ is and what it does is the first step in having a command over the subject.

There are many methods for using EQ, and there are several types of equalizers available to help you achieve desirable results. It is important that you are familiar with the different terms common to all equalizers. This will help boost your confidence when you work with a new plug-in or any piece of outboard gear that has EQ. If you apply what you already know about EQ to any new piece of gear, the new piece a gear isn't nearly as intimidating.

Here are some key features of, and terms related to, equalizers. Keep in mind that this is a brief overview of EQ. There are many fact-filled resources available to you if you would like to learn about EQ in depth. The objective of this overview is to help you acquire a better understanding of EQ and make educated choices when using any of the many EQ plug-ins that are available today.

Frequency Spectrum

A frequency spectrum analyzer is a visual gauge that allows you to see the overall frequency content of a signal. Using spectrum analysis can help you train your ears visually.

Many EQ plug-ins don't have spectrum analysis, but they usually have a frequency spectrum graph and different visual aides to show you where and how you are affecting the signal you are manipulating.

Frequency Curve

The frequency curve of any signal is measured by its overall frequency content. When viewed through a spectrum analyzer, you have the ability to see exactly which frequencies are present in a signal.

This helps you make better decisions when boosting or cutting different ranges of frequencies. Ultimately, using your ear is your best bet when trying to achieve a certain type of sound. One of the most important pieces of advice I can give you about trying to get an instrument to sound a particular way is to either already have the sound in your head or have a reference sound that you are trying match. If you can close your eyes and hear the sound you are going for, knowing the basic principles of EQ will help you a great deal when you are trying to harness it. Of course, you can twist the knobs and move the sliders on an EQ until you find a sound you like, but if you find yourself frustrated with this technique, try doing the things discussed in this section.

You will notice that boosting or cutting the same frequency on various instruments has a different effect on each instrument's sound and frequency curve. This is because different instruments have different fundamental frequencies. Every instrument or sound has a fundamental frequency range. Applying EQ within this fundamental range will have the most impact on the sound that is being EQ'd. There are also other excitable frequencies on a given instrument, and those are called lower or upper harmonics. Listed below is a table of frequencies and descriptive terms that will help you when you are applying EQ to a mix.

GENERAL DESCRIPTIVE FREQUENCIES TABLE

Bass Guitar	Bottom, 50–80 Hz; fullness, 120 Hz; attack, 800 Hz; slap, 2.5 kHz
Kick Drum	Thump, 65–90 Hz; boxiness, 350 Hz; beater, 3–5 kHz; pillow smack, 9–12 kHz
Snare	Fatness, 120–240 Hz; shotgun pop, 800 Hz–1 kHz; crack, 3–5 kHz; snap, 9–12 kHz
Toms	Fullness, 180–360 Hz; attack, 5–7 kHz; snap 8–10 kHz
Floor Tom	Fullness, 80–120 Hz; attack, 5 kHz; snap 8–10 kHz
Hi-Hat and Cymbals	Clang, 200–350 Hz; harshness, 3–5 kHz; sparkle, 8–10 kHz
Electric Guitar	4 × 12 cabinet thump, 120 Hz; fullness, 240–600 Hz; presence, 1.5–2.5 kHz
Acoustic Guitar	Full body, 80–120 Hz; richness 200–400 Hz; presence, 2–5 kHz; sparkle, 7–10 kHz
Organ	Fullness, 80–120 Hz; body, 240 Hz; presence, 2–5 kHz
Piano	Fullness, 80 Hz; boxiness, 200–360 Hz; presence, 2.5–5 kHz; sheen, 7–10 kHz
Horns	Fullness, 120–240 Hz; piercing, 5 kHz
Voice	Chest, 120Hz; boom, 240 Hz; presence, 3–5 kHz; sibilance, 5–8 kHz; air, 10–15 kHz
Strings	Body, 240 Hz; scratchiness, 7–10 kHz
Conga	Tone, 200 Hz; smack, 3–5 kHz

COMMON EQ PARAMETERS

Having a firm grasp of all of the important features of the many types of equalizers available to you will give you a lot more control when you are trying to achieve the sound you hear in your head. Listed below are the essentials that you should dedicate to memory as soon as possible. They will instantly improve your mixes and help you obtain the exact sound you are going for.

Bands

Bands are the divisions of the frequency spectrum into equal sections, with each band spanning a particular range of frequencies. Usually they are broken into four sections that are named Lows, Low-Mids, High-Mids, and Highs. Since there are a few different types of equalization, there may be as little as one band or as many as 32 or more. Here are the parameters most commonly found on equalizers.

Target

The target frequency may be either the center point or the starting point of a range of frequencies being boosted or cut.

Bandwidth

This feature determines which frequencies that are immediately surrounding the target frequency are affected when a boost or cut is applied to the signal. The ranges of frequencies are affected equally above and below the target frequency. The letter "Q" is used to represent bandwidth.

Gain

This parameter determines how many decibels of the selected frequency are added to or removed from the signal that is being altered.

Bell, Peak, and Notch

These are descriptive words for shapes made in the frequency curve by boosting or cutting a target frequency and the surrounding bandwidth. A wide bandwidth results in a smooth, broad (or bell) curve, while a narrow bandwidth forces the gain to happen inside a more confined region, resulting in a more sharply sloping peak shape (if boosted) or notch shape (if cut) in the spectrum.

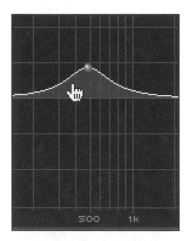

Active and Passive

An active EQ can add or remove gain from a signal, while a passive EQ can only remove gain. Therefore, any EQ with boost and cut options on the gain control will be an active EQ. A passive EQ will have only a cut or a minus option.

Graphic EQ

A graphic equalizer will always have several preselected target frequency choices and a fixed Q for each band. This is the type of EQ traditionally seen in home or car stereos, and it looks like a group of vertical slots with a slider that is able to move up and down in each slot. Each slot represents one band and is labeled with the target frequency measured in hertz or kilohertz. The bandwidth of each band is predetermined and nonadjustable. A graphic EQ may have one or several bands, but the only available manipulation is to boost or cut the target frequency of each band. You boost or cut frequencies by moving each slider up or down from the center position. A graphic EQ with many bands assigned to frequencies equally distributed across the spectrum is useful for smoothly shaping the contour of the entire range of frequencies present in a signal. The frequencies assigned to the bands of such a graphic EQ are commonly spaced at intervals of one-third of an octave and are called one-third-octave filters.

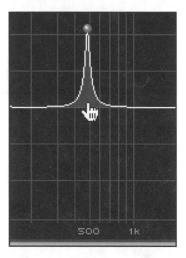

Parametric EQ

A parametric equalizer allows the adjustment of all three parameters within each band. This is the type of EQ found on many professional recording consoles and in many modern plug-ins. The traditional parametric EQ divides the spectrum into four overlapping bands: they are called "highs," "high mids," "low mids," and "lows."

The sweep, or target frequency, control is labeled in hertz or kilohertz. It allows the selection of the target frequency within the range of frequencies included in that band.

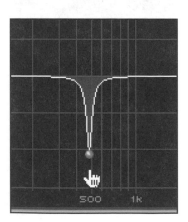

The bandwidth control is often labeled with a Q and is often indicated by a bell-shaped curve at one end of the control's range and a peak-shaped curve at the other end.

The gain control, usually labeled with a plus sign on the boost side of the control range and a minus sign on the cut side, determines how much boost or cut will be applied to the selected frequency range.

Shelving EQ

A shelving EQ still allows the user to select a target frequency within the band. However, instead of affecting frequencies both above and below the target within a bandwidth, the boost or cut applied to the band begins with the target frequency and continues equally to boost or cut all the frequencies from the target frequency on up or down, depending on the band you are using.

With high-shelving EQ, the boost or cut is applied from the target frequency all the way up to 20 kHz. With low-shelving EQ, the boost or cut is applied from the target frequency all the way down to 20 Hz. The range of frequencies affected by shelving EQ is determined by the distance from the target frequency to the extreme outer end of the spectrum. Bandwidth, or Q, does not apply to shelving EQ. Many professional recording consoles and software plug-ins have an option that allows the high and low band of the parametric EQ to be switched between parametric and shelving modes.

The symbol for shelving EQ looks like a little fork. The "handle" is the unaffected part of the spectrum, while the broad part of the fork is the sudden change level at the target frequency. The symbol for high-shelving EQ is open to the right (toward the high end of the spectrum line), while the symbol for the low-shelving EQ is open toward the left (toward the low end of the spectrum). Because midrange bands of an EQ do not extend to the ends of the audible spectrum, the idea of shelving EQ cannot apply to the midrange bands.

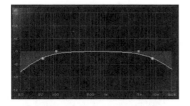

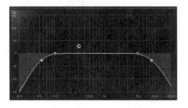

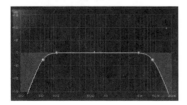

Highpass and Lowpass Filters

High- and lowpass filters are passive EQs. They remove, or filter out, part of the frequency content of the signal as it passes through. A highpass filter allows high frequencies to pass through it, while low frequencies are filtered out. A lowpass filter allows low frequencies to pass through it, while it filters out high frequencies.

The frequencies above or below the target frequency are filtered out at a fixed rate and are measured in decibels per octave, such as 6 or 12 dB per octave. The standard term for rating these filter slopes is known as a filter's *order*. Here's an example of how this terminology is used: A first-order filter will reduce a signal's amplitude by 6 dB for every octave above or below the target frequency; a second-order filter will reduce a signal's amplitude by 12 dB per octave; and so on. This filtering of the signal produces a spectrum shape, which tails off in a slanting line, or slope, from the target frequency to the end of the spectrum in either direction. The severity of the slope is determined by which order filter is used.

COMPRESSOR/LIMITERS

Compressing and limiting dynamic processors work to control the dynamic range of a signal. Compression should be used when the desired effect is to have control over the signal's amplitude level in order to make the amplitude of the source more consistent, thus allowing you to raise the overall volume of the signal. For instance, it can make a vocal much more intelligible, or a kick drum or bass guitar part more consistent, thus creating more energy when it is called for.

Limiting is a compressor with a very high ratio. Typically, a ratio from 10:1 to 19:1 is considered standard limiting, and any ratio above 20:1 is known as brickwall limiting. Brickwall limiting uses a fast attack time and a very high ratio. Therefore, it usually does not produce a good sound. However, it is beneficial when used as a safety precaution in live situations because it stops the peak transients dead, and therefore there is no chance of them damaging the equipment. Some engineers like to use brickwall limiting during the recording process to send the highest input levels possible to the multitrack without distorting. This is a personal choice, so do as you please; this is not one of my personal favorites for studio recording purposes.

Parallel Drum Compression

Parallel drum compression (aka New York compression) is when you blend a highly compressed track with an original drum mix that is uncompressed. This gives your drum tracks the feeling of having more power, and the technique commonly used in many genres of music. Creating parallel drum compression can sometimes be challenging due to the track delay caused by some of the nicer CPU-intensive plug-ins. The best way I've found to avoid phase issues created by track delay is to use busing to outsmart the system and make track latency a nonissue. Try this: create two new stereo aux inputs and name them DrmCmp and DrmUncmp. Set the inputs to receive the DrmBus sends and the DrmCmp send. Then highlight the track names of all the drums in the mix, enter the keyboard shortcut Shift + Option, and set the outputs to DrmBus.

Next, use the keyboard shortcut Shift + Option + Control and set a secondary output to the "DrmCmp" bus. This sends two copies of the drum mix's outputs to two separate bus inputs on the corresponding aux input tracks. Since you won't be hearing the original drum mix outputs through the main outs anymore, set the inputs for each new input you created to Solo Safe by Command-clicking on the Solo button. This allows the drums to be heard anytime, even when soloing other instruments. Finally, add a compressor to both aux input tracks. The key is to bypass the first one, and use the second one only to really compress one set of the stereo drum mix. When you have the same compressor on both aux inputs, you create the same amount of latency with each of them. Bypassing the first compressor allows you to hear the uncompressed drums but still create the same amount of track delay that the heavily

compressed drum track on the second aux input has. Now you can blend the two together with no concern of having phase issues. This will be demonstrated in the QuickTime tutorials associated with this chapter.

GATES

A gate is a processor that is used to block out unwanted background noise of an audio track, so that sounds are essentially muted and only the desired "primary" sound is heard. An example of this would be if you had a kick drum track, and the microphone on the kick drum were to pick up some of the snare sounds during the recording process.

A FEW MORE KEY INGREDIENTS

In this next section we will go over some advanced routing techniques for using a feature on a gate commonly referred to as a key input, which allows you to make various creative enhancements to your mix. The exercise below shows you a practical application for using the key input on a gate processor. I always suggest trying this technique on whatever you can think of and not just for the traditional technique described below. Be creative!

Key Inputs for Triggering Gates

Using key inputs, or using the sidechain of a dynamic processor, is a trick that's been around for decades. This type of processing is used in many applications, and I will show one of the most common ways to use the key input of a gate as an example here. It is a fairly simple process that will help you understand the concept so that you can then use it more creatively when the situation calls for it. The principal goal of this exercise is to add some *oomph* to the kick drum by blending it with a low-frequency sine wave. This is achieved by using the aux sends to send a copy of the kick drum to the key input of a gate that

is attached to oscillator. Every time the key input on the gated oscillator track receives the aux send copy of the kick drum, the gate will open up and allow the sound of the oscillator to come through. Create a mono aux track and go to its inserts, and then select the Signal Generator plug-in from the Other Plug-in folder. When the Signal Generator plug-in appears, you have a few decisions to make. Set the frequency slider to 220 Hz and its level to −7 dB, and the preselected sine wave will work just fine.

Once you hear the 200 Hz tone, use the insert on the same channel and choose Expander/Gate Dyn 3 from the Dynamics folder. When the plug-in appears, use the Librarian and select the Kick Gate SC factory preset.

Now set the Threshold parameter to −5 and the gate should close, making the sound of the oscillator disappear. Next go to the kick track, select the send, and choose bus 1 to send a copy of the kick down aux send 1. When the Send fader appears on the screen, set its fader level to +5.

Now you are halfway done. Go back to the Gate plug-in. On the upper-left side of the Gate plug-in there is an icon resembling a key. Click on the drop-down menu just to the right of the icon where it says "no key input," and select bus 1.

Now look to the right-hand side of the gate, and you will see another key under the Side-Chain section of the gate. Turn it on, and you will hear the oscillator open every time the kick track hits.

You have just used the sidechain of a gate to trigger a gated oscillator with a kick drum signal that's being bused to it. Now you can set the release time of the gate to allow it to stay open for as long or short a time as you desire. Finally, go back to the Signal Generator plug-in and set the frequency to 63 Hz or lower. (Setting it to around 49 Hz sounds good on this particular kick.) You have essentially created a new kick drum, and you can use it to blend in with your original kick drum to enhance the fullness of the overall kick drum sound.

Use the Room

Learning to trigger a gated signal generator using sidechain inputs can be fun, but that's only the tip of the iceberg for this type of signal routing. Try playing with the same idea but use the room sounds as sources to be triggered at their sidechain input by the kick, snare, and tom tracks. The trick is to set the range of the gated room sounds properly, so that you can still hear the rooms in the mix but there is a little extra room on the kick, snare, and toms when they hit. I'm a huge fan of big-room sounds, but I've found myself washing out my drums with too much room sound overall. However, this method of triggering them through the sidechain inputs of a gate makes them sit very nicely in the mix. Use the release time to set the decay of the room sounds. Be creative! This is a nice alternative to putting a reverb on the kick, snare, and toms, when you have perfectly good room reverb to use already. And it's the reverb of the room you recorded your drums in to begin with. Cool! Use 'em if ya got 'em.

Sidechain Compression on a Vocal

Many of the newer compressors have a feature called look-ahead compression. If, however, you are using other compressors from your plug-ins that do not have look-ahead compression as an option, you can achieve the same thing by using the techniques discussed in this chapter. The concept behind look-ahead compression is to have the ability to use some nice vintage compression emulation. Unfortunately, many vintage compression units react a little bit too slowly for the vocal, causing the vocal to have a "pumping" or "breathing" effect. To work around this situation, you can use an aux send from a vocal copy that can't be heard and that is nudged back in time in order to trigger the sidechain input of the compressor that is instantiated on the original vocal track before the actual original vocal passes through it. This allows the compressor to already be open by the time the lead vocal enters it, therefore working around the "pumping" or "breathing" effect.

To do this, make a duplicate of your vocal on another track and send it to a random bus so it is not heard.

Then nudge it back so it is slightly ahead of the original vocal. So far, all you have done is move the copy back in time and make it inaudible. Next, go to the new vocal that can't be heard and send it down a bus. Go to the lead vocal compressor and set its key input to the corresponding bus. Now you can move the duplicate vocal around the timeline until it is triggering the key input on the lead vocal's compressor just right. The result is a much smoother compression, especially at higher compression settings. It's a nice choice to use for creating consistency for the lead vocal's overall level. Make sure that you pay close attention to the release time so the gate doesn't close too fast. Also remember that it's opening early because it is being triggered by another vocal, so it will close earlier for the same reason. A longer release time will do the trick.

STUTTER EDITS

Creating stutter edits can be a fun and creative tool to use when you are mixing. There are many ways to accomplish this effect. This is just one of the many ways to quickly create stutter edits. Let's say that you have an instrument or a voice that is sustaining a long note or chord. The principle behind a stutter edit is to insert silence into a sustaining part, thus creating a *stut-ta-ta-ter* in the audio. A pretty cool effect.

To do this, create a new audio track next to the sustaining part. Zoom in on the beginning of the sustaining region and highlight a section of the new track. Create some silence using the Consolidate Selection command (Option + Shift + 3).

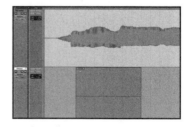

Set the Grid to 16th notes. Now delete the first 16th note of the silence, leave the second 16th note of silence, and select everything after that and delete it. Now you should have a 16th note of actual silence and a 16th note of audio silence.

Highlight them both and use the Repeat command (Command + R) to repeat the two parts as many times as necessary.

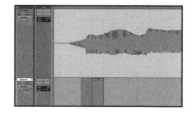

Now you should have several slices of actual silence and created silence along the entire timeline next to the sustaining track.

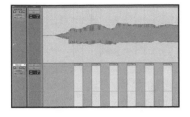

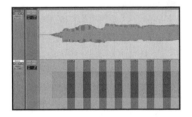

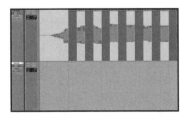

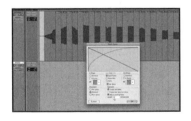

Click on the Grabber tool, and then select the Object grabber.

Make a grab selection around all of the silence slices and move them on top of the sustaining track.

You should now have inserted silence in 16th-note durations throughout the entire sustaining source, and thus created a stutter edit. The edits are cut hard, so you will want to create crossfades for all of the silence you have inserted into the track. Simply highlight the track with the stutter edits, and then use the Fades command (Command + F) to create a batch fade.

Now when the stutter edit track is played back, the edits aren't so harsh and have more of a tremolo effect.

TIME-BASED EFFECTS

Unlike dynamic effects that manipulate the audio source by increasing or decreasing various gain parameters, time-based effects alter the audio with time manipulation. Effects such as reverb, delay, multitap delay, ping-pong delay, flanging, chorus, and pitch-shifting are all considered time-based effects.

The way that time-based effects differ from gain-based ones is that time-based effects typically aren't applied directly to the audio source. To use time-based effects, send a copy of your audio via its aux sends to the corresponding input of an auxiliary track that has an effect on it, and then blend the aux, or wet, fader with the original dry signal to achieve the desired balance between the two of them. The send from the original dry audio is sent postfader, so once you have a nice blend between wet and dry, you can maintain the integrity of this blend when the dry fader is being moved up or down.

Saving Plug-in Settings

It is easy to save your plug-in settings so that you can recall them anytime, on any session. This is especially useful if you have particular settings you like to use for different instruments. Once you have your plug-in set up the way you like it, click on the

Settings menu and select the desired setting's preference. Your choices are Set Plug-in Default To User Settings or Set Plug-in Default To Factory Settings; Save Plug-in Settings To Root Settings Folder or Save Plug-in Settings To Session Folder; and finally, Set Root Settings Folder. Selecting Save Plug-in Settings To Session Folder will put your plug-in settings in your Session folder. Selecting Set Root Settings Folder allows you to put your saved settings anywhere you desire. The default Root Settings folder is in the Plug-in Settings folder on the main hard drive under Library, Application Support, and then Digidesign.

Once you've selected exactly where you would like to save your settings to, choose the Save Setting As option, name them, and you are done. To retrieve your settings, click on the Settings Librarian folder and choose them from either the session's Settings folder or from the Root folder. Saved Root folder settings do not appear inside their own folder; instead, they appear directly in the Settings Librarian menu.

AUTOMATION

Automation is yet another creative tool to make your mixes sound just how you hear them in your head. It is used for making subtle volume changes in various instruments during certain sections of the song. Creative panning techniques and even automating plug-ins is not only common but also very easy to achieve in Pro Tools. In version 8, Digidesign added some great new features that will be covered in this section of the book. First let's learn how to enable or disable the Automation features in Pro Tools.

Enable and Disable

To enable or disable certain parameters that can be automated, go to the Window menu and select the Automation option, or you can use the keyboard shortcut Command + 4. Notice that when the dialog box appears you can write-enable seven different parameters or temporarily suspend any automation that has already been written by choosing the Suspend option.

MODES OF AUTOMATION

Now let's look at the standard Automation modes in Pro Tools, learn how to use them, and discover what they give you the ability to do. They all have their own unique purpose and you will need to determine what suites your needs at any particular time during the automation process.

Automation Off

Off mode turns off all automatable parameters including volume, pan, and mute; send volume, send pan, and send mute; plug-in controls; and MIDI volume, pan, and mute. When you are in Off mode, automation information for these parameters is ignored. Automation can be switched from Off automation to another automation mode during playback or recording.

Read Automation

Read mode plays any automation that has been previously written to the track.

Write Automation

Write mode starts automating from the time playback starts to the time it stops. It erases any previously written automation for the duration of the pass.

Touch Automation

Touch mode writes automation only while an automatable parameter is being touched or clicked on with the mouse. When a fader is released automation is no longer being written, and the fader returns to its previous automated position at a rate determined by the AutoMatch settings in the Preference menu under Mixing.

Latch Automation

Latch automation is just like Touch automation in that it starts automating when a control is touched. But unlike Touch, writing of automation does not stop until you stop the transport or "punch out" of the automation pass by changing the automation mode to Read or Touch.

VIEWING AUTOMATION

One of the best features of Pro Tools automation is having the ability to automate everything with a graphical view. You simply use your standard edit tools to apply and manipulate graphic automation. You will notice that every time you automate something, a new playlist is created in the Track view, giving you the ability to visually confirm what you have automated. It also gives you the ability to modify automation using your eyes and not just your ears. To view the automation you have written, click on the Track View selector, and from there you will see the various view types. If you have written automation on plug-ins, the parameter of the plug-in will show up on this list also.

DRAWING AUTOMATION

You can use the Pencil tool to create automation events on an audio or MIDI track. The Pencil tool can be set to draw various shapes for automation. Some of the more popular choices include Free Hand, which allows you to freely draw automation according to the movement of the mouse. The shape will have enough breakpoints so the automation plays back smoothly. If you are using the Pencil tool with MIDI, the shape is in a series of steps, using the resolution settings you select from the MIDI Preferences page. Triangle is another popular shape that draws a sawtooth pattern that repeats based on the Grid value. This is cool if you are looking for a gradual fade from left to right, or vice versa. The square shape for Pencil tool automation is really cool if you are looking for hard-panning automation that never lets the source touch the center field or anywhere in between. Each move is hard left or hard right, based on a rate determined by

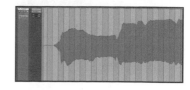

the Grid value. There are other Pencil tool shapes, so experiment with them until you find the effect you are looking for.

DELETING AUTOMATION

There are a few methods for deleting automation. You can delete each individual breakpoint by holding down the Option key and using the Pencil tool to click on each individual breakpoint. You will notice that the Pencil tool turns upside down, leaving you with the eraser end when the Option key is selected. You can remove several breakpoints at once by highlighting a range of breakpoints with the Selector tool, and then pressing the Delete key. To remove all automation from the displayed track type, triple-click with the Selector tool to highlight all breakpoints, and press the Delete key. Finally, to remove all automation data on all automation playlists on a track, use the Selector tool and use the Select All command (Command + A), and then press Control + Delete.

THINNING AUTOMATION

By default, Pro Tools writes automation information using the maximum amount of breakpoints for the most accurate representation of the moved recorded. Many times, this density of breakpoint is overkill, and the same effect can be achieved when using fewer breakpoints. Having fewer breakpoints uses less CPU and allows you to optimize your resources.

You can set the automatic Smooth And Thin Data After Pass parameters from the Mixing Preferences window. You can also choose the degree of thinning. Selecting Some usually yields acceptable results.

If you write automation with the maximum amount of breakpoints, you can always smooth and thin automation after a pass. The degree of thinning you selected in the Mixing Preferences window will be used by selecting the range of automation you would like to smooth and thin; then go to the Edit window and select the Thin Automation option, or you can use the keyboard shortcut Command + Option + T.

PRO TOOLS 8
AUTOMATION FEATURES

Learning how to use yes the different modes of automation is nice when you are working on a nice control surface and you really like the feel of automating on faders, but drawing in automation is generally much quicker and very accurate. The new Automation and Controller Lanes features let you edit track automation and controller data without changing the Track view. You automate and edit automation just the way you did before these options were available, by drawing in automation with various Pencil and Trimmer tools. You can still set your automation information to snap to a grid when in Grid mode. The main difference is being able to see everything all at once. Pro Tools has made so many things so visually pleasing in its latest software version that things have become much easier to use. I suggest playing around and really getting creative with the way you automate your tracks. Use the techniques mentioned above and take advantage of the Automation and Controller Lanes. To access these new features, click on the new Show Hide Automation Arrow at the bottom of the Track Color Code strip in the Edit window. They look just the way they did in the MIDI Editor, and new lanes can be added and taken away by using the Plus and Minus keys. So get to work and be creative. You are limited only to what you can hear in your head.

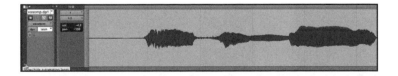

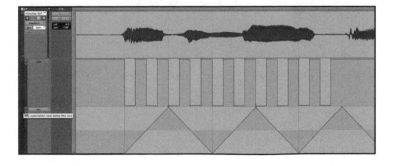

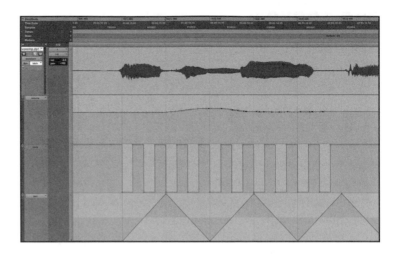

PLUG-IN AUTOMATION

Plug-in automation is very powerful and should be experimented with a lot. It has many useful purposes, so start thinking about it. To apply automation to a plug-in, hold down all three modifiers (Command + Option + Control), and click on the parameter in the plug-in you would like to automate.

If you would like to apply automation to any parameter in the plug-in, hold down all three modifiers and press the Auto button on the plug-in. Parameters that have been selected for automation will be indicated by a green or red emphasis near or surrounding the plug-in's parameter. Red means that you are in a writable automation mode, and green indicates you are in Read mode.

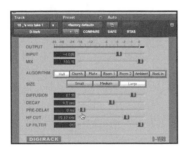

BOUNCING TO DISK FOR INSTANT GRATIFICATION

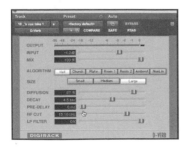

Here is how you quickly make a music CD that you can play on any consumer-level CD/DVD player. Select the length of audio you would like to "bounce to disk." Go to the File menu and select the Bounce To option and choose Disk, or you can use the keyboard shortcut Command + Option + B. When the Bounce dialog box appears, choose Bounce Source: 1–2 (Stereo); File Type: WAV; Format: Stereo Interleaved; Resolution: 24; and

Sample Rate: 44.1 kHz. Then choose Convert After Bounce. Once all of these selections have been made, select the Bounce option on the lower right of the Bounce dialog box. The Save dialog box will appear, and you will have to choose a destination for the file you are bouncing to disk. I suggest that you make a bounce folder in a location you can conveniently get to, anytime you desire. Name the bounce file and select Save.

Bounce to Disk Details

Once your mix is at the final stages and it is ready to be mixed-down to a stereo format that can be played on consumer CD players, you have a few options for completing this process. In Pro Tools under the File menu, there is an option called Bounce to Disk.

This option provides you with several choices you can make when bouncing your mix to a 2-track format. You can choose your Bounce Source, or which outputs will be acknowledged when you are bouncing. In other words, if you choose 1–2 as your Bounce Source and any of your tracks are being sent to outputs other than 1 and 2, those tracks will not be part of the 2-track file when you perform your bounce.

The next choice you have to make is which file type you would like your bounce to become once the process is complete. The standard choices are SDII, WAV, and AIFF. If you have upgraded your Pro Tools software with the Music Production Toolkit, you will have the option of converting your bounces to MP3, QuickTime, or Sound Resource. These are primarily for Internet use. The best advice I can give you is to keep your file type the same as the audio content in your mix. If the files in your session are AIFF, then use the AIFF option. If they are WAV, then use WAV. The key is to do as little conversion as possible, to maintain the integrity of the original audio. This will give you the purest bounce.

Format, resolution, and sampling-rate choices are very important. If you have recently finished the mix and you are going to master the final mix, you will want to choose the Multiple Mono format and keep the bit resolution and sampling rate as high as possible. This way, when you import your bounced mix into another Pro Tools session or any other program with mastering capabilities, your bit resolution and sampling rate remain the same, and the file format will not need to be converted upon import.

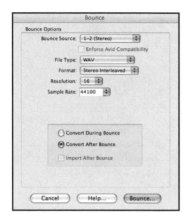

If you choose Stereo Interleaved, you will be able to burn your bounced mix to a standard CD and play it back in any consumer CD player, as long as you choose 16-bit and 44.1 kHz. However, you'll more than likely want to master your mix so that the overall frequency curve is well balanced and the overall volume level of your mix is as loud as the average professional CD you buy from your local or online CD retailer. The final option is whether you would like to convert during or after your bounce. You should generally choose Convert After Bounce. This option takes longer, but it ensures you the best level of automation playback accuracy.

MASTERING

Mastering is a form of audio postproduction. It's the process of preparing and transferring audio from a final mix to a master storage device. This is the final 2-track version of the final mix, and the master file is what is considered ready for duplication. Although analog masters are still being used by a few engineers who specialize in analog mastering, digital masters are becoming the final format of choice.

Since the 1950s, mastering has played an important role in the fidelity of the final product that is mass-produced for the consumer. It is usually done by a highly skilled mastering engineer, and it is widely recognized that a good mastering can make or break a commercial pop recording. Since so many advancements have been made in digital technology, it is now possible to have decent masters done without the high-dollar equipment. However, it is hard to put a price tag on a good set of mastering-engineer ears. Mastering engineers are paid top dollar for what they do and have unique skills. They know how to manipulate a final mix to achieve a professional product. Using professional mastering houses and mastering engineers may not be inexpensive, but more than likely a pro will give you the results you are looking for.

Almost every DAW software program is considered capable of producing masters. The key is having a good set of ears and knowing what you are trying to achieve. The process of mastering usually consists of equalization, compression, multiband compression, limiting, noise reduction, ambience creation, and dithering. The process of mastering will vary depending on the needs of the audio content. Examples of possible situations to address during the mastering process include, but are not limited to, creating a master DAW session and importing the final-mix audio, editing minor flaws, adjusting the stereo width, equalizing audio between several tracks so that they sound as though they were recorded and mixed on the same planet, adjusting overall volume levels between the audio tracks, and adjusting the peak limiting.

THE MASTERING SESSION

Create a new session in Pro Tools and make sure that you maintain the file format, bit depth, and sampling rate of the audio you are importing so you minimize or alleviate the conversion process. Once the session is created, you need to import the final mix into the session using the keyboard shortcut Command + Shift + I.

It is crucial that you use a reference mix to help you gain perspective on what you are trying to accomplish. When you are trying to create something that sounds professional, use a reference that has been mastered by a professional and distributed for consumer use. This way, you have something to shoot for. Many times people just put a little EQ and then a limiter on the final mix, and then call it good. Well, when you do that, you basically just make the track very loud, and you make it sound good to *your* ears, in *your* room. The probability of it transferring to every average CD playback system is very low. However, if you at least use a proven professional reference, you may be able to come close to matching the way a professional CD sounds.

There are many incredible mastering plug-ins available on the market today. Most software companies have bundles specifically for mastering audio that include spectrum analysis, stereo-imaging processors, linear-phase multiband EQ and compression, mastering limiters, and so on. All of these things are great tools to have and there is plenty of information on how to use these plug-ins well, but for the purpose of this book, we will go over only a typical scenario for mastering at home—one that will give you acceptable results on a modest budget.

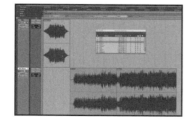

Once you have imported the final mix and a professional reference, line them up so that they aren't playing at the same time. Now listen through the songs, and set memory locations on every section of each song. I suggest using 1 through 19 on the final mix and 20 through 29 for the reference. This will allow you to quickly audition the different sections of the song with a couple of keyboard commands, and A/B between your mix and the reference mix. Remember to use Period (.) + the number, and then Period by itself, yes to quickly toggle between the different sections of each song.

If you have a spectrum analyzer, put it on the last insert of both tracks and use it! The goal is to get your frequency curve to be similar to the reference.

The Chain of Command

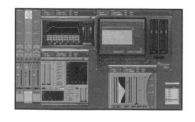

Typically, you would have a nice EQ for frequency-curve matching, a sidechain limiter for taming the low end, a multiband compressor, and finally, an overall limiter. This will give you ample control over the frequency curve and allow proper gain staging to achieve competitive volume and similar overall frequency-curve content when compared to the reference.

Use the EQ at the top of the chain to try to match the frequency curve of the reference mix by critically listening to the lows, low mids, high mids, and highs. Focus on each bandwidth and adjust accordingly. Use the sidechain compressor in the next slot to find the frequency or small range of frequencies that have a lot of bass response (not necessarily bad bass response, just a lot of it). Set the sidechain compressor up as a limiter, and really crush the narrow bandwidth of "hyper" bass frequencies until you have several decibels of gain reduction. Then use the make-up gain to bring the hyper bass back up in volume, but with more control and continuity with the rest of the lows. Use the multiband compressor to iron out the mids and highs. Finally, use the limiter on the final insert to bring the overall volume of the track up. If you have done your first inserts justice, you should be able to bring down the threshold on the limiter quite a bit before you hear breakup. Set the final output on the limiter to 0 dBfs for the loudest possible result, and make sure you have the Dither function turned on and set properly.

The Master Bus

Once you are totally satisfied with your master and you think it is competitive with your reference mix, create a new stereo audio track and set the output of the final mix to an open stereo bus. Then set the inputs of the new stereo audio track to receive the final mix on its corresponding bus. Record-enable the new stereo audio track and name it.

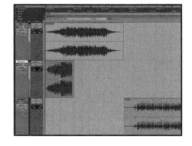

Press Record and print your final mix. Once the recording is complete and your final master is printed, you can clean up the front and the back of the track and apply the desired fade time if necessary.

THE FINAL DESTINATION

When everything has been done and the fades are just right, duplicate the playlist so you have a copy of the original master and consolidate the selection so the intro silence, the outro fade, and the outro silence is consolidated with the selection. Now go to the Regions list, and you should see your final master mix consolidation track already highlighted. Use the List drop-down

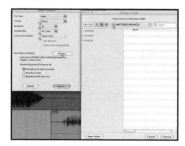

menu or the keyboard shortcut Command + Shift + K to export the final mix.

Choose the final destination for the mix and give it the proper name. Set the file type to WAV, the format to Stereo Interleaved, the bit depth to 16, and the sampling rate to 44.1 kHz, and then select Export.

Now you can use this file to burn discs from any disc-burning program, and you will have a mastered final mix to enjoy.

FINAL THOUGHTS

This final chapter has covered essential and advanced techniques for mixing and mastering with Pro Tools software. Since there is so much information in this chapter, it is in your best interest to read it more than once, and dedicate the information, terms, and techniques described in this chapter to memory as soon as possible. As a result, your mixes will get much better much faster, and have you coming a lot closer to achieving the exact sounds you are hearing in your head with each new mix you work on. Mixing and mastering are both art forms that take several years of experience, experimentation, patience, and a lot of trial and error to achieve the desired result consistently. There may be many times you will be fulfilling someone else's needs or mixing on Pro Tools to suit their taste, so being able to translate their descriptions of the sounds they hear in their heads, into what actually comes out of the speakers, is very important if you are an aspiring engineer. This can be a difficult skill to develop but an important quality to have if you want to be a great mix engineer. However, with the right amount of time, determination, and a blessed set of ears, you'll get there. Just keep refining your skills and learn from previous mistakes. I suggest having this book around while you are mixing and mastering to use as a reference. It will help you remember the many options that are available to you when using Pro Tools, and remind you how to use the many tools you'll need to use to create the mix of your dreams, and to become a real power user.

POWER TIPS SUMMARY
FOR CHAPTER 9

1. There are several ways to enhance your computer's performance when mixing your audio. Try to remember to always use the smallest component of a plug-in: for example, if you need only a 3-band EQ, use the 4-band EQ and not the 7-band EQ. If you have any send meters being viewed, turn them off unless you absolutely need them. Use the Automation Thinning feature whenever possible.

2. You can use the Windows Configuration list in coordination with the Memory Locations window to quickly go from editing views to mixing views (with every floating-window option you would like to see) with a click of the mouse. Once you have several window configurations stored, you can make them part of your custom View Marker locations by adding them to the General Properties settings selection when creating your view markers.

3. Creating custom I/O settings and Send settings can really keep things organized and easy to remember. To set your custom I/O and send settings, go to the Setup menu and select the I/O option. To modify the name of the input, output, or send, be sure to click on the appropriate tab, and then click on the field of the name you would like to modify. It is usually more precise to build custom settings from scratch by deleting all paths first, and then creating specific new ones that suit your needs.

4. Try to refrain from using dynamic processing on the master fader while you mix. Instead, adjust the volume fader of different instruments in your mix to prevent overloading the main bus. This is definitely subjective, but if you can get a well-balanced mix without using any compression on the master fader, you may be able a keep a fair portion of dynamics in your overall mix even after it is mastered.

5. Using a frequency spectrum analyzer on the master fader can help when carving out frequencies from particular instruments to make room for other instruments in your mix. Applying

spectrum analysis to the master fader lets you see individual frequency analysis when using the solo features, or you can see the frequency curve of your overall mix.

6. Remember to turn the target off in any plug-in or floating window that you would like to remain open after you select another plug-in or floating window. This allows the previous one to remain open, so that you can customize the window configuration in any way you like.

7. To achieve "look-ahead" compression from a plug-in that does not have this feature, remember to duplicate the track, set the outputs to a random bus so it is not heard, then use the sends to trigger the key input of the compressor on the original track. This concept works well for false triggers on gates, however there is no better gate than simply editing out what you don't want to hear.

8. Once you have your plug-in set up the way you like it, click on the Settings menu and select the desired settings preference. Your choices are to set the plug-in default to either User Settings or Factory Settings; then, to save the plug-ins settings to either the Root Settings Folder or the Session Folder; and finally, Set Root Settings Folder. Selecting Save To Session Folder will put your plug-in settings in your Session folder. Selecting Set Root Settings Folder allows you to put your saved settings anywhere you desire.

9. When using automation, you can select the Pro Tools Preference, Smooth And Thin Data After Pass parameter from the Mixing Preferences window. Setting Degree Of Thinning to Some usually yields acceptable results.

10. Once you have imported the final mix and a professional reference, line them up so that they aren't playing at the same time. Set memory locations on every section of each song. Use these markers to quickly audition different sections of each song and A/B between your mix and the reference mix. Remember to use Period (·) + *the number*, and then Period by itself, to quickly toggle between the different sections of each song.

KEYBOARD SHORTCUT
SUMMARY FOR CHAPTER 9

Hopefully you have memorized as many of these commands as you can. We have gone over quite a few, but there are still more. Please continue to learn these keyboard shortcuts. Knowing them will prove to be a real convenience once you get used to using them.

KEYBOARD SHORTCUT	FUNCTION
Option + C	Clears all peak indicators
Command + Option + M	Toggles Narrow Mix and Wide Mix views
Command + Shift + A	Selects All from Regions list
Command + Shift + R	Renames Region
Command + Shift + I	Imports Audio
Command + A	Global command for Select All
Command + 4 (numeric keypad)	Shows and hides Automation Enable
Commmand + U	Shows and hides Strip Silence
Command + Shift + K	Exports Region as File
. (decimal point) + Number + *	Selects Window Configuration settings
Ctl + Opt + Cmd-click on Plug-in Parameter	Sets Read or Write status for automation
Ctl + Opt + Cmd-click on Signal Indication Meter	Selects Narrow or Wide view for meter
Control + Option + Command + W	Shows and hides all floating windows
Control + Option + J	Shows and hides the Windows Configurations list

PRO TOOLS TUNE-UP
FOR CHAPTER 9

1. The _____ is very similar to the Memory Locations list. However, this list recalls all floating windows and screen arrangements.

2. _____ is a feature that allows you to quickly edit out unwanted background noise without having to manually edit the whole track.

3. This Strip Silence parameter _____ takes away the background noise, leaving only regions with the desired audio on the track.

4. If you have a lot of dense editing on your tracks, your hard drive may not be able to access the audio fast enough to play back properly. To ensure proper playback of densely edited tracks, you should consider _____ the track to make it a whole file, therefore enhancing playback performance.

5. To make a copy of your session for archiving and portability, go to the File menu and select the Save Copy In option. To ensure that the audio files are copied with your backup, choose the _____ option from the Items To Copy menu.

6. The _____ is the gathering place for all audio in your session and serves as a meter or visual gauge for the volume level for the sum of all audio in your session. This is a postsend fader.

7. A _____ is a visual gauge that allows you to see the overall frequency content of a signal. It is a great reference when trying to match a frequency curve.

8. _____ allows tonal control of the frequency content of an audio signal.

9. The _____ may be either the center point or the starting point of a range of frequencies being boost or cut.

10. A _____ is designed to control the dynamic range of an audio signal.

11. A _____ is a dynamic processor that is commonly used to block out unwanted background audio in an audio track.

12. Processors such as reverb, delay, flanging, chorus, and pitch-shift are all known as _____ effects.

13. Gain-based plug-ins are usually inserted on a channel to replace the original signal with a more desirable signal. Time-based effects are used primarily on an auxiliary input, and they receive a copy of the original signal. The two sounds are blended together to achieve a nice balance. In order to keep the integrity of the blend when moving your original audio fader, you must set its Send to act as a _____.

14. The five modes of Pro Tools Automation are

    a. Automation Off
    b. Read
    c. _____
    d. Touch
    e. Latch

15. The _____ tool is used to draw various shapes for automation.

16. To delete individual breakpoints when using View Automation, select the Pencil tool and click on the unwanted breakpoints while holding _____.

17. To delete automation from every playlist, you must click on the track you would like to remove automation from, use the Select All command, and then press the _____ keys.

18. Since Pro Tools uses the maximum number of breakpoints when writing automation data, once the automation has been written it is important to use the _____ option to remove unnecessary breakpoints.

19. Holding down all three modifier keys (Command + Option + Control) and clicking on the plug-in parameter you would like to automate toggles the Read and Write status of that particular parameter. Once automation is activated on the plug-in, a green or red indicator will let you know which status you are in. Green indicates _____, and red means _____.

20. When performing a quick bounce to disk that is ready for consumer playback, set the parameters in the Bounce to Disk dialog box to WAV, _____, and 16-bit. These settings will allow you to burn CDs that are audible on consumer digital audio playback devices.

21. When creating a mix file that is ready for mastering, leave all settings on their original settings, and then select a file format of _____ to ensure that there is no conversion of your audio when importing to the mastering session.

22. When mastering your final mix, it is crucial that you use a _____ to help you gain perspective on what you are trying to accomplish. When you are trying to create something that sounds professional, use one that has been mastered by a professional and has been distributed for consumer use.

23. There is no set rule on how to master a mix, but a typical signal chain for mastering would be a nice EQ for frequency-curve matching, followed by a sidechain limiter for taming the low end, a multiband compressor, and finally, an overall limiter. The limiter is used at the very end of the chain to make sure the mix is at its maximum _____ before distorting the main outputs.

24. When printing your final mastered mix, it is important to apply _____ to the audio file. This ensures that you will get the best-quality conversion when going from 24-bit to 16-bit resolution.

25. Use the Regions List drop-down menu and select the Export Region As File option, or use the keyboard shortcut _____ to export the final mix.

Answer Key for Pro Tools Tune-ups

CHAPTER 2

1. amplitude, frequency, and waveform.
2. decibels
3. 120 dB
4. frequencies
5. Hertz
6. kilohertz
7. 20 kHz—20 kHz.
8. lower
9. one octave
10. waveform
11. simple and complex
12. complex
13. microphones
14. condenser
15. frequency response
16. frequency curve
17. analog to digital conversion.
18. 44.1 kHz.
19. two times
20. 96 dB, –144 dB
21. host
22. plug-in.
23. RTAS or Real Time Audio Suite
24. delay
25. authorize

CHAPTER 3

1. Create Blank Session
2. saved or stored
3. dedicated
4. a. Sample Rate
   b. Bit Depth
   c. File Format
5. 44 kHz.

6. BWF (WAV)
7. PTF
8. Audio Files
9. Fades File
10. lower
11. RTAS plug-ins
12. Lowering
13. File menu
14. Track menu
15. Help menu
16. Mix Window, Edit Window
17. a. Shuffle
    b. Slip
    c. Spot
    d. Grid
18. Grid Mode
19. a. Selector
    b. Grabber
    c. Trimmer
    d. fade-ins, fade-outs, and crossfades
20. Windows
21. View menu
22. Track List, Regions List
23. 10
24. 10
25. a. Audio tracks
    b. MIDI tracks
    c. Aux inputs
    d. Instrument tracks
    e. Master Faders

CHAPTER 4

1. audio
2. RTAS
3. operation
4. nudge value

5. tilde (ˋ)
6. bars:beats
7. Regions/Markers
8. plus and minus
9. plus sign
10. track name
11. click and drag
12. a. Instrument track
    b. MIDI track
    c. Audio track
    d. Auxilliary track
    e. Master Fader
13. hide and make inactive
14. right click
15. MIDI studio
16. MIDI time code
17. instrument
18. instrument
19. four
20. the patch list browser
21. transpose
22. MIDI thru
23. route its outputs
24. ReWire
25. preferences

CHAPTER 5

1. a. Record Mode
   b. Destructive Record Mode
   c. Loop Record Mode
   d. Quick Punch
2. Options
3. Loop Record
4. six
5. three
6. Command + K
7. Option + K

8. Command + G
9. Pre-fader
10. Track menu
11. Metronome
12. Quantize
13. Interface
14. Input Only
15. Harmonic
16. factory presets
17. compression
18. inserts
19. time-based
20. aux input track
21. fit to window
22. Save As

CHAPTER 6

1. Windows
2. AudioSuite
3. highlight your selection
4. individual
5. right click
6. option + control
7. CPU resources.
8. Command + G.
9. Command + Shift + G.
10. Color Pallete
11. remove or delete.
12. double click
13. grooves, fills.
14. mute, blue
15. Kit, Style, and Mix
16. Style Editor
17. Wurlitzer
18. Setup Section
19. Learn
20. Edit
21. Command + 5
22. Option
23. Enter
24. Selection, None
25. Option + F

CHAPTER 7

1. Command + Shift + W
2. Import Session Data
3. Group List Keyboard Focus.
4. standard tape deck
5. Link Timeline and Edit Selection
6. loop playback
7. two independent playback
8. region group
9. Command + Option + U
10. Automatically Create New Playlists
11. duplicate playlist
12. Identify Beat
13. Beat Detective
14. Groove Template Extraction
15. Collection mode
16. Bar/Beat Marker Generation
17. Region Conform
18. Edit Smoothing
19. editing application
20. enhanced resolution

CHAPTER 8

1. Varispeed.
2. tick-based
3. Real Time Processing Mode.
4. Warp
5. Analysis view.
6. Accordion Warp.
7. Elastic Properties
8. the Event Operation
9. Conform to Tempo
10. Spacebar Toggles File Preview
11. Regions view.
12. placement in the timeline
13. Control + Option + (+/-)
14. human element
15. applied evenly
16. blue diamond

17. Trimmer Tool
18. Regions view
19. Real Time properties.
20. "rubber-banding"

CHAPTER 9

1. Windows Configuration List
2. Strip Silence
3. Strip
4. Consolidating
5. All Audio Files
6. Master Fader
7. Frequency Spectrum Analyzer
8. Equalization
9. target frequency
10. Compressor/Limiter
11. gate
12. time-based
13. Post-Fader Send.
14. a. Automation Off
    b. Read
    c. Write
    d. Touch
    e. Latch
15. Pencil
16. Option.
17. Control and Delete
18. Thin Automation
19. Read, Write.
20. Stereo Interleaved
21. Multiple Mono
22. reference mix
23. volume level
24. dithering
25. Command + Shift + K

Index